TICOM:

The Hunt for Hitler's Codebreakers

Randy Rezabek

Copyright ©2016 by Randy Rezabek

Published by the author

Rochester, N.Y.

In honor of:
The dean of cryptologic historians
David Kahn
And the last man standing
Selmer S. Norlan

Acknowledgments:

To David Kahn, Ralph Erskine, Chris Triantafyllopoulos, and Frode Weierud for their feedback and encouragement.

Rene Stein, librarian at the National Cryptologic Museum, a friend to all cryptology historians, and the staff of The National Archives (College Park) for being there.

Leslie Monthan, copy editor and Navy shipmate.

Table of Contents

Preface: The Last Great Secret of World War II ... 1
Introduction : The Role of Signals Intelligence in the Second World War ... 3
1. Beginnings ... 12
2. Spoils of War ... 29
3. TICOM in Burgscheidungen ... 63
4. Fruits of Victory ... 93
5. Success ... 116
6. Captured Intact ... 147
7. Mopping Up ... 179
8. Postscript ... 216
Appendix: The codes and ciphers of WWII ... 225
Notes ... 237

Preface:
The Last Great Secret of World War II

TICOM was declared to be "the last great secret of the Second World War" by bestselling author James Bamford in his 2001 book, *Body of Secrets*. It was a statement that launched conspiracy theories supposing that TICOM hid blockbuster political secrets that threatened the continued security of the republic, even 50 years later.

Unfortunately, or perhaps fortunately, reality is never as dramatic as paranoid imaginations assume. Over the last twenty years the slow dripping of TICOM's secrets into the public realm provided no bombshells. TICOM revealed the identities of German cryptologists who continued their careers working for the west during the cold war who had to be protected from the spymasters of the Soviet bloc. Details of Soviet wartime codes and communication techniques learned from the Germans were, of course, relevant in the late forties. Moreover, the working alliance and scale of British and American Signal intelligence efforts was continued on a formal basis into the cold war, and this needed to be masked from their adversaries. Furthermore, a domestic political consideration was the desire to hide the "fact of signal intelligence" from a public that had no "need to know".

But by the end of the cold war in 1992, these points were irrelevant. Yet, according to Bamford, the director of NSA was compelled in 1992 to extend its top secret/codeword classification to 2012, the longest allowed by law.

Preface

There is no documentary evidence justifying the decision; perhaps it was just a matter of old habits dying hard for an agency whose secrets were the source of its power. After all, no one in the NSA was ever fired for not revealing secrets. Why TICOM remained classified into the 21st century is perhaps its greatest secret.

Here is the story; you can decide for yourself.

Introduction:
The Role of Signals Intelligence in the Second World War

The Second World War provided a catalyst for the scientific and technological developments that characterize the modern world, With the exception of perhaps the atomic bomb; no other innovation had a greater or more profound impact than Signals Intelligence. The 1939-45 efforts in communications electronics, code breaking, information processing, automation and organization helped create what is now known as the information age.

Until the twentieth century, military intelligence was a backwater of military strategy, treated with indifference or contempt by Clausewitz, who theorized that the commander should be offensive minded and had little need for detailed information about the enemy who would give way through force of will and arms. Furthermore, dealing with spies was ungentlemanly and dishonorable. Moreover, classic military history up to then had few examples of the successful use of intelligence in winning battles.

All that began to change with the twentieth century. New technologies such as the aircraft and photography allowed for the collection of detailed objective information, and the increasing use of radio enabled eavesdropping on the enemy's intention. The cataclysm of modern industrial war, with the very survival of nations at stake, soon erased any concerns about the honorability of the practice.

The First World War soon taught commanders the value of intelligence; it could not only help win battles, it could affect strategy. German General Ludendorff's radiomen intercepted unencrypted Russian signals outlining the movements of their armies into eastern Prussia. Based

Introduction

upon this information, Ludendorff outmaneuvered the Russians, defeated them at Tannenberg and changed the course of the war in the east. The British Admiralty, after discovering almost by accident that they could receive the signals of the German High Seas fleet in England, and aided by a fortuitous gift from the Russian of a captured codebook, were able to build a first class intelligence bureau, Room 40, which tracked the movements of the German Fleet, allowing its every move to be blocked. And in what was the most important case of code breaking in history, that of the Zimmerman telegram, the war was ultimately won. Interception of the signals, determining the direction they came from, and breaking the codes they communicated provided information of greater saliency and at a greater speed than had ever before been experience in war.

The British learned the lesson, in the early 1920s they salvaged the remnants of both their Army and Navy code breaking agencies and organized them as the Government Code and Cypher School, under the auspices of the Foreign Office. Here they kept the black arts of cryptanalysis alive through the lean years of the depression. Other powers, including Soviet Union, Germany, Italy, France and Japan kept their hands in the game. The United States did too, but its efforts, divided between the Army and the Navy, allowed interservice rivalries to get in the way.

The advent of the Second World War created an explosive growth in the size, scope, and range of signals intelligence, especially in Britain and America. By 1945, the practice had evolved into a whole cycle of interlinked activities, now known as the" intelligence cycle": interception, direction finding, traffic analysis, decryption, translation and intelligence processing, culminating with the secure communications of the results to customers in the field.

TICOM: The Hunt for Hitler's Codebreakers

The basic gist of Signals intelligence was interception, for the most part conducted by the various military services. The opposing armies had both permanent and mobile intercept units, focused on enemy military traffic, the Air Forces had equivalent stations, and Navies had both land based and ship based intercept capabilities. Interception of enemy signals was not an easy process, search and identification of new signals on various, ever changing frequencies was an ongoing process, and all call signs and operator chat had to be copied accuracy, with the encoded signals themselves sounding like random gibberish to the intercept operators. Allied intercept stations were spread through the world, from England and Washington DC, to Two Rock Ranch in California, to Corregidor, Melbourne, Singapore, Cairo, Deli and points in-between. Conditions were often primitive and at times dangerous; a German signals intelligence unit was caught up in the fighting in North Africa and destroyed, and later the Russians captured a whole German SIGINT Regiment in the Kurland Pocket. American naval cryptologists were evacuated by submarine from Corregidor just ahead of the Japanese, and a few years later suffered kamikaze attacks while serving onboard the carriers of the Pacific fleet. British intercept operators of the 'Y' service served on every front and in every condition from the heat of the desert, to the rainy humidity of Ceylon, to the mountains of India.

Correlating with interception was the practice of direction finding. Known since before the First World War, the adaption of high frequency radios by the world's military services in the 20s and 30s led to more sophisticated DF techniques known as High Frequency Direction Finding (Huff-Duff). This allowed for smaller antennas and more portable sets, which were organized into networks to generate cross bearings. These cross bearings could be used to identify the location of a transmitter. Interception stations, identifying an interesting signal, could alert the DF network, and calculate the physical location of the transmitter. This proved

Introduction

especially valuable to tracking ships and aircraft, and during the war was heavily used by both the British/Americans and Germans.

The information gathered by interception and DF networks was then compiled and studied by traffic analysis. Studying the call signs, message preambles, traffic load and physical location of signals, they could identify enemy units, their movements, and even make accurate guesses as to their intentions. These three steps, interception, DF and traffic analysis was often referred to as 'radio intelligence'. Even before the content of enemy messages could be read, radio intelligence could provided field commanders with critical information, the enemy's order of battle.

Of course, knowing the content of all these intercepted signals through decryption is the icing on the cake of SIGINT. Information about the concerns, debates and decisions of the enemy, especially at the high level of strategy, allows opponents to predict and prepare for the resulting actions. The importance of the results, along with the sheer intellectual challenge of cryptanalysis, has been the drama that historians and now the public have embraced in the story of SIGINT.

Cryptanalysis became so important that every belligerent had dedicated organizations for that purpose. The British, because of their desperation at the beginning of the war and with the personal support of Winston Churchill, took a unified and centralized approach to code breaking via the Government Code and Cypher School, which grew into a behemoth organization of almost 10,000 employees at Bletchley Park, and included outstations in Cairo, Deli, and Ceylon. Its American partners, the US Army's Signal Intelligence Service and the US Navy's OP-20-G also became massive, with central code breaking centers in Washington DC and overseas at Hawaii, Australia and eventually, Guam. For their part, the Germans were much more decentralized with separate agencies for the Army, Navy, Air Force, for the Armed Services as a whole, for the Foreign Office and the Nazi Party itself. This had the effect of diluting the effort and generating competition and turf battles which did serious harm to the quality of their code breaking effort.

But cryptanalysis in itself is not enough; intelligence must be processed to be useful. The raw decrypts had to be translated from the enemy's native language, not a simple process, especially if it is as complex as Japanese or Russian. Even the German communications, which used many military and technical terms, acronyms and abbreviations, required a specialized vocabulary beyond that taught in British or American universities. And even when accurately translated, specialized intelligence officers had to interpret the *meaning* of a message. If commander what's-his-name is suddenly transferred to unit so-and-so to a backwater base does this indicated a buildup, a change of tactics, or a shift in strategy? Signals Intelligence is very much a complex puzzle, and each message is a small piece of a much bigger picture. Bletchley Park used intelligence officers from the various services to staff the various interpretation units, Hut 3 for Military and Air intelligence, Hut 4 for Naval. These officers painstakingly cross-indexed each message, cataloging every instance of an individual's name, place name, unit information, equipment nomenclature, or any other fact revealed in the traffic. Cards were created from millions of messages broken during the war; by 1945 Bletchley Park had what was probably the most extensive database of the pre-computer age. Each new message was then augmented with the intelligence officer's comments and corrections, providing the proper context for interpretation by the high command.

Introduction

The Germans, too had a system for evaluation, with each SIGINT agency having specialized departments, and each major SIGINT Regiment in the field having an evaluation company, utilizing techniques similar to the British, but not as centralized or thorough.

However, no matter the completeness, accuracy or thoroughness of the system, intelligence is worthless if it cannot be communicated quickly and securely to the appropriate commanders and decision makers. The British realized this early, and developed special teletype and radio circuits to the service ministries and the field commands to communicate ULTRA intelligence. The British, and later their American allies, had the problem of distance, with armed forces throughout Europe, the Mediterranean, Far East and Pacific to service. The Secret Intelligence Service (MI6) developed a separate communications department, Section VIII under Brigadier Richard Gambier-Parry in 1938 to create a worldwide, secure network, originally to communicate among its various agents throughout Europe, but adopted by the GC&CS during the war to pass ULTRA intelligence.[1] To service these links they formed "Special Liaison Units/Special Communications Units' (commonly referred to as SLUs). The Special Liaison component consisted of a half dozen RAF code clerks to encipher and decipher the ULTRA traffic while the Special Communications component were Royal Signals radiomen who actually worked the circuit. The units enciphered all ULTRA communications either with the British TYPEX machine, never broken by the Germans, or by one-time-pads. A junior officer who was responsible for communicating the information to the authorized commander and for maintaining security commanded them. This system, set up by Group Captain Fred Winterbotham, eventually had detachments at every Allied command from Army and Army Group up to the Ministry level.[2]

The US Army in Europe adopted this same system with one exception, the addition of an American "Special Liaison Officer" to act as the go-between the British unit and their U.S.

commanders. This SLO did the actual briefing and interpretation of ULTRA intelligence to such commanders as Eisenhower, Bradley and Patton. Security was tight, with only the commanding general and their G-2 authorized to know about ULTRA, and it was the SLO's responsibility to enforce the strict regulations regarding distribution, short-term storage and the timely destruction of such information. Most of the G-2 staffs at the higher levels down to Corps level were ignorant of ULTRA, and none below that level, even among the tactical SIGINT battalions, were aware of its existence.

Each German SIGINT regiment had a dedicated communications platoon to fulfill this role. Utilizing landlines when possible and radio circuits when not, the Germans passed raw data and finished evaluations up and down the chain of command from Berlin to the Corps level. However, the British had broken, unknown to the Germans, both the Enigma machine and the SZ 40/42 teletype that they used for secure communications, and they were providing their enemies with as rich a source of intelligence as they themselves had. For example, most of the information the Anglo-Americans had about events on the Russian front came from the Germans, not their Soviet allies.

As valuable as Radio Intelligence was to the field commander, the breaking of codes and ciphers was the epitome for the intelligence officer; only cryptanalysis can read the enemy's intentions.

World War II saw the use of a plethora of codes and ciphers used by the belligerents in a variety of settings. From simple frontline hand encrypted messages which only needed a day or two of security to machine generated ciphers used at the strategic level, cryptanalysts had their work cut out for them. The greatest challenge of the front line ciphers (codenamed PEARL and

Introduction

CIRO-PEARL by the allies) was the sheer number and volume of them; they were normally handled by forward crypto units such as the American Signal Security Detachment 'D', or by the evaluation companies of the German KONA signal intelligence regiments. Higher level communications, such as messages generated from the German ENGIMA machine and the encrypted teletype machines the SZ-40/42 and the T-52 received a vast amount of manpower and effort from the Allies, a story told in the various histories of ULTRA. In turn, the Germans soon gave up on breaking high level ciphers, concentrating instead on more profitable fields of effort, such as tactical signals and merchant shipping codes. What the Soviet's were up to is still largely a mystery, but given their level of war effort it must have been considerable; there is some evidence that they had read ENIGMA. But the highest, most secure form of communications was the use of one-time pads. A labor intensive and inefficient process, they were used often by the Russians and less frequently by the Allies, however, they were not as invulnerable as thought, the slightest misuse could open a door to enemy cryptanalysts.[*]

With the exception of the Manhattan project, whose existence was reveled to the world in a most speculator way on August 6, 1945, ULTRA was the greatest secret of World War II. Secrecy has been inherent to SIGINT since its beginnings for the simple reason that any evidence that the enemy's communications were being decrypted would force a complete change in their codes and ciphers, wiping out years of hard work, and forcing a new start from scratch for the cryptanalysis. With the stakes so high in the midst of a global war, any break in the flow of this high level intelligence could be a disaster.

Those tens of thousands of people who worked in this secret world, the need for security was drummed into them so intensively with threats of court marshals, two years imprisonment

---

[*] Se Appendix 1 for a more complete description of codes and ciphers.

for minor violations to the death penalty for treason, that for decades afterwards the secret was kept even from spouses. One wife stated "The saddest thing for me was that my beloved husband died in 1975 and so he never knew. It became public in 1977." Even after the public revelations of ULTRA, former employees were hesitant, "It's strange – I want to buy a video of Bletchley Park to send to friends in Australia but still have the feeling I shouldn't do it."[3]

As recounted already, only a select few within the military high command had access to this knowledge. And with victory in sight, the burning question was "What does the enemy know?" Given the western allies own level of effort and success with signals intelligence, a worst case scenario had to be assumed. How successful were the Germans in breaking allied codes? Had they developed any new techniques or technologies in cryptanalysis? Had they shared this knowledge with the Japanese's? And as events wound toward their conclusion in the spring of 1945 a new strategic concern emerged: what about the Russians? How much did the Germans know about Soviet codes and communications?

To seek answer to these questions, TICOM was born

1. Beginnings

In the summer of 1944, with allied forces ashore in Normandy, Allied strategists began to seriously plan for the next big step, the defeat of Germany. In Washington, the war department and the Navy were in discussions about a "post war pinch project" capturing German SIGINT material. In London the director of the Government Code and Cipher School (GC&CS) Commander Edward Travis and his deputy Nigel de Grey met with Colonel George A. Bicher, the senior U.S. signals intelligence officer in the European Theatre of Operations, to discuss a joint Anglo-American operation.

Bicher was a West Point graduate and a career Signal Corps officer, who after previous service in the Philippines had commanded the Second Signal Service Company (the Army's signal intercept outfit) in 1939, and was in Hawaii during the Pearl Harbor attack. In 1942, he was transferred to the staff of the Chief Signal Officer of the newly established European Theater of Operations, United States Army (ETOUSA). As director of the Signal Intelligence Division (SID) he was the senior American SIGINT officer in Europe, responsible for the transportation, training and assignment to the combat commands of tactical Radio Intelligence companies and battalions. Signal Security Detachment 'D' which supported 12th Army Group was attached to his headquarters. In addition he supervised the three detachments in the UK working with ULTRA intelligence, including the 6813th which worked directly with the British at Benchley Park. Shortly after these initial meetings, Bicher requested that the War Department approve and support this joint operation.

Meanwhile, Travis decided to appoint a joint committee to organize and supervise this effort, to be known as the Target Intelligence Committee, TICOM. He appointed the youthful but highly respected Harry Hinsley as chairman. Hinsley had been attending St. John's College,

Cambridge on a history scholarship when he was recruited to BP at the outbreak of the war. Assigned to Hut 4, which developed ULTRA intelligence on the German Navy, he conducted traffic analysis studies that identified the Kriegsmarine's communication networks and organizational structure. Base upon this source, he predicted the invasion of Norway; however the young civilian was not taken seriously by the Admiralty. Only in June 1940, after Hinsley warned that the German battlecruisers *Scharnhorst* and *Gneisenau* were sorting off of Norway, to be followed shortly afterward of the sinking of the Royal Navy's aircraft carrier *HMS Glorious*, did the Admiralty began to listen to him. By the following spring, BP had broken into the naval Enigma of the surface fleet, allowing Hut 4 to trace the movements and plans of the *Bismarck*. Afterward Hinsley, by this time the head of Hut 4, instigated a plan to seize lone German weather ships in the North Sea, which were known to use the Enigma cipher machine. The result of these operations allowed BP to make its first breaks into the U-boat cipher systems. In late 1943, Travis chose Hinsley to accompany him to Washington to negotiate the BRUSA Agreement with the US Navy. Known and respected on both sides of the Atlantic, Hinsley was expected to provide strong leadership of the committee.[4]

Bicher received his reply on August 7th when the Chief of Staff, General George Marshal, sent formal orders to General Eisenhower, as commander of both SHAEF and ETOUSA, to support the TICOM mission. In addition, the Commander in Chief of the US Navy, Admiral Ernest King, decided to participate in TICOM, ordering a liaison officer from OP-20-G, Lieutenant Commander Robert B. Ely to London to supervise the Navy's participation. Eisenhower made Bicher's role formal on October 9th, writing to him that: "As Director, Signal Intelligence Division, Office of the Chief Signal Officer, ETOUSA, you are ... to effect the

1. Beginnings

necessary liaison with the British authorities on this matter to formulate plans to carry out the wishes of the Chief of Staff, U.S. Army, for presentation to this Headquarters. [5]

Bircher was formulating plans, indeed. Based upon preliminary discussions with BP, he had already handed a "Joint American Proposal for Exploitation of German Signal Intelligence Targets" to De Grey. In it he proposed identifying two classes of targets; Class 'A', tactical SIGINT targets such as the field units of the German Army, Navy and Air Force which could be expected to be overrun in the normal course of events. Class 'B' targets were those of "extraordinary importance or unusual circumstances" such as the headquarters of the various crypto agencies, which would be subject to special assault forces in order to prevent the destruction of materials or equipment by the enemy. Bircher recommended forming the organization in four groups; a Target Intelligence Group (basically the TICOM committee and supporting offices at BP) to provide high level direction and later dissemination of the captured materials; a Target Occupation Group, SIGINT officers on secondment to the major combat commands to act as advisors on the capture of SIGINT targets; Target Reporting Teams, drawn largely from BP personnel, who would go out to the field and secure and inventory the class "B" targets; and a Target Expert Group, again largely drawn from BP, of experts in the various forms SIGINT who would do the follow up exploitation.

By this time the Allies had broken out of Normandy, captured Paris, and had raced across France to the borders of the Reich. Expectations were high that the war would be over by Christmas. However as the Germans retreated their lines of communications shortened and their resistance stiffened. Montgomery's daring airborne operation "Market Garden" ended in defeat and 21st Army Group bogged down in fighting among the canals and dikes of Holland. First

Army spent months in brutal fighting in the Hürtgen Forest, chewing up three divisions. Patten's drive was blocked at Metz, and 6th Army Group in the south, after initial success in Lorraine and the capture of Strasbourg, ran into stubborn resistance in the Colmar Pocket. Then on December 16th the Germans counterattacked through the Ardennes, sending the allied armies reeling.

Meanwhile, far from the front, the TICOM committee began its work. Lieutenant Commander Ely arrived in London in mid-September, and awaited a meeting with Bicher. The Colonel, who had moved with the ETOUSA headquarters to Paris, was making frequent trips back to the U.K. for meetings. Ely was the OP-20-G expert on the Enigma, and was responsible for designing the logic of the US bombe. He was no stranger to BP, having been one of the first Americans to visit there in June '42 with Joe Eachus to work with their code breakers. Now back, Ely went up to BP for preliminary meetings, first meeting with Captain Edward Hastings, Deputy Director, and Hinsley to get their views of the project.

Returning to London, Ely had his first brief meeting with Bicher on 20 September. They met again on Friday to compare notes on their understanding of the project; Ely explained that although captures of naval SIGINT material during the Normandy campaign had been satisfactory, they were made afloat or in the coastal areas, often utilizing deployed Naval Intelligence officers or relying on the Admiralty's 30 Assault Unit. Now that the battle had moved inland, the naval effort needed be coordinated more carefully with the Army. Due to the limited number of its Radio Intelligence personnel in theater, the Navy felt it could contribute more in the collection of target information and later the recording and dissemination of captured documents. Its actual participation in field operations would be limited. In the first week of October, Ely flew to Paris for further meetings with Bicher, beginning a series of frequent trips to the SID Headquarters. Ely presented a copy of his initial report to OP-20-G outlining these

1. Beginnings

points to Bicher. That afternoon they went to brief Brigadier General Thomas J. Betts, the Deputy G-2 of SHAEF, and head of the CIOS target sub-committee, who was in a hospital after being wounded by antiaircraft fire during a recent flight.

"The Colonel explained that our ideas were along the lines set out in my report; that the British were working up a similar plan; that we would attempt to merge them, or at least make them as nearly identical as possible....The General then said to get on with the plans, that he would assist in getting proper instructions to the combatant T forces; and that he would assist on coordinating our mission with others....He indicated that the possibility that the T force might be airborne...."[6] This was a reference to Operation ECLIPSE, which would soon dominate TICOM's planning.

Starting in November, the planners at SHAEF were busy reworking the plans for Operation ECLIPSE the occupation of defeated Germany. Much effort was now being expended on one contingency for ECLIPSE, an airborne assault deep into Germany. The operational planning for the operation had been given to the First Allied Airborne Army. The FAAA ground element consisted of the US XVIII Airborne Corps (82nd, 101st and 17th Airborne divisions), and the British I Airborne Corps (1st and 6th Airborne Divisions, 1st SAS Brigade, 1st Polish Parachute Brigade and the 52nd Air Landing Division). Two simultaneous Airborne assaults were planned, one against Berlin to be led by XVIII Airborne Corps and the other against Kiel by the British I Airborne Corps. Although the main purpose was military, the capture of enemy intelligence centers and headquarters was the second highest priority of the operation, for which a special command, T-Force Berlin, was created within SHAEF. This command was responsible for organizing and commanding the intelligence assault missions for ECLIPSE.

TICOM: The Hunt for Hitler's Codebreakers

The TICOM committee began its formal meetings in early October. Joining the committee, in addition to those already mentioned, were Ely's old friend Lieutenant Joe Eachus, OP-20-G liaison officer to Hut 8, along with fellow U.S. Naval officer Lieutenant John Coolidge. Representing the U.S. Army were Major Roy D. Johnson, longtime liaison officer and first commander of the 6813 Signals Security Detachment, and Major William F. Edgerton, former acting Chief of the General Cryptanalytic Branch at Arlington Hall and since August working at SIXTA at BP. Additional British members joining were Lieutenant Commander Dudley Smith, former Personal Assistant to Travis, and current Head of Security of Allied Cyphers; Wing Commander Oscar Oeser, Senior Air Adviser, who had formed a section to establish Enigma processing priorities, and coordinated Hut 3 Fish processing requirements; and the colorful Commander Geoffrey Tandy.

Tandy was a prewar expert in Forestry and Marine Biology, and a noted radio broadcaster in the 30s; he was a good friend of the poet T.S. Elliott. Commissioned in the RNVR at the outbreak of the war he was posted to BP in November 1939, according to a popular story by a mistake. His interest in botany with a specialty in 'cryptogaphy', the study of certain classes of plant life such as algae, ferns, lichens and mosses which have no apparent means of reproduction, was misread as 'cryptology'. Tandy was no expert in codes, although he was an accomplished linguist and his research skills were also of great value. Several sodden notebooks holding vital clues to the German code were recovered from sunken U-boats, but they seemed damaged beyond recovery. Tandy, however, knew exactly what to do, for the problem was not so different from preserving marine algae. Obtaining special absorbent papers from the museum,

1. Beginnings

Tandy dried the sodden pages and made them readable, an important contribution to deciphering the Enigma Cipher. Later he was appointed head of Naval Section 6, technical intelligence.

Initial work of the committee consisted of reviewing the paper prepared by de Grey and Bicher, which besides policy recommendations, identified six main Class 'B' targets: OKW/*Chi* in the Wilmersdorf district of Berlin; the OKH Inspektorat 7/VI of the Army located at Juterbog; the Chi Stelle of the Luftwaffe at the Wildpark, Potsdam; the Naval SIGINT center at Eberswalde which included the cryptanalytic B-Dienst; another Army unit, the OKH/LNA which controlled all the field SIGINT units, located at the big OKH headquarters at Zossen, and the location of the Kriegsmarine SLK (Naval Operations Staff) in Lanke. Among the policy recommendations adopted was the creation of an executive committee consisting of de Grey, Bicher and Ely to give final approval of all formal recommendations. Other items they considered was the need for continuous monitoring and identification of Class 'B' targets, reviewing ad advising on the handling of captured materials, and the selection and training of field personnel, and the liaison problems with SHAEF and the combat commands.[7]

At least 14 TICOM meetings were held between October and the following March. The committee systemically tackled the many issues facing TICOM over the next few months. First, policy was created and directives issued to the target reporting officers (TROs) as to their roles and responsibilities in the field. They were to go in with the T-Forces to seize and then secure German SIGINT class "B" sites, isolate them from all others, including other allied intelligence groups, identify all captured personnel and inventory all captured equipment, and freeze the sites until they could be exploited by follow on teams of TICOM experts. Decision matrixes and reporting formats were devised to manage the whole target reporting process.

Developing intelligence on all their prime targets was an ongoing effort. A subcommittee was charged with developing information on all six of the class "B" targets. In addition to looking through BP's extensive catalog of old ULTRA intercepts, they ordered photo reconnaissance coverage of the targets, and contacted MI-8 for the latest maps and geographic information available. The result was a series of target folders that were as detailed as the limits of allied intelligence could provide. For instance, the target folder for the OKW/*Chi* headquarters in Berlin-Wilmersdorf included a complete description of the setting of the building and the surrounding neighborhood, locations of the local railroad station and police station, and estimates of the building's defenses. They even found a German POW who had worked at OKW/*Chi* who could provide a description and a sketch of the layout of the building. This intelligence needed to be shared with SHAEF, especially the T-Force staff, so any information from the ULTRA sourced had to be rewritten to be disguised so it could be downgraded to Top Secret. They were also aided greatly with the periodically circulation of the Combine Intelligence Objective's Subcommittee (CIOS) Black List of wanted German personalities.

Liaison with SHAEF and the field armies was a difficult problem, from both a security and a political perspective. Only a small handful of officers at the Army Group and Armies were cleared for ULTRA, usually the commanding general, his chief of staff, and his senior intelligence officer. Even among the SIGINT field battalions and companies, ULTRA was forbidden knowledge. TICOM would be limited on what they could explain about their mission to the local commanders, politically not an envious position to be in when facing a busy Corps commander pushing his way into Germany. TICOM officers, mainly through Bicher's office, began building relationships with key players, particularly T-Force Berlin, which agreed to give the TICOM mission their top priority.

1. Beginnings

Although the T-Forces were created by a SHAEF directive signed by Eisenhower shortly after the Normandy landings, they did not come into force until Allied ground forces began to enter Germany. Each Army group was ordered to create a staff to "identify, secure, guard and exploit valuable and special information, including documents, equipment and persons of value to the Allied armies". In the American Army Groups T-Forces coordinated local combat forces in securing targets identified by the CIOS in London or other targets identified locally. Once secured, the T-Forces were to guard the targets until specialist personnel were called in to evaluate and exploit the target. Their staffs were fairly small, for instance the 6th AG T-Force staff constituted just 9 officers and 43 enlisted personnel

The British took a different approach, designating specific combat units to T-Force duties. In Montgomery's 21st AG, the Chemical Warfare officer, Brigadier G.H.C. Pennycook, was named the commander of T-Force. After the crossing of the Rhine there was little employment for his CW troops, so he transferred 5 companies, mainly for the use of their transport, to T-Force. He was also given three veteran combat battalions, the 5th Kings Regiment, the 1st Buckinghamshire, and later the 30th Battalion of the Royal Berkshire Regiment, to be augmented with the Admiralty's veteran intelligence commando Number 30 Assault Unit. 30 AU had had considerable success with their operations in the Mediterranean and during the Normandy invasion; they would serve as the model for the rest of T-Force.[8]

The T-Forces Berlin staff was created by Eisenhower in early October and Colonel D'Alery Fechet was named the commander. Fechet, who won a DSC in the first war, had been called out of retirement to serve in North Africa as commander of the 16th Infantry Regiment, was wounded and was invalided out of active service (for the second time in his career) and sent to staff duty in England. After serving on Bradley's staff in France, he ended up at SHAEF G-2.

His appointment came with the responsibility for capturing all the enemy intelligence targets in Berlin, so he became TICOM's main contact for ECLIPSE planning. His staff consisted of just himself and his executive and operational officers. By December 5th, T-Force was formalizing its plans with TICOM; they proposed that TICOM not enter Berlin until the main body of allied ground forces were within 14 days of occupying the city. The combat element of T-Force supporting TICOM would consist of five battalions, four against the city proper and one reserved for the suburbs. These combat forces would "seize and freeze" all of the assigned intelligence targets with TICOM targets the highest priority. Other specialist forces scheduled to be assigned to T-Force included demolition experts, fire-fighters, and mine-disposal experts, with four interrogation teams and eight microfilm teams attached to headquarters. T-Force also required that TICOM form their TROs into teams, train them, and brief them well in advance of any action.[9]

SHAEF agreed to give TICOM TROs complete control of the exploitation of the targets, and were authorized to send captured materials directly back to BP without going through the normal channels, and all other allied personnel were to be kept out of the target.

With the policy decisions made and the U.S. Navy's role in TICOM firmly established, Ely was order home at the end of December, leaving his able deputy Lieutenant Joe Eachus in charge.

Despite the German offensive through the Ardennes which broke out on December 16th, planning progressed and the TICOM committee began its selection of the TROs, the officers who would enter the front lines. By the end of January, a list of eligible TROs was compiled, mainly from BP ranks, largely from Hut 3, Hut 6 and SIXTA, but also including a large representation from the naval section and a few representatives from MI 8 and ETOUSA. From

1. Beginnings

this list teams were selected for each of the six targets, each team consisting of eight TROs, except for OKW/*Chi* team which was twice as large. As promised, they were balanced out between British and American members. Each team identified two officers that would be on 48 hour notice for immediate deployment.[10] Among the team commanders were the British officers Commander Bacon and Wing Commander Oeser, and American Army officers Majors Wiliam F. Edgerton and Bill Bundy, commander of the 6813 SSD. Among the naval members Lieutenant Joe Eachus, now head of the US Navy delegation to TICOM, and Royal Navy Commander A.M.S. Mackenzie each got a team

Of the six teams formed two were slated to capture the OKW/Chi locations at Wilmersdorf and Juterbog. A third was scheduled to capture the Luftwaffe's Chi Stelle at the Wildpark, Potsdam. Another was targeted against the SIGINT center at OKH headquarters at Zossen. Each of the main Kreigsmarine targets, the communications intelligence Funkaufklaerung at Eberswalde and the naval high command center at Lanke were assigned a team.

A compulsory part time training program was devised for all TROs, beginning on Monday March 19th. The training, accomplished in two hour blocks so as to not overly interfere with TROs regular duty was to total 27 hours over a two week period. Topics covered included procedures for handling of POWs, recognition of German Codes and Ciphers, including recording of the settings of any Enigma machines captured, handling of documents, priorities of target exploitation under varying condition, and communication procedures. Briefings were given on the intelligence available on OKW/*Chi*, Naval, Army and Air Force targets. Since almost all TROs had fought the war from behind a desk, and had not had any military training since induction, lessons in map reading, booby traps, grenades, small arms and unarmed combat were worked into the schedule. A three day field exercise consisting of a march overland to Woodstock was devised to teach them how to operate in the field.

The handling of captured documents had been sore point to Benchley Park. The previous year during the North African campaign, BP received a report that a German POW, from a Luftwaffe signals unit, while being marched back to a prisoner cage, had spotted some of their classified documents sitting unattended in a crate in an olive grove on the road to Tunis. This incident was serious enough that BP sent Wing Commander Oeser out to the Mediterranean to investigate the whole process for handling captured documents. Captured documents in the field were turned over to battalion intelligence officers, who as non-specialists may not realize the value of certain types of materials. SIGINT documents are almost always captured with other types of documents or in conjunction with other types of electronic equipment, such as radars, and were often not properly evaluated. Oeser complained that some documents captured in Cosimo, Sicily that were of use to GC&CS were not turned over for two months. There was much confusion and little clear direction as to the accounting and routing of classified documents in the Mediterranean. Oeser recommended that a captured documents department must be inter-allied, inter-service, be endorsed and backed by the various services' directors of intelligence, be mobile and have adequate photographic services to duplicate all captures, and be led by a trained intelligence officer familiar with SIGINT and knowledgeable of the problems and methods of GC&CS. The purpose of the unit should not be evaluation of the materials but rather the speedy duplication and routing back to the concerned agencies.[11] Now more than a year later the problems were recognized by a sub-committee of the Joint Intelligence Committee who warned that too many officers were authorized to remove documents, no effective registration

1. Beginnings

process existed, a danger of single documents becoming separated from larger groups en route, and documents coming from different sources often being mixed together generating confusion.[12]

T-Force at SHAEF issued a policy to all of its Army Group detachments ordering that all captured crypto materials, such as code books, signal plans, frequency lists, etc. be turned over to the nearest Signal Intelligence unit, to be transported by SIGINT channels back to a special documentation handling unit at BP. This unit was modeled after a special Admiralty unit at Bletchley named NID 12a which had been set up to handle crypto material captured by 30 AU. There they were given a library number based upon classification, titles were listed and translated along with the place of origin, and accession list was written and circulated. All non-crypto naval intelligence material was returned to the Admiralty in London to be made available for circulation to appropriate agencies.[13] TICOM set up a document sub-committee with representation by the various services, and they proceeded to work steadily throughout the summer, processing and translating documents until TICOM was disbanded in late November.

Now, with the prospect of floods of documentation falling into Allied hand with the defeat of Germany, the problem was compounded by rivalries among the different intelligence agencies as to who rightfully possessed what types of documents. Soon after the surrender differences broke out between the Army and Navy as to determination of which documents were of interest to the separate services and what to do with documents of mutual interest. US Army Signal Security Service chief General Preston Corderman agreed with Bicher's suggestion that all documents be filmed to enable sharing in the future. A photography unit from the U.S Navy, consisting of an officer and eight cameramen, was assigned to micro-film this material.[14]

Planning for ECLIPSE had accelerated in the winter but it was now becoming problematic. The main difficulty was lack of airlift. In mid-January bids were requested from the various agencies desiring to be in the airborne assault. Specialists were limited to 45 pounds of personal baggage and were expected to provide their own arms, ammunition and three days rations. TICOM estimated that they needed 56 TROs and 10 communicators in on the initial airlift. The psychological warfare division was requesting seats for 25 personnel on the first day, to be followed by an additional 165 people within the first week. Even the Public Relations Task Force wanted room for up to 50 officers and war correspondents, with over a dozen lifted on the first day. There were also administrators for the Commander, Berlin District who were needed almost immediately to take over German government ministries needed to keep the city functioning.

Yet at the end of January, First Allied Airborne Army operations division stated that IX Troop carrier command, which FAAA relied on for air lift, and the RAF's 38 and 46 Groups, which provided air lift to the British Forces, "...cannot mount a British division and an American division, nor can they mount two American divisions." All three of these groups "... can mount about 45% of two divisions." Furthermore a total of 22 airfields would need to be captured to support the airlift. The US Strategic Air Force was reluctant to release the other troop transport wing, the 302nd, because it was needed to maintain supply and transport for the rest of the Air Forces in Western Europe. It was also not trained for airborne operations. Furthermore, FAAA planners had assumed that the heavy bomber force could be diverted to flying supplies to the Airborne forces, but allied intelligence had determined that only one airfield in the greater Berlin area could handle the heavy four engine aircraft. [15]

1. Beginnings

SHAEF had originally envisioned two simultaneous airborne attacks, one against Berlin by the XVIII Airborne Corps and another against Kiel by the I British Airborne Corps. Each attack would have two commanders, a land commander and an air commander. The Kiel operation was designed to accomplish the 21st Army Groups ECLIPSE mission, to occupy Schleswig-Holstein and secure the German ports on the North Sea and on the Baltic. However some of the high command began having doubts, with the staff of Allied Commander Naval Expeditionary Forces (ACNXF) in early March questioning the justification for the Kiel operation citing the fact that 6 Airborne Division was already engaged in ground action and would have to be withdrawn, that operations were moving fast enough that a ground attack would probably be as quick as an airborne assault and that current air lift was needed to support the fast moving armies.[16]

Eisenhower, with the lingering memories of the disastrous airborne operation at Arnhem, also faced a divided command, a lack of airlift, and a changing political landscape. The Yalta conference in February confirmed the division of Germany into occupation zones. Berlin would be far in the Soviet Zone although the city itself would be divided up among the allied powers. By this time intelligence was indicating that the Wehrmacht's various high commands were evacuating Berlin, scattering to the north and the south of Germany. Thus any strategic necessity for the rapid capture of Berlin became moot. Uncertainty of the level of German resistance and the potential of American forces clashing with the Russians advancing in Berlin convinced Eisenhower to call the airborne operations off at the end of March. Despite adamant opposition to the decision by Churchill and some of Eisenhower's own generals such as Patton, this decision was the prudent one. A few weeks later the Red Army entered Berlin and suffered 100,000 casualties in a week of heavy fighting.

Despite the months of careful planning being negated, the sudden change in direction actually had a number of advantages for TICOM.

The German High Command's evacuation from Berlin, including their intelligence agencies, had scattered the targets far and wide; time was needed to pinpoint where they may have moved. In early April Allied intelligence had managed to trace the movement of the naval crypto agency to the radio station at Neumuenster, and the collective movement of the Army's GdNA and of OKW/*Chi* to the Army signal school at Halle.

Communications were a particular concern, given that all their activities would be classified Top Secret ULTRA, the ordinary communications channels of the army would not suffice. Under the ECLIPSE planning, the TICOM teams would have acquired a special signals team for each group. Limitations of available airlift, not to mention shortages of radio operators and code clerks with ULTRA clearance soon made the plan problematic. When the ECLIPSE plan was cancelled and TICOM realized that their teams would go in overland, it was decided that a single radio operator borrowed from the local Army Group SLU would suffice, with the TICOM officers acting as their own code clerks utilizing one-time pads, rather than bulky crypto machines.

Transportation was another issue, in the ECLIPSE plan the Airborne would have flown in by glider. This of course was limited, and the TICOM teams were expected to beg, borrow or steal local transport as needed. When the plan shifted into a land assault, BP was able to provide jeeps and 2.5 ton trucks, either ferried across the channel by LST, or borrowed from the ETOUSA motor pool.

1. Beginnings

TICOM quickly regrouped. Class 'B' targets, previously fixed objectives, now had to be treated as targets of opportunity, requiring a more flexible response. Their liaison with SHAEF and the Army Groups had to be expanded; intelligence staffs across the western front had to be briefed as to TICOM targets. Channels of communication had to be established from the field to TICOM, mainly through Bicher's office in Paris. Although the six main targets had moved geographically, the teams designated and briefed for them were still intact. They were now standing by, waiting for developments on the continent.

2. Spoils of War

After a bitter and hard fought winter, spring was finally drying out the northern German plains. General Montgomery's 21 Army Group crossed the Rhine on 21 March in a massive operation. This battle, combined with the other American crossings by First and Third Armies was the initiation of the final phase of the European war. When Operation Eclipse was called off by Eisenhower in April, 21 Army Group axis was redirected from Berlin northwest towards Lübeck, with the goal of cutting off and isolating Schleswig-Holstein and its port cities from the rest of Germany. These cities became the prime target of Number 30 Assault Unit, and TICOM would be along for the ride.

T-Force headquarters were near Montgomery's at Venlo, Netherlands, and in mid-April Commander A.M.S. Mackenzie, the OIC of TICOM Team 6, was sent there to brief Colonel Humphrey Quill, RM, commander of Number 30 Assault Unit on TICOM's mission and to arrange transportation and communications with 21 AG

Mackenzie, a veteran of BP who had served in Hut 4 in the Naval Section since June 1940, had been selected to lead the team formed under the "Eclipse" plan to capture the German Naval Intelligence Headquarters at Eberswalde and Lanke. Now that those organizations had evacuated Berlin, ULTRA confirmed that they would be located in the territories being attacked by 21 Army Group in Schleswig-Holstein.

30 AU (Originally No. 30 Commando) was the Admiralty's intelligence assault unit, and was, the brainchild of the Personal Assistant to the Director of Naval Intelligence, Commander Ian Fleming.[17] 30 AU, consisting of both RN personnel and Royal Marine commandos, had had a colorful and often controversial career in both the Mediterranean theater and during the battles

in France. Reorganized and refitted after the French campaign, and now headquartered close to the front, they formed a key part of 21 Army Group's T-Force.

Shortly after the landings in Normandy, SHAEF issued a directive to the Army groups to form special T-Forces to "identify, secure, guard and exploit valuable and special information, including documents, equipment and persons of value to the Allied armies." [18] Each Army Group appointed a T-Force commander; in the American armies this usually consisted of a small staff that coordinated local ground forces when an intelligence target was located. The British, perhaps inspired by the Admiralty's success with 30 AU, pulled two veteran infantry battalions out of the line, the 5th Battalion of the Kings Regiment, the 1st Oxs and Bucks, a handful of spare chemical warfare troops, some Special Air Service (SAS) troopers and of course 30 AU itself, and assigned them exclusively to T-Force duties. The Kings Regiment supported the 2nd British Army, the Oxs and Bucks supported the 1st Canadian Army, while 30 AU ranged widely in search of various naval targets.

Mackenzie had flown out to Venlo to brief Colonel Quill on TICOM's mission and to arrange transportation and communications with 21 AG. He was no sooner back in England when he was ordered to deploy his team, now consisting of Lieutenant John Nuelsen, USNR, his second in command, and four other junior naval officers, two British and two Americans back to Venlo.[19] Arriving on April 15 the TICOM advance party set up their communications in a local monastery, and awaited the arrival of a truck and a jeep shipped to Antwerp. For the next two weeks they settled in and awaited developments, scouting for possible targets.

2. Spoils of War

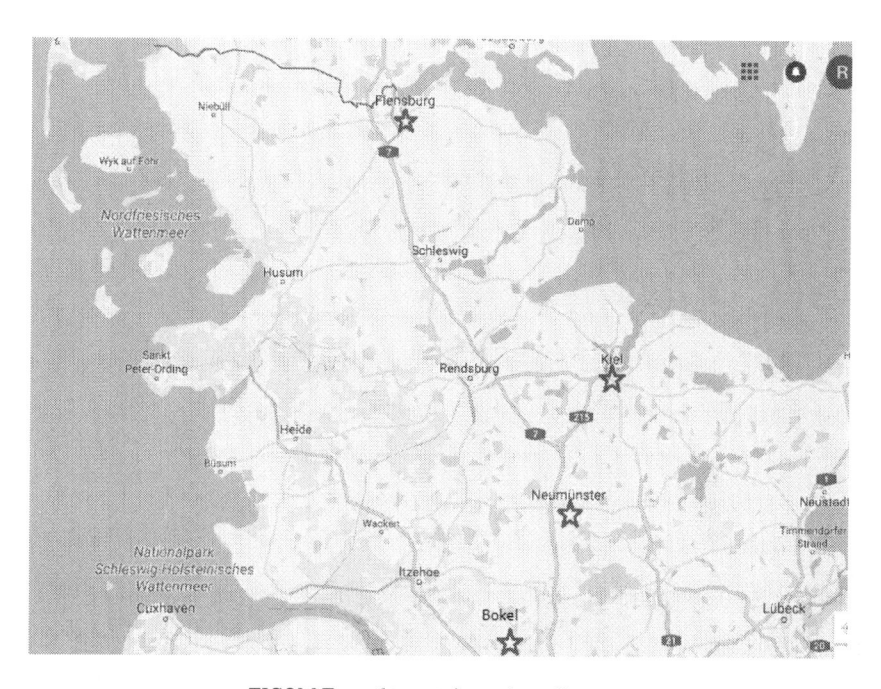

TICOM Team 6 targets in northern Germany

On the day Mackenzie and his TICOM detachment arrived in Venlo, a 30 AU team under Lieutenant Commander "Sancho" Glanville captured the Kreigsmarine's naval archive at Tambach Castle in central Germany. After spending 10 days following a convoluted route based upon some leads from a captured document, Glanville and his 8-man team came to roost at the Schloss, deep in Thuringia in the Third US Army's area. Approaching the 17th century castle at night, Glanville and his men peered into the ground floor windows and saw bookshelves stuffed with official documents. Glanville found an unlocked door and simply walked in with drawn pistol, and demanded the surrender of the small handful of guards. Among the bag of prisoners were three aging Rear Admirals, protectors of the Kriegmarine's historical archive, which consisted of a complete set of operational reports, ship's logs, war diaries, technical reports and administrative minutes dating back to 1870; in all almost five tons of materials. It was one of the greatest intelligence coups of the Second World War. The only resistance came from Fräulein Andröde, a member of the German women's naval auxiliary who attempted to set fire to the contents until rudely prevented by one of the Marines.[20]

By the end of April, the British had engaged in a hard fought battle for the port city of Bremen, with 30 AU's team 4 becoming the first British troops to enter the town and its team commander, Lieutenant Commander Job accepting the surrender from the acting Burgomaster, while also capturing a NARVIK class destroyer in the Harbor. Other British forces pushed across northern Germany to cross the Elbe and seal off the Jutland Peninsula at Lübeck. By May 3, British forces entered the shattered city of Hamburg which surrendered without a shot. During this period TICOM officers made unsuccessful trips to Gröningen and Sulingen in search of some reported targets, and were tipped off by GC&CS to be on the lookout for a new bigram table codenamed "Flusslauf" due to be issued to German forces on May 5th. The Kriegsmarine used frequently issued bigram tables to encode the indicator settings for the Naval Enigma, and without a capture, it would take BP weeks of effort to reconstruct the table through cryptanalysis. It would black out Naval ULTRA during the critical final weeks of the war.

Mackenzie began to move some of his people further forward to Osnabrück, where 30 AU had an advanced base. More intelligence was sent from Bletchley Park; the receiving station for the experimental "Kurier" burst communications that the Germans had been developing for U-Boat communications had been located at Bokel, near Neumünster, along with confirmation that the German Naval War staff (SKL) had moved to Flensburg.

2. Spoils of War

Now the final action of the war took place, the occupation of Kiel, and T-Force with 30 AU were in the van. With the fall of Hamburg, T-Force was able to consolidate its scattered forces and was order to prepare an assault on this strategically important port city. There was serious concern among the Allied high command that the Soviets would try to occupy the Jutland peninsula and Denmark either by land or by amphibious assault. On May 1 the local T-Force commander, Major Tony Hibbert was ordered to prevent this by occupying Kiel and its important targets as soon as possible. His scratch force consisted of two companies of infantry from the King's regiment, some engineers, elements of the SAS, and 30 AU, in all about 500 men. However, a ceasefire had been declared while the Germans were signing the surrender of their northern forces to Field Marshal Montgomery, and all allied units had been ordered to remain frozen in place. Hibbert needed permission from VIII Corps to move through the lines. At Corps headquarters, Hibbert was refused permission, despite his argument that his orders came from sources higher than the local Army commander. As the story goes, Hibbert spent the rest of the evening plying the duty officer with a bottle of scotch until the boozy, tired officer signed the permission chit.[21] This was good enough for Hibbert, and he order T-Force to advance the next morning.

At 0700 T-Force crossed the front line at Bad Segeberg, past bewildered German troops, who were uncertain what to do. The 60 mile trip north soon became a dash between competing elements of the force, with the jeeps of 30 AU, flying the white ensign of the Royal Navy, trying to pass the vehicles of the Kingsmen and the SAS. One of the participants, Harry Henshaw later recalled:

"We had a race into Kiel with the Marine Commandos – part of the way there; there was a very nasty accident. One of the jeeps – with the Marines or SAS in it – began to overtake us.

There was a burning 88mm gun, still blazing in the road – it had been shot up. So we had to move over but that left no room in the road. So they ran off the road and drove smack into a tree. Their four bodies were hanging over the side. But of course we couldn't stop. I suppose their own people looked after them but I think they were dead."[22]

The column soon passed Neumenünster the site of a major naval radio station. This powerful station had been a key international radio link for the Kriegsmarine since before the First World War, and had housed both an intercept and decryption station for German Naval Intelligence. Recently reported as the location of the B-Dienst, it was one of TICOM's prime targets. The next day, the 6th of May, Colonel Quill drove up from Lübeck accompanied by TICOM officer Lieutenant Nuelsen. The site was now manned with a small German skeleton staff under a junior naval officer. A quick inspection showed 4/SKL III had evacuated the site the day before the cease fire, leaving behind a few documents and considerable amount of equipment. Nuelsen ordered that the site frozen, the German officer to be held responsible for security, and that the quarters be prepared to act as the temporary HQ for the TICOM forward party.

Meanwhile, the main body of T-Force made their way into Kiel. Crossing into the outskirts of the heavily bombed city in a morning drizzle, the small T-Force were outnumbered in a city of 40,000 German civilians and a garrison consisting of some 12,000 fully armed Germans, one cruiser in dry dock and one upside down in the harbour, and a number of U-boats and smaller craft, uncertain if they had all gotten the word of the surrender. Tony Hibbert and his driver drove along the edge of the Kiel Fjord to the Naval Academy, where he presented himself to the headquarters. The German naval commander had not received official word of the surrender; Hibbert prevailed upon him to put a call through to Admiral Dönitz in Flensburg.

2. Spoils of War

With the news confirmed, the Germans allowed the British forces to secure the port and city. Meanwhile, Commander Dunstan Curtis, in charge of the 30 AU component of T-Force, led his men to the H. Walter KG company's industrial works and occupied it. In the process of seizing the company headquarters, they captured Dr. Hellmuth Walter himself. Walter was one of Germany's leading industrialists, inventor of hydrogen peroxide engines used in both the V-2 rocket and in the Kriegsmarine's Type XXVI state of the art U-boats, which were currently under construction in the yards.

The next day, Curtis took a party of three dozen of his men to Friedrichsort, a suburb of Kiel, to seize a lighthouse and a radio station, which contained a complete set of charts of the Western Baltic minefields. They finished the day's work by driving another 20 miles northwest to capture the Kreigsmarine Torpedo Experiment/Trials Institute at Eckernförde.

2

At 0141 the next morning, in Reims, France, at the headquarters of General Eisenhower, Dönitz's representatives, General Jodl and Admiral Freideburg, signed the unconditional surrender of the German nation. Operations were set to end at 2301 on 8May. Jodl had brought a large staff with him to the negotiations, including a number of senior signals officers, who were immediately detained for interrogation by SHAEF intelligence.

Later that morning Lieutenant Nuelsen returned to Neumünster Y station with half of 30 AU's 'A' troop, of Royal Marines to begin the process of securing the site and converting it to TICOM's advance headquarters. Quill and Neulsen made a quick trip to the naval hospital in Plön, where SKL had spent a few days. Finding some miscellaneous documents, they ordered the site sealed, and after dropping Nuelsen back at Neumünster, Quill made his first trip into Kiel. The entire target area was still unoccupied by Allied troops. That day another 30 AU team in Bremerhaven captured a German destroyer in the port, the Z 29, with all its confidential materials. The next day, V-E Day, found Team 6 was scattered across northern Germany. With the impending surrender, the TICOM committee realized that there would be a number of additional German Army signal sites and personnel available for exploitation, so they decided to reinforce Team 6 with a number of military SIGINT experts, who were currently en-route, and would show up later that day.

Mackenzie was in Menden with awaiting the arrival of the captured documents from Bremerhaven. "It was found to contain absolutely everything except 'Flusslauf', Mackenzie later reported, "the reason for the absence of the current bigram tables being that Z 29 (the captured destroyer) was refitting and was not due to be ready for sea for a matter of three weeks." It was a bitter disappointment. However, Neulsen in Neumünster had a more successful day, settling in to begin the onsite exploitation, joined by Lieutenant Commander Griffiths, who had been sent out from BP to augment Team 6 and Ensign Phillips, accompanied by Major Evans. Evans was the 30 AU officer charged with the responsibility to escort and protect TICOM. That morning, Griffiths, Phillips and Evans drove 15 miles north to the village of Bokel to find the "Kurier" receiving station where they found the station manned by a German naval officer, and two NCOs, specialists in Kurier operations, still there. That afternoon, two officers belonging to the B-Dienst showed up at the station, unaware that it was in Allied hands. They were carrying a written order from OKM authorizing them to dismantle and bring back to Flensburg the wireless intercept recorders that were the heart of the system. Immediately

2. Spoils of War

surrounded by the Royal Marines they were informed of their new status as POWs, and were quickly removed to Kiel and put into the custody of 30 AU at the Waltherwerke.

The "Kurier" was a revolutionary burst communications system developed by the Germans in an attempt to evade Allied direction finders. Growing allied success in D/F had become a serious concern for the Kreigsmarine by the mid-point of the war. Their first response was to emphasize the use of short signals (*Kurzsignal*) by U-Boats to communicate tactical information such as course, enemy reports, position grids or weather reports. Based upon extensive codebooks, which contained tables that converted complete reports into a four-letter group, each Kurzsignal had a strict format to communicate the message. These four letter groups were further encrypted using the Enigma machine prior to transmission, which limited broadcasts to less than a minute.

In the spring of 1943, Dr. Berndt of the Telefunken firm proposed a method to further compress these signals to what would now be referred to as burst encoding, as a further counter measure against Direction Finding. The first trials of the system, codenamed "Kurier" were prototyped in the summer of 1943. After another year of development, the first sea trials conducted in the summer of 1944, failed due to the levels of humidity and temperature in the U-Boat's radio room. This problem was overcome by fitting a synchronous electric motor to the device to precisely time the revolutions of the "Geber", the KGZ 44/2 pulse generator. The Geber was an aluminum disk 25 centimeters wide with a series of 85 small adjustable iron bars around the perimeter that could be set to create a pulse when the disk rotated over a magnetic head. Each pulse was 1 millisecond long and there was a 3 milliseconds gap between each pulse. One bar pushed in represented a dot, two bars pushed in adjacent to each other represented a dash, and an unset bar represented a pause between pulses. The Geber could be programmed to send a three letter group (the indicator) followed by a four letter group, (the Kurzsignal) within 460 milliseconds. This was a serious threat to Allied Naval intelligence, as no Kurier signals were ever successfully located through direction finding. However, a captured copy of the German "U-Boat Communication's Regulations, 1942" mentioned the phase "Short Signal Procedure Kurier", alerting Allied intelligence to be on the lookout for further evidence. Additional information, from ULTRA, led to an intelligence assessment that a radical new system for U-Boat communications was under development. By November, it was known that the Germans were testing the system in the Baltic, and after an intense effort, the British first intercepted the signals in December. TICOM's capture of the station at Bokel on May 8 was just in time, blocking the destruction or removal of the equipment by a few hours.

The receiving station was equipped with three Phillips CR 101 receivers, each with its own antenna and all tuned to the same offset U-Boat frequency according to a complex broadcast schedule. The incoming signals, converted into pulses on a CRT were then photographed onto film, to be decoded upon development. The system, given a top priority, was still in development when the war caught up to it. The original receiving station at Bornau, in Eastern Germany, was forced to relocate when the Russians approached in the spring of 1945. Evacuated to Bokel, it went operational on April 27th, 1945. Only a few days later, on 2 May, OKM ordered its destruction, which was accomplished with sledgehammers and with the resulting pieces buried. This was the only complete receiving apparatus but manufacturing had begun and parts were probably still in the Berlin area. The other half of the system, the Geber sending unit was captured from a Type XXI U-Boat at Bergen, Norway in June.[23]

2. Spoils of War

3

On Wednesday, 9 May, Mackenzie having picked up his newly arrived military officers moved the Team 6 rear party to Minden. Neulsen with his advance party went to Kiel to report to Colonel Quill. Quill, anxious to find out what happened to OKM decided to take a scouting party to Flensburg. Taking a Humber scout car, and accompanied by some of his officers and the TICOM members Nuelsen and Griffiths, he drove the 60 miles north.[24]

In the final days before the surrender, Flensburg had become the final refuge of Admiral Dönitz and what remained of the German government. One day after the surrender, the situation was still tense with refugees, recently freed forced laborers and thousands of still armed German troops in the region. Entering the city by mid-day they sought out the mayor, who put them in contact with the local Kriegsmarine commander and Dönitz's chief of staff.[25] They took the party to the OKM headquarters, now located at the Naval Academy near Glücksburg. Lieutenant Nuelsen requested a written outline of the German's signals organization and a roster of its key personnel, only to be told that this data had already been turned over to the SHAEF interrogators in Rimes. Nuelsen then thought of asking OKM to issue a directive to all their officers that all information was to be made available to the Allied representatives. With night rapidly approaching, Quill's party was sent by the Germans to the Hamburg-Amerika liner "Patria" moored in the harbor, now serving as a barracks ship for Dönitz and his staff. They were well fed and politely entertained. Next morning Quill took his party on a brief "goodwill" tour across the Danish border before returning to Kiel. They had been the first allied troops to enter this final capital of the Third Reich.

The following week Mackenzie stayed behind in at the Minden H.Q. to meet with representatives from the 12th Army Group to inform them of TICOM operations in their area and to warn them about Team 6's "pirate" SCU transmitter. Three of the recently arrived TICOM army officers, Morrison, Laptook and Kirby, were sent up to Neumünster to help with the exploitation of that station. The team had found both a T-52a and a T-52e, German encrypted teletype machines codenamed 'Sturgeon', four tape recording machines and associated equipment. Over the next few weeks another 47 Enigma machines, two Hagelins, a Hellschreiber fax device, a T-52d and two more T-52es's along with an SG 41 cipher machine from the Abwehr were brought in and held.[26]

On the weekend, Lieutenant Neulsen went down to Minden to meet with Mackenzie and it was decided that he should go back to GC&CS to personally brief the TICOM committee. The next morning the Team's Humber scout car was cleaned out, having been loaded down with miscellaneous documents and manuals from a German mine laying base and Neulsen left for Venlo. As Mackenzie later reported "During the afternoon this material was examined, mainly out of curiosity; and, to the very great surprise of the whole party, the first handbook that came out was "Flusslauf"." The material was immediately photocopied, and Mackenzie and an aid drove 5 ½ hours through the night to catch Neulsen at the airfield to courier the bigram tables back to BP. After spending the night, Mackenzie returned to moved the rear HQ forward to Neumünster, where for the first time the whole of team 6 was together.

Now that Neumünster, Bokel, and "Flusslauf" were secured, Mackenzie turned his attention to his primary target, the B-Dienst in Flensburg.

4

At this point the team was forbidden, for security reasons, to directly interrogate Germans about their cryptologic activities, rather their primary purpose was to identify personnel and their

2. Spoils of War

locations. Furthermore, in tracing 4 SKL's journey from Eberswalde, through Aurich and Neumünster, then to Flensburg, Mackenzie suspected that they may have buried documents in dumps rather than destroy everything. With the Allied Control Commission not yet fully in charge, there was always the danger that the members of these intelligence agencies would simply drift away towards home. Summing up the situation, Mackenzie later reported that he

> "…decided that as soon as we could get any idea of the exact whereabouts of 4/SKL, we would try to get in touch with them on our own. I decided that for the time being we would keep the Team at Neumünster and operate from there, even though it was a good two hours' run from Flensburg. The reason for this was that the half troop of Marines under Major Evans could best be accommodated there and they afforded a valuable protection for the equipment that we were collecting to send back to GCHQ[†]
>
> Also Neumünster was near to Bokel. The fact that we had discovered the Bokel target, which was obviously of immense value to DSD, left us in a position where we had to nurse it till some officer of the Signals Division could be found to take it over."[27]

[†] Government Communications Headquarters, at this point it was a cover name for GC&CS in Bletchley Park, but after the war it became its official name.

The next day Mackenzie took Evans, Griffiths and Horsfield with him to Kiel to meet with the staff of the newly arrived Allied Flag-Officer-in-Charge. There he ran into Commander Frank Beasley, RN, a former member of Bletchley Park, now serving as the staff intelligence officer. Later, at 30 AU headquarters at the Waltherwerke, he was introduced to Lieutenant Connell, RNVR, of the Field Interrogation Unit, who also expressed an interest in getting to Flensburg as soon as possible. The two men agreed to meet on the 18th and go up together. However, upon Mackenzie's return the next day he found that Connell had already left. Taking Captain Horsfield with him, they drove to Flensburg arriving around lunchtime, and proceeded to the Naval Training Academy where they knew OKM had relocated. Finding a building that had both a British and a German sentry guarding the door, they went in and immediately ran into Connell, who had just learned that the all of 4 SKL (Naval Communications) was located at the nearby Signal School.

At the school, the party introduced themselves to the 4 SKL commander, Konteradmiral (Rear Admiral) Krauss. With Connell acting as translator, they explained their general requirements for information, and Krauss immediately agreed to cooperate. He described the main divisions of his organization, 4 SKL/II was the intercept service (what the British called the 'Y' service) under Captain Lucan, with 4 SKL/III as the cryptanalytic section (known by its pre-war name as the B-Dienst) under Captain Kupfer. Mackenzie explained that their main business was with Captain Kupfer but that they would also be interested in talking with Captain Lucan about his 'Y' service. A further meeting was arranged with the two officers for Saturday.

"This meeting with Admiral Krauss was of the greatest importance for the future success of the operation. While walking along the corridor, Lieutenant Connell asked me how we intended to take these interviews. I felt myself that the only thing to do was to

2. Spoils of War

follow the lead of Admiral Krauss, that is to say, if he proved amenable we would be pleasant and helpful, if he proved obstructive, we would be just as unpleasant as he was. As it turned out, he was rather scared and very polite, and so were we, and from this original meeting the whole tone of the future relationship between TICOM Team 6 and 4 SKL/ III was set." Mackenzie later recounted.[28]

Mackenzie returned to Neumünster to see how Griffiths was getting along with the plans to fly the Bokel prisoners back to the U.K. However, a signal arrived that night from TICOM announcing a change in policy. Due to the surrender, the interrogation centers in London were overflowing. Authorization to interrogate prisoners in the field was impending. Luckily, a signals officer from the Admiralty had shown up that day while investigating the area and, informed of the Bokel discovery, he was able to conduct a full three-hour debriefing of the prisoners.

While the rest of the TICOM team was finishing up the sorting and packing of the captured equipment at Neumünster, Mackenzie along with Major Evans, and Captain Horsfield returned to Flensburg for the second meeting with 4 SKL. The TICOM military representatives Major Morrison and Lieutenant Kirby followed to begin scouting out any OKW/*Chi* members in the area. The meeting proved productive, the team met Captains Lucan and Kupfer, who were asked to prepare diagrams of their organizations. Lucan was described as "politely difficult, while Captain Kupfer appeared very willing to cooperate".[29] A plan for preliminary interrogations was worked out, and the admiral agreed for a couple of rooms to be set aside in the Hansa building for TICOM's use. Agreeing to give the two Captains time to draw their organizational charts, Mackenzie scheduled a follow up meeting for the 21st. Colonel Quill had just returned from the U.K. that day and called a team meeting the next day in Kiel. At the meeting Quill announced that he had been discussing with the Admiralty plans to wrap up 30 AU's activities and return the unit to the U.K. for demobilization. He recommended that TICOM finish up in Neumünster as soon as possible, and then move its HQ to Eckernförde, where 30 AU had its advanced headquarters. Since Eckernförde was only an hour from Flensburg and it would make the commute much easier, Mackenzie readily agreed.

On the Monday, joined by the recently returned Lieutenant Nuelsen, the party went back to Flensburg to inspect the charts prepared for them by the Captains. Mackenzie decided that the information was important enough for the charts to be immediately photographed and flown back to BP. Based upon the charts, individuals were identified for detailed interrogations and plans laid to locate any missing bodies. They decided to begin the detailed interrogations on the morning of the 23rd, in two days time. Everyone was back in Neumünster that night to finish loading the trucks and closing out operations the next day.

Mackenzie decided that he and Nuelsen should return to Flensburg and spend the night on the accommodation ship the "Caribia" in order to be fresh for the morning interrogations. However, that evening they were informed that all personnel were confined to the ship until further notice, the scuttlebutt being that Admiral Dönitz was scheduled to arrive for a meeting on board the "Patria" the next morning with the Allied Control Commission. Dönitz and his staff arrived at 10:00 am; all other personnel were held incognito on board the ships until about 11:30, when they were released. Now late for their critical meeting, Mackenzie and Nuelsen, with Connell as their translator set off for the Signal School only to find Flensburg in an uproar. When Dönitz showed up that morning for his meeting, the Allied authorities had arrested him and his government was dissolved. Meanwhile, British troops had moved into occupy the city and they were busy rounding up all German troops and civilian officials and putting them into holding

2. Spoils of War

pens. Alarmed, Mackenzie rushed across town to find out what had happened to his charges. This could be disastrous for TICOM, for not only damaging to the prisoner's morale and endangering the cooperative relationship TICOM had been trying to build, there was also the very real danger that the unit could be broken up and its personnel sucked up into the bureaucracy and lost in the system. At the gate to the signal school, a British corporal who mistook them for German naval officers returning to work challenged them. It took some forceful English to persuade him otherwise and he directed the party up the street to Brigade headquarters. There the Brigadier told him that they had no idea where 4 SKL would be, but if Kupfer or any of his men were on the official black lists, they surely would be sent to the PW concentration camp at Lüneburg. Facing that dead end, Mackenzie next went to the office of the FOIC (The British Flag Officer in Charge) and got the naval adviser to the Allied Control Commission to agree to order the release of the 4 SKL personnel if they could be found. Connell was sent in a car with a loudspeaker to trawl the crowds calling for Captain Kupfer. By this method, they managed to round up most of the Signal School personnel and concentrate them in a football field by 1:00 pm. They sat there throughout the afternoon without rations, waiting for released. Mackenzie found Kupfer and reassured him that everything would be all right, arranging to begin the interrogations again the next day back in the Signal School.

The next day Nuelsen, got there early and spent an hour having a quite talk with Kupfer, calming the situation and getting everyone back on track. When Mackenzie and Connell showed up they were taken down to the room reserved for them, and the formal interrogations finally began. At last, Allied intelligence was to get a firsthand description of what was Germany's most deadly SIGINT effort. The plan for the interrogation team was to "act dumb", pretend that they knew little of the Signals Intelligence business and draw the Germans out. This first interrogation was critical because the B-Dienst Chief Cryptanalyst Oberregierungsrat (Senior Specialist) Wilhelm Tranow, was the star of the interrogation. In addition Amtsrat (Senior Administrative Officer) Wilhelm Schwabe, an expert on Russian Naval ciphers, was included. Captain Kupfer even provided two shorthand stenographers for the transcription. The interrogation went well:

> "We started the ball rolling by asking Ob.Reg.Rat Tranow to give us an outline of the building up and working of his party. He started on a long historical description and, after a little prompting to begin with; he soon got into his stride and merely needed steering in the right direction. The stenographer took it all down, and we only had to sit back and listen. When Tranow had finished, the others all spoke in turn, giving detailed accounts of what they had done and answering all questions quite frankly, even going out of their way to explain points which they thought would not be clear to us in our "non-expert" capacity. Several times during the interrogation we enquired after dumps of material that might have been made at any point in the moves from Eberswalde to Aurich, to Neumünster, to Flensburg, but they all stated definitely that but for the original archive dump in Berlin, of which Captain Kupfer gave us the address, everything except Hollerith machinery had been destroyed."[30]

Congratulating themselves for a fine start, Mackenzie, Nuelsen and Connell retired for the night.

However, before the next day's interrogations could start, Captain Kupfer asked to have a private word with Mackenzie. Sensing something was up; Mackenzie was worried that he might have suffered a change of heart. Kupfer sheepishly admitted that he had lied the day before; they had after all buried some documentary materials while on the road. Two dumps in fact, one near

2. Spoils of War

Neumünster and another on the Elbe near Torgau in the Russian zone. He provided Mackenzie with the address and names of local contacts for the dumps. The day was spent with Kupfer explaining the workings of the intelligence side of his operations, and Captain Lucan with three of his 4 SKL/II officers briefed the TICOM team on the "Y service side of their organization.

5

Germany's Naval SIGINT service was founded almost by accident during the First World War. German Army radiomen, finding themselves with little to do after the belligerent armies dug into static trench warfare, began searching for any signals that were detectable. They discovered that they were able to monitor Royal Navy traffic from the Dover Patrol, most of it in the clear. This information was passed to the Naval Staff in Berlin, who realized that a system of dedicated monitoring stations in Belgium and France could be used for intelligence purposes. An "Observation Service" (*Beobachtungsdienst* or B-Dienst) was created to exploit this opportunity. As the practice of enciphering messages became more common, the B-Dienst also developed skills in cryptanalysis. The service proved its value to the Naval Staff during the war by tracking British cruiser squadrons, convoy sailings, and assisting in the breakthrough of German raiders.

The end of the war and the impounding and later scuttling of the fleet almost ended the German Navy. Cutbacks eliminated the B-Dienst, but by the end of 1919, the admirals realized that an effective intelligence organization was as necessary in peacetime as it was in war. The service, reestablished under its former commander Kapitänleutnant (Lieutenant Commander) Martin Braune, had only six civil service employees. However, one of them was Wilhelm Tranow, former naval radioman and veteran of the wartime B-Dienst, who had originally demonstrated his talent by breaking a top-secret coded message sent to his own ship when his officers had trouble decrypting it.

A lack of budget, frequent rotation of its naval officer commanders, and lack of support by the higher-level naval staff meant that the B-Dienst struggled to survive the lean years of the 1920s. As a cost cutting measure, in 1928 the service moved to Kiel where it was headquartered with the Inspector of Torpedoes and Mines, further limiting its influence. The tide turned in 1934, when a reorganization of the naval high command brought the B-Dienst back to Berlin as one of the three elements of the Office of Communications and Intelligence. The appointment of an energetic new chief, Kapitänleutnant Heinz Bonatz, resulted in the addition of additional men and listening posts to the service and enabled the B-Dienst to put teams aboard ships.

During the 1930s the Navy developed two chains of costal radio stations, a North Sea chain anchored at Borkum in the west, which then ran to Nordholz, near Cuxhaven in the center and terminating at List in the west. The Baltic chain started at Falshöf near Flensburg on the Danish border, ran through the naval base at Kiel and along the Baltic coast to Pillau, in the then far eastern end of Prussia. Wilhemshaven acted as control center for these chains. Each station was equipped with state of the art receivers, transmitters and direction finders, all interconnected with landline telephone and teletype lines. By the start of the war, the Kriegsmarine had a modern and efficient radio intelligence interception system, one that eventually proved critical in the coming naval war.

Wilhelm Tranow kept busy during the 1930s. Now appointed head of the English language cryptanalysis section he led the attack on the codes and ciphers of the Royal Navy, solving their 5-digit Naval code in 1935 by comparing the encoded messages with merchant ship movements reported in Lloyd's Weekly Shipping Report. Historian David Kahn later wrote "...(this) success, and the attacks in 1937 on four other English, five French, four Russian and three Danish cryptosystems enlarged the B-Dienst. The 30 men in its Berlin Central in 1936

2. Spoils of War

became 90 by the summer of 1939.' Monitoring foreign naval exercises and experience in the Spanish Civil War further added to the reputation of the B-Dienst.

Mobilization at the start of the war expanded the service. For the first time academics and businessmen with language skills were recruited as reserve officers, and a six week training course was established. Within a few years, the B-Dienst had expanded to over 6,000 staff. A reorganization of the Naval Staff at the beginning of the war, followed by a further reorganization with the appointment of Dönitz as Grand Admiral, resulted in the B-Dienst becoming the third division of the fourth branch of the Maritime Warfare Command, the *Seekriegsleitung* (i.e. 4 SKL/III, the name referred to by TICOM).

Heinz Bonatz was superseded in January 1944 by Kapitän zur See Max Kupfer, who remained in command until his capture by TICOM at the end of the war. Tranow was critical to the agency's success, his solving of the Broadcast to Allied Merchant Ship Code (BAMS) enabled the B-Dienst to track and predict Allied convey movements, which allowed Dönitz to direct his murderous U-Boat wolf packs into them. In terms of results, this was the Germany's most effective use of SIGINT in the war. Tranow was described by Davis Kahn as:

"A man so bursting with energy that he sometimes seemed to skip instead of walk, he was a middle-level civilian official for the Navy. He had been doing the same work since WWI, steadily advancing in grade. He was one of those rarities in bureaucracies: a man who both performed the technical of his job in exemplary fashion and administered the men under him effectively. He was tall and erect, with firm features and a compelling way of thinking. But the most impressive thing about him was his memory, his brain." [31]

The B-Dienst in the pre-war period had an inherent advantage over its land bound colleagues. Foreign army units, with the exception of annual field exercises, generated little radio traffic. Foreign Navies, and the Merchant Marines they protected, generated a vast amount of radio traffic during their normal operations. By 1937, the naval intercept service was providing 700 messages a day. This provided the B-Dienst a large amount of material to study. Among Tranow's accomplishments in the late '30s was the reconstruction of the Royal Navy Administrative Code., a five-figure code reciphered on a subtractor table. This code transmitted routine information relating to personnel and technical transactions; it allowed the B-Dienst to track the readiness of the Royal Navy's heavy units. Although the British changed their systems in the first month of the war, Tarnow's group was able to reconstruct the Admin Code in about 8 days and read the bulk of the traffic sent in this code.

Tranow now described to his interrogators the seesaw back and forth battle between British code makers and German code breakers that, in many ways, paralleled the Battle of the Atlantic itself.

The British Merchant Navy Code introduced in January 1940, was cracked within three months aided by the capture of the codebook at Bergen during the Norwegian campaign. This code, which stayed in effect until April 1942, allowed the Germans the ability to read a majority of the messages sent to Atlantic convoys. It was superseded by the Merchant Ships (BAMS) Code, which at times was broken by the B-Dienst on a depth of two with the aid of another captured codebook. By this time, due to their skill in deciphering British subtraction systems, they could read the system currently. This was the most deadly of Tarnow's accomplishments, it allowed the U-Boat command to identify, track, and read the instructions of allied convoys to deadly effect. Some 72,200 Allied naval and merchant seamen lost their lives, in no small account due to the efforts of the B-Dienst.

2. Spoils of War

The four-figure Naval Code #1, called MUNICH by the Germans, was the Royal Navy's most commonly used code. Introduced on 20 August 1940 for confidential level messages and intended to replace the old Administrative code, it was based upon a new book. It was almost identical in design to Naval Cypher #1, which made the traffic difficult for the Germans to distinguish from Naval Cypher. This was superseded by Naval Code #2, brought into force in January 1942. A copy of this book captured at Tobruk, aided the Germans in reading the code through 1942, but in March 1943, the British introduced Code #3 and, in addition, started to use a stencil subtractor with it in December of that year. The B-Dienst put an immense effort to analyze the stencil system, at one point employed 250 people on the problem. By early 1944, they were able to read some back traffic on an older version of the book, but could never read traffic currently.

The most important British system as far as the B-Dienst was concerned was the Naval Cypher, an officers only code used to transmit secret and above level messages. Early success against the Administrative Code freed up personnel to attack the new tables for the Naval Cypher, and they were able to read parts of it by October 1939. This system was a four-digit superenciphered code, which used a variety of encipherment tables for different geographic areas. Tranow's section, concentrating on the North Sea and Atlantic area, were able to break the indicators, and by January 1940 they were reading 40-50% of the traffic, which was used to great advantage a few months later during the Norway operations. In August, the British changed all their systems to four figure codes, making the sorting and identification of British traffic more difficult, however, after six weeks effort Tranow and his section were able to read it again. The British threw in another difficulty a year later when they started enciphering their indicators (which gave the page and line references to the reciphering tables), forcing the Germans to work out a secondary encipherment system to break into the primary system. This slowed down the Germans for four weeks until they figured out the new indicators, although they had to double the staff working on this problem. In October of 1941, a new code book the Naval Cypher #3, a joint Anglo-American system used by the convoy escorts and shore stations, was introduced. However, the British reintroduced an old five-figure indicator system for use with this code, which gave the B-Dienst a break into the system and by mid-1942, they could read 80% of the traffic, including the Admiralty's daily U-Boat summary. The security of Naval Cypher #3 had been increased by more frequent changes to the reciphering tables, and this put increased stress on the manpower needs of Tranow's section. However, #3 continued to be used until June 1943, giving the Germans an advantage during the big convoy battles of that spring.[32]

However, hints through ULTRA and security studies of the convoy attacks tipped the Allies off about the Germans success against their long subtraction ciphers. A new Naval Cypher #5, introduced in June, used a stencil-subtractor frame system for encipherment developed by John Tiltman at GC&CS. This system changed the key for the stencil daily, and although the B-Dienst attacked it vigorously with the aid of Hollerith machines, and was able, in theory to reconstruct its basic principles, but in fact, they were never able to read it, and they ceased all work on it in January 1945. In addition, increased use of one-time pads and adoption of the Combined Cipher machine for inner-allied use dried up this source of intelligence for the Kriegsmarine.

The continuing manpower crisis in Germany, due to declining military success, sapped the B-Dienst as personnel were transferred to combat units. The heavy bombing of Berlin in November 1943, which damaged or destroyed so many of Germany's military and government agencies, also destroyed most of the B-Dienst's records and forced them to move to Eberswalde,

2. Spoils of War

a small village some 25 miles northeast of Berlin. Again forced to move by the Russian advance in the spring of 1945, they went first to Aurich, in northern Germany, then onto the naval radio station at Neumünster, quickly followed by a final move to the Signal School at Flensburg, where TICOM caught up with them. In his interrogations by the allies, Admiral Dönitz credited the B-Dienst with contributing half the operational intelligence that the Kriegsmarine used in fighting the war. It was a record unmatched by any other German intelligence agency.

6

From the time of the German collapse to these first interrogations, Kupfer had kept his men busy monitoring the international news broadcasts and producing a daily news summary for the benefit of senior members of OKM. Mackenzie saw the value in keeping the 4 SKL/III people occupied, and it would give him an excuse to keep the unit together and out of the influence of other, more hard core prisoners. Mackenzie suggested an expansion of this effort by publishing an English language version for use by the Control Commission, which had the advantage of keeping the translators and cryptanalysts busy. "Almost immediately, Captain Kupfer, who is a keen propagandist, began to expand this idea to cover a news service to the main German Naval bases, and started to write a paper on the value of a news service as a deterrent to rumor and subversive influences."[33] This idea was sold to the Control Commission, who probably saw the advantages of controlling the flow of information to their former enemies, and the news service became official.

One disadvantage of keeping 4 OKW/III at the Signal School was that word soon got through to the other allied intelligence agencies who began demanding access to the prisoners. "We had observed that many of the senior German Naval officers, when contacted by people who were either interrogating them on subjects not their own, or interrogating them on their own subjects but with an imperfect background, were badly affected and tended to resent interrogation in any form." Mackenzie viewed this as not only an annoyance, but also as a security risk. He returned to the Control Commission and got them to promise to leave the B-Dienst alone, and to steer any curious spectators away. During this period, there was a series of cross communications with TICOM back at BP, which complicated the situation. At Rimes, Lieutenant Colonel Jack Brown, a GC&CS liaison officer to SHAEF met a Lieutenant Morgenroth of the Kriegsmarine who had worked at 4 SKL/III, but was now serving as an interpreter. Morgenroth gave Brown a short list, from memory, of people he had known at the B-Dienst. This list made it back to BP, and became the basis for TICOM's Brown list of wanted personnel. However, it was badly flawed, and Mackenzie, knowing that his own organizational charts and names gathered in their first interrogations had been sent back, assumed that BP knew this. However, this data was misfiled and had not been translated or processed. This was to cause further problems a few days later.

On 29 May, the team was informed by TICOM that no further prisoners could be flown to the U.K., instead Jack Brown was seeing if it would be possible to transfer the prisoners as a group to 21 Army Group PW camp at Lüneberg. However, he was informed that it would take up to three weeks to make room and arrange transport. In addition, Morgenroth's list was still creating difficulties and Group Captain Winterbotham had ordered six officers on the list to the U.K. One of them was Kupfer, and Mackenzie feared his absence would negatively affect the rest of the Flensburg group. Another foul up occurred when an army officer sent by CSDIC[3] at 12 AG to the *Patria* to collect the six prisoners failed to contact Lieutenant Kirby, who was on the ship at that time. Instead, this officer was intercepted by representatives of the Control

---
[3] Combined Services Detailed Interrogation Center

2. Spoils of War

Commission, who sent him packing. Complicating the situation, the signal TICOM sent to Team 6 demanding an explanation was mangled in the decoding. It took two days to sort out the confusion, assisted by Nuelsen, who was back at GC&CS on yet another liaison trip. By then TICOM signaled that they had decided to abandon the old policy forbidding in-depth field interrogations and that soon a special interrogation team under Commander Dudley Smith would be sent out from BP.

Over the next week or so Mackenzie kept the B-Dienst personnel busy with the news service. The Control Commission decided to close down the signal school by Tuesday 12 June, but that 4 SKL/III would be kept together and moved to the OKM buildings at Schloss Glücksburg for the field interrogations. Captain Lucan's intercept service 4 SKL/II was to be dissolved and Mackenzie provided the names of eight officers from the group recommended to be retained for further questioning.

7

Now that the in-depth interrogations were to begin, Mackenzie decided that events had advanced to the point that he could return to the U.K., leaving recently returned Nuelsen in charge of the team. He paid a final visit to the Allied Control Commission, and successfully argued that 4 SKL/III should either be kept intact and not mixed into the regular PW population, or be released. It was imperative that the Kreigsmarine cryptologists continued to be available until every last drop of intelligence was drained from them. The group was kept in Flensburg for a few more weeks until most of them were transferred to DUSTBIN, the recently established interrogation center at Kransberg Castle, 25 miles north of Frankfurt. On the 9th June Mackenzie made his goodbyes and he flew back and reported in to TICOM at BP. Lieutenant Nuelsen, made sure the final materials and gear were packed, ready for shipment home, then moved the remaining members of the team up from Eckernförde to Flensburg, setting up shop onboard the *Patria*. The BP Interrogation team finally arrived on Tuesday 15 June.

Lieutenant Commander Russell Dudley-Smith headed the mission. He was also an old-timer, serving at BP since 1940 in Hut 8, had been the Personal Assistant to GC&CS Director Commander Travis for two years and was currently the Head of Security of Allied Ciphers section. Accompanying him as members of the interrogation team were such BP notables as Major John N. Seaman, US Army Security Agency liaison officer to GC&CS, Dr. R.C. Prichard, linguist in the Military Section, and Major G.W. Morgan, head of the Bletchley Park Research Section.[34]

Over the next three weeks, the interrogation team, with the help of Team 6, questioned 35 members of the B-Dienst, ranking from Admiral Krauss, the Director of Naval Communications, to Funkmeister (Radioman) Luft, who worked on Merchant Marine codes. Building on the information already provided by Tranow, a number of experts were interrogated at length about their specialties.

Lieutenant Frowein, Specialist on analysis of German ciphers, was interrogated at length on one of TICOM's most intriguing questions: Did the Germans suspect that the Engima had been compromised, and if so, why didn't they do anything about it? Hans-Joachim Frowein, a cryptanalyst, was detailed to 4 SKL/II in mid 1944 for six months to study the security of the German Naval Enigma. Dönitz, after suffering the heavy U-Boat losses of 1943–44, suspected something was amiss and ordered this enquiry. Frowein started with a small staff of two officers and ten men, which was constantly whittled down in size due to personnel demands during this period,

2. Spoils of War

"My particular task was to discover whether the inner setting (wheel order) and stecker could be recovered from a crib of 25 letters. I started with no knowledge of the Enigma machine, and I was able to show that this was possible." he told TICOM. Studying the wheel turnovers, frequency counts of the cipher text and calculating all of the 600 potential tests for the stecker, he developed techniques that in many ways parallel the methods invented by BP at the beginning of the war. The official reaction to the findings of the investigation was the immediate decision that only wheels with two turnovers should be allowed to be used in the right hand position. This was introduced at the beginning of December 1944. It reduced the possible permutations of the wheel order, but increased the security of the machine against this particular weakness."[35]

Although Frowein was awarded the War Merit Cross for this research on the Enigma, it had little effect on practice.

These studies were theoretical in nature; they were never applied on real traffic. They therefore never discovered the various tricks, such as cribs or Banburismus, or the means of automation, that came from practice. There was an element of denial on the part of the Germans, believing that the thousands of personnel and complex organization necessary to break the Enigma were beyond the resources of their enemies. Also, replacing the Enigma required the need to not only develop a new system, but to develop the keying system and materials, their distribution, the training of the cipher personnel, and for security reasons, the necessity to introduce the new system worldwide on the same day made this practically impossible. Additionally, there was no hard, definitive evidence that the Enigma had been broken. With the deteriorating military situation in 1944 -45, and with far greater problems to worry about, it was far easier for the German leadership to ignore the issue.[36]

Another issue of interest to TICOM was the Kriegsmarine's use of soluble printing inks and papers.[37] Perhaps because of institutional memories of the *Magdeburg* incident of 1914, the Kriegsmarine began looking for a way to ensure that their crypto materials could be easily destroyed in event of capture or sinking.[38] The solution lay in the development of water soluble inks, which by January 1940 they began to produce under contract with both the National Printing Office and various commercial firms in Berlin. Further experimentation with papers showed that ordinary rough blotter paper used by printers would dissolve in water. For no particular reason, the paper was pink and used in conjunction with red ink. After six months of production, SKL II added a trick, they created dummy text in a colorless ink that would visually resolve when wet, confusing any enemy that might view it before it fully dissolved. Documents were printed on a standard commercial press modified with rubber type, and two examples of this machine and their inks were present in Flensburg. All back cipher material had been destroyed in the various moves across Germany, by the time SKL/II got to Flensburg, they only kept the back keys for the previous month, which were destroyed when dated.

There was a Hollerith machine component at 4 SKL/III, under the direction of Dip. Ing. Schmalz. Their Hollerith machines were apparently made under license in Germany, and were used to make "brute force" attacks on the British Naval Cypher to find depths by double repeats, and to make catalogs of likely enciphered code groups. 4 SKL/III's variety of equipment included 30 card punchers, a half dozen each of sorters and collators and seven tabulators. Five percent of their Hollerith capacity was spent compiling code tables for the KM's own use.[39]

Relations with the Japanese were few and in one instance, 4 SKL/III gave the Japanese data on the British Naval Cypher No. 3 and in returned received some strips and setting for the

2. Spoils of War

US strip cipher, however, no intelligence was exchanged. Lieutenant Morgenroth, the naval crypto officer accompanying the surrender party at Reims had been selected to accompany a special interservice SIGINT liaison party to Japan. The plan was for him, Captain Optiz and Oberleutnant Schubert of GdNA, to travel via U-Boat, but the trip kept being delayed. They were poorly prepared, only one of them able to speak Japanese, and so little was known about the Japanese crypto service that did not know where to go in Japan or whom to contact. Luckily, for them, the war ended before they could sail.[40]

If insight into Japanese SIGINT operations was a disappointment for TICOM, information about the Russian Navy provided by the B-Dienst proved to be far more interesting. In 1943, in a show of solidarity with their co-belligerent, both Churchill and Roosevelt ordered their intelligence agencies not monitor the Soviet Union. That and the much higher priority of Axis Comint limited the knowledge of Soviet activities in allied intelligence. In fact, the primary source of military intelligence from the eastern front was the Germans themselves in the form of ULTRA intercepts. Amsrat Wilhelm Schwabe and Oberfunkmeister (Senior radioman) Alfons Warzecha, specialists on Russian Naval ciphers, were in Flensburg assigned to 4 SKL at the surrender, and were interrogated by the team. They explained that the Soviet communications divided according to fleet, Baltic, North and Black Sea. The main systems were similar, four and five figure systems for heavy units and shore station, and 2, 3, and 4-figure systems for small ships.

In the Baltic, the main pre-war system was a five-figure codebook superenciphered with a limited 300-group subtractor, changed daily. After the start of the war this system was replaced with a 4-figure simple subtractor derived from a clear text of a book entitled "History of the Communist Party", with a complex system of indicators. Later, further five figure systems were introduced which were only partially solved by the Germans. Some of these main systems were in effect one-time pads, using a key thought to be a subtractor book, 100 groups per page with each page containing an indicator. Each sending station was allocated a number of pages, which were struck off and destroyed as used. However, from July to September of 1944, one Soviet station, Chabarovo, ran short of these indictor pages and reused each from 2 to 10 times. This allowed the B-Dienst to intercept a number of depths and was able to partially read the traffic until October when the problem was apparently rectified by the Russians.

The small ship systems were 4-figure codes based upon a 22 page book, enciphered with a bigram substitution table. This system codenamed GRAUDENZ proved to be the most productive code for the Germans in the Baltic. In the Black Sea there were two four-figure subtractor systems one with an underlying alphabetic book and the other with a hatted book. Originally, the same subtractor table was used which changed every three to five days. This was later replaced by a five-figure system that was not attacked because by that point priority had shifted to Baltic and Northerly traffic.

In the North Sea, a three-figure code enciphered on a simple three-column substitution table used for recognition signals was usually sent two days in advance, which allowed the Germans to cleverly exploit them. The German planes, on approaching a Russian airfield would give the correct signal, and the field would be lighted up, illuminating it as a target. This code was also used for reporting ship positions.[41]

When originally set up in the summer of 1944, the Soviet Union was not an official target of TICOM, but by the spring of the following year Allied intelligence became increasingly alarmed over events involving the Russians. The Germans were much more experienced dealing with Russian communications, and their body of knowledge about Soviet tactical signals were

2. Spoils of War

falling into the hands of TICOM, giving Anglo-American intelligence a kick-start in the cold war.

Upon conclusion of the B-Dienst interrogations, it was decided to keep holding 23 of the prisoners for further questioning, including SKL/III commanding officer Kupfer, Chief Cryptologist Tranow, Russian experts Schwabe and Warzecha, and most of the personnel experienced with breaking of English codes and ciphers. They were soon shipped to DUSTBIN. However, for Team 6 and the interrogators their work was far from done, they still had to deal with OKW/*Chi*.

3. TICOM in Burgscheidungen

Diplomatic code breaking of was the raison d'être for the development of the secret arts of cryptanalysis ever since renaissance princes established 'Black Chambers' as a means to spy on their rivals. As principalities evolved into nation-states, their foreign ministers continued this practice, extending it into the electronic realm with the development of the telegraph. Although given a late start due to the delayed development of a centralized state, Germany's Foreign Ministry the *Auswärtiges Amt* was no exception. Its cipher bureau had been established prior to the First World War and its code breaking success far outs hone its code making weakness, exemplified by the Zimmerman telegram. Its most unique feature was its consistency, despite defeat in WWI and the political chaos of the 1920s, the tiny bureau kept functioning. It developed the greatest depth of experience of any of the Nazi era crypto bureaus; in 1945 it still had on its roles a number of employees hired during the First World War. Little of this was known to Allied intelligence in the spring of 1945; it was assumed that, like all major powers, foreign diplomatic communications were being intercepted by the Germans, until hard confirmation was dropped into the lap of TICOM.

1

On the 24th of April, Colonel Bicher in Paris received a phone call that electrified the whole office of the Signals Intelligence Division; an entire German crypto organization had been captured intact in Central Germany.

"One day we got this frantic call," Bicher's intelligence officer Lieutenant Colonel Paul E. Neff recounted in a postwar interview."They had run across these people, Germans, who had been in the cryptographic business, signals intelligence, all of them. Bongo…" 'These people' turned out to be the German Foreign Office Cryptanalytic Bureau, known as Pers ZS.[42]

While TICOM was making its initial deployment to Venlo, the US First Army began its drive eastward to the Elbe River. Its rapidly advancing armored divisions bypassed any pockets of resistance and overran vast swatches of Saxony, capturing Leipzig. On April 18th, a representative of the First Army military government, 2nd Lieutenant Alfred G. Fenn, entered the small village of Burgscheidungen, 20 miles west of the city near the Harz Mountains, on a solo mission to make contact with local officials to inform them of their status and establish the authority of the occupation. He was introduced to the owner of the local schloss, Graf von der Schulenberg and his interpreter, Fraulein Asta Friedrichs. Although the two were somewhat evasive, he learned that a section of the German Foreign Office was located there. After continuing his rounds of the area, he returned three days later for a follow up interview. This time he met with Friedrichs and one of her superiors, Dr. Hans Rohrbach, who requested to talk privately with him. They told Fenn that they were they were part of the Cryptologic section of the Auswärtiges Amt (German Foreign Office), specifically its Cryptanalytic Bureau, and that they were willing to cooperate. Lieutenant Fenn handled them gently at first and extracted the whole outline of their work from them; then left them with a warning now that they and their work was known to Allied authorities, any destruction of files would be punished by death.

Without any forces of his own to occupy or guard the unit, Fenn returned to his headquarters and reported the incident up the chain of command. His report passed to Colonel Haskell H. Cleaves, the Signal Officer of V Corps, who took the initiate to "freeze" the target and post a detachment from 102nd Cavalry Regiment to guard the village. His intention was not only keep the Germans there but also to prevent any straying American troops or roving civilians

3. TICOM in Burgscheidungen

from looting it. Cleaves drove to the village and met with Friedrichs and Rohrbach, and then made his call to Paris.

2

After the scattering of the German intelligence agencies and the cancellation of the Berlin operation, Bicher had collected a pool of TICOM officers as an advanced echelon at his office in Paris. Upon receipt of this call he assigned Lieutenant Colonel Neff, his staff intelligence officer, to form a team from this pool and designated it Team 3. Along with Neff, he assigned British Intelligence Corps Lieutenant Colonel Geoffrey Evans as chief interrogator, along with Major William P. Bundy, Captain D. M. MacIntyre of the US Army, and Captain R.W. Adams. Evans worked at Hut 3 at Bletchley Park as a linguist, Bundy (who years later would become Assistant Secretary of State in the Johnson administration) worked in Hut 6 and was commander of the American contingent at BP, and MacIntyre was from SIXTA. The group departed the next day

Lieutenant Colonel Paul Neff and Major Charles J. Donahue of Bicher's intelligence section in their office in Paris; Neff commanded Team 3 and Donahue was the OIC of Team 2.

and spent two days driving across France and Germany, via Verdun, Wiesbaden, Weimar and Naumburg, arriving in Burgscheidungen on the morning of April 27.

Neff immediately began sorting out the situation. Initial interrogations and examination of the seized documents revealed the history and structure of Pers Z branch. Its Chief was Kurt Selchow, who held the rank of *Gesandte* (Minister), and had headed the branch since its founding in 1919. He was not present, apparently departing for Salzburg in March. Under him were four departments: an Administration department, a Communications Department, and a Cryptographic office known as Pers Chi, responsible for developing the Foreign Office's own codes, and most importantly Pers ZS, the cryptanalytic branch that broke the diplomatic codes of foreign powers. Pers ZS in turn was divided into two subsections, a mathematical subsection, under the direction of Dr. Werner Kunze, which was responsible for stripping off the ciphers of the intercepted messages, and a Linguistic-Cryptanalytic section, under the direction of Dr. Adolf Paschke, that was responsible for book building and translations of the underlying codes. Both men were reported to be up the road at the village of Zschepplin, site of the mathematical sections temporary office. Some quick detective work revealed that both had been arrested two days before and were on their way to a First Army POW cage. It was a TICOM security policy to keep their prisoners separate from other captives (and their handlers) to avoid any "contamination". Neff and Adams managed to chase them down and intercept the truck and remove the two Germans into their own custody.

"I remember going through this G-2 and the Provost Marshall and racing in my jeep after a truck that was taking these people to a detention center.' Neff later recounted. " Stopping the darn truck, getting these two guys off the truck, signing for them, putting them in my jeep, driving them 50 kilometers or something back to my castle, [and] putting them in with their

3. TICOM in Burgscheidungen

friends. And this guy (Paschke) gave them bloody hell for talking at all. Gave them hell for not having burned all their papers that they were supposed to. He was a real menace. I'm glad we had him, but he was really a menace. I put him in solitary."[43]

Now that key personnel were accounted for, the team divided their efforts. Neff provided the overall supervision and drafted all signals, which required a daily 35-mile currier run to First Army Headquarters. Evans handled the interrogation and gathered facts; Bundy concerned himself with sorting and packaging the documents, and ensuring security. MacIntyre was responsible for logistics and with Adams made most of the follow up side trips investigating secondary targets. Two enlisted men on the team, Sergeants Marx and Loram, utilized their German language skills to deal with the locals and asset in the field trips.

Allied intelligence had little information on the Pers ZS organization and was not even certain of its existence until Burgscheidungen was captured. With Paschke and Kunze in hand, field interrogations began with the intention of discovering the basic history and structure of Pers ZS. This Foreign Office Intelligence Section was the oldest, but smallest of the German services, employing between 180-200 personnel in 1945. Pers ZS traces its roots back to the Political Intelligence Bureau of the Foreign Office in the immediate post WWI period. Thus Pers ZS, although small in number, was highly experienced. Their principal effort was the cryptanalysts of foreign diplomatic codes and ciphers, attacking the diplomatic systems of approximately 50 countries. Despite its small size it was able to read substantial segments of the medium grade systems of a number of major powers including England, the United States, France, Italy, China and Japan. According to TICOM, Pers ZS "evidenced an extraordinary degree of competence".

Meanwhile, Evans continued his initial interrogations. They were all conducted in German with the goal of identifying additional SIGINT targets, indentifying specific individuals and their likely whereabouts, and developing a basic sketch of the organizational structure of Pers ZS and other German crypto agencies.

Dr. Hans Rohrbach, the first Pers ZS cryptanalyst to meet the Americans, was a professor and chair of Mathematics at Charles University, who, since the beginning of the war had acted as a consultant to Pers ZS. He traveled from Prague to Berlin frequently, and just happened to be with the group at Burgscheidungen when it was overrun by the American army. Since Selchow was absent and Paschke and Kunze were in Zsohepplin when Lieutenant Fenn showed up, Rohrback took the initiative to make contact, not because of any position of authority within the organization but because he was the only one present with the common sense not to panic.

The two primary sources of information were the two department heads, Paschke and Kunze. Paschke had been an army cryptographer during the First World War and joined the Foreign Office shortly after the establishment of the Political Intelligence Bureau in 1919. Born in St. Petersburg, he was recruited into the army's cryptanalysis service due to his knowledge of Russian. Although trained as a lawyer, he found cryptanalysis interesting and challenging enough to stick with it after the war. A talented linguist, he also knew English and Italian and rose to be head of the linguistic-cryptanalytic section. In 1933, he joined the Nazi party. Kunze, who joined the Foreign Office at about the same time as Paschke, had a doctorate in mathematics from Heidelberg, had also served as a cryptanalyst in the army during the war working on British codes. After the war, he used his mathematical knowledge to strip the superenecipherment from a French diplomatic code. He later worked on Japanese machine ciphers, solving the Red

3. TICOM in Burgscheidungen

machine, which the Germans were able to read until 1939 when the Japanese switched to the Purple machine. Based upon these achievements, he became head of the mathematical section and therefore was Paschke's peer.[44] Therefore, Pers ZS' cryptanalytic effort, divided between a mathematical subsection and a linguistic-cryptanalytic subsection, was further divided into approximately 9 groups organized along geographical and linguistic lines.

Also in the bag at Burgscheidungen was Senior Specialist Rudolf Schauffer, who was the senior cryptanalyst in the Linguistic section. Although senior to Paschke, and once listed as head of the section, by 1945 he functioned as a subsection head. Originally, a mathematician, his primary interest was theoretical research rather than operational, Schauffer along with two colleagues invented the one-time pad system used by the Foreign Office since the early 1920s. Working independently and without knowledge of the American Vernam cipher he and his colleagues discovered that the use of truly random numbers to encipher codes could not be broken if they were used only once between sender and receiver. The primary problem with using these one-time pads was the immense about of labor and time needed to generate enough random numbers. A machine, similar to a printing press, was devised to print sheets of random numbers. However, this machine was pseudo-random, rather than truly random, and generated a repeating pattern, after an extremely long series. This pattern was discovered and exploited by the U.S. Army Signal Intelligence Service and by the end of the war they were able to read the bulk of this traffic.[45] By then Schauffer had yielded his authority to the more forceful Paschke by default, and was more concerned with the writing and editing of an in-house private periodical entitled "Scriften des Sonderdienates" concerned with cryptologic methodology. In addition to his mathematical background, he knew Japanese and Chinese and headed that subsection.

These three senior members mapped out the history of the organization to TICOM. Pers ZS established with an initial strength of 20 – 30 people in 1918, grew to around 50 employees in 1930, and to a wartime peak of 180 – 200 personnel. By 1940 Pers ZS was large enough to occupy quarters in three buildings in the Berlin area; in Dahlem at the Königin-Luise-Stiftung, Podbielskiallee 78; at Jagerstrasse 12 III, and in a few rooms in the Ethnographic Museum at Prinz Albrecht and Koeniggraetzer Street. At the end of 1943, Pers ZS, like the other German intelligence agencies, was forced to evacuate these locations due to the bombings. The branch was split into three groups, with a small section remaining in Berlin and the crypto-linguistic and mathematical sections moving into separated locations in southeastern Germany. In the spring of 1945, as the Russians advanced, the groups were further splintered and moved into the Burgscheidungen area. Allied intelligence had little information on the Pers ZS organization until it was captured. Until that point, a German Foreign Office cryptanalytic effort was suspected but not confirmed.[46]

Pers ZS therefore became the second German SIGINT organization captured intact with documents, equipment and personnel. In addition to personnel, TICOM discovered a considerable amount of documents stored in filing cabinets and recovered many Hollerith machines used by Pers SZ. TICOM was very careful in the handling of its prisoners, insuring that they be treated well, and being careful to keep them separated from other Nazi POWs to avoid influencing their attitudes.

3

The primary problem facing Nuff was security. It was TICOM's policy for their TROs to use pseudonyms when interrogating their prisoners in the field, and to keep their own mission as obscure as possible in order to prevent the Germans from inferring the depth and nature of the Allies knowledge of their enemy's crypto systems. Even before they arrived, both Fenn and Colonel Cleaves told the prisoners' that their debriefing would be by their opposite numbers, and

3. TICOM in Burgscheidungen

upon meeting, Cleaves introduced the team by name. "From that point on the members of the team adopted aliases and did their utmost to impress the fake names up on the Germans. This proved a difficult front to maintain…and it is likely that the Germans knew our right names at all times and were probably deriving a little quiet amusement from the attempt to conceal them." Neff recounted another problem with this plan to maintain autonomy, "There had been some servants in the castle who were still there, so they were doing our laundry because you know in the military your name is on everything. They knew all our names. Everybody knew all our names before we knew our own names." [47]

But the biggest security problem was political. With the surrender fast approaching, Nuff and his team knew that, based upon decisions made at Yalta, the Burgscheidungen area would be turned over to the Russians within a few weeks. Furthermore, under the four-power agreement, the Soviets could insist on access to the PWs and captured materials. It was therefore imperative that the existence of Pers ZS be kept from them. Not only would the entire organization need to be moved west, but also the Graf's extensive household of relatives and servants, some 40 odd in number, and any local civilians that had had contact with the Foreign Office personnel. Essentially, the bulk of the villages of Burgscheidungen and Zsohepplin would have to be relocated, in order to remove the evidence from the Russians. "…only a handful of ladies, mostly old and some sick were left at Zsohepplin, and none at all at the Burg. The standard used was a rough and ready one to some extent; wives were taken but the mistress of one of those evacuated to England was left in Zsohepplin."[48]

TICOM: The Hunt for Hitler's Codebreakers

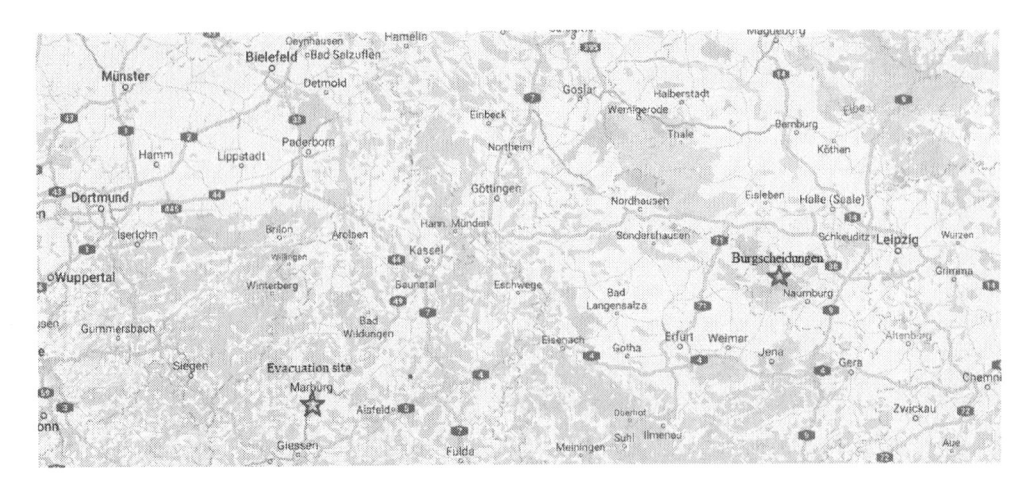

Location of Pers ZS in Central Germany May 1945

A contemporary view of Schloss Burgscheidungen. (X-Weinzer, Wikimedia Commons)

With the approaching surrender decisions needed to be made about the dispersion of the Foreign Office personnel. As Nuff explained in a postwar interview, "…but, my problem became

3. TICOM in Burgscheidungen

what are we going to do with them? Because they apparently had a lot of good information. I couldn't hang on this way very long …. "

He went up to the First Army SIGINT officer to teletype Bicher, recommending "What we really ought to do, if we're going to get the most out of this crowd is to get them somewhere where they can be taken care of (I got a few people that are very sick) and still enable us to keep our hands on them. The only suggestion I have that makes any sense to me at all and it may not be practical, is to ship them out of here to England --ship them over to London. Bicher said I'll look into that."

But elements in the British government objected to enemy civilians entering the U.K. "Apparently they had a hard time when this thing hit London because they couldn't decide what to do. They had to clear it [up to] the Attorney General or whatever he's called over there. Is it legal to do?"[49]

While TICOM at BP and the British government debated these issues, Neff started formulating a plan for the evacuation, and work continued for the team. A visit to Halle/Nietleben in a search for additional transportation resulted in a command car and the promise that the various U.S. radio intelligence companies in the area would dig up further vehicles for equipment and personnel transportation. Bundy got busy sorting and identifying the documents. Not wanting to alarm the prisoners as to the priority of the "pinch", Bundy tried to appear leisurely as he searched for documents under their noses. Documents were not impounded immediately but were left in the work room for a day or two before being removed to a more secure area of the schloss. Initial inventory revealed 170 steel file cases, most of them in a locked basement, along with five crates of work material and personal luggage. Avoiding the necessity of a room-by-room search of the castle, and not seeing any evidence to the contrary, the team took the word of the prisoners that all of the material had been turned over to them. In the following days, the files were quickly examined to determine if they were relevant cryptographic material, graded as priority A or B, and were inventoried in a blue notebook. Obvious cryptographic documents, non-cryptographic documents stamped "Geheim", and three packing crates containing one-time pads were all graded 'A'. Lack of sealing wax or baling wire prevented the team from following standard procedures for securing the material for shipment, so it was decided to keep it in the original steel cabinets but provide a special watch over them during transit.

Meanwhile, on May 1st, Evans and Adams made their first trip to Zschepplin. There they found three additional prisoners from the Pers ZS detachment, Dr. Wilhelm Brandes, Dr. Helmut Grunsky and Karl Zastrow, and a trailer of Hollerith machinery. Wilhelm Brandes was Head the group for France, Belgium, Holland, and Switzerland. Another veteran from World War I he had joined Pers ZS in 1920, and held the civil service rank of Senior Specialist. Dr. Grunsky was a group head in Kunze's mathematical-cryptanalytic subsection; he had contracted acute tuberculosis and was sent to the hospital when he arrived in England. Zastrow was an expert in U.S. systems, an experienced book breaker who had worked for Pers Z for 27 years, and had worked on the American diplomatic A1, B1, C1 and Brown codes. Although a gifted analyst, he was described as absent-minded and a poor administrator, he never advanced into the higher grades despite his long continuous service, which dated from 1918.[50]

The cache of Hollerith machinery consisted of key punches, sorters, a collator, reproduces, a multiplier and a tabulator, all standard business equipment for statistical analysis. The machines appeared brand new but had been rendered inoperational with cut wiring and

3. TICOM in Burgscheidungen

removable parts discarded. The team did a detailed study of the machines and did not find anything unique.

The next day Captain Adams went to the town of Muehlhausen, 85 miles west of Burgscheidungen, to pick up Dr. Roy, Pers Z's head of personnel and administration. His knowledge of the department's operations was of course limited having no knowledge of cryptology, and having already developed a detailed picture of the organization, Evans separated him from the others and sent him back into the normal channels to be processed.[51] That day the heavy transportation requested by the team arrived.

By now the diplomatic problems had been sorted out and an airlift for the priority prisoners had been scheduled for pickup at the nearby airfield of Kölleda. Major Caddick from BP arrived to act as chief courier and supervised the final packing of the materials and documents for transport to the airfield.

On Thursday the prisoners were taken to the edge of Kölleda and given a picnic of K-rations. They had not been told that they were being flown out, so they waited all day out of sight while the rest of the TICOM team waited impatiently. No one had bothered to signal them that the planes had been delayed in Paris due to the weather. The next day the same drill happened, and Captain MacIntyre, responsible for the escort of the prisoners, had another anxious day. Finally on Saturday morning the word came through about the weather situation and the flight was postponed until Monday, the 6th.

Over the weekend, the Team returned to Zschepplin with troops from the US Army's Counter-Intelligence corps to round up any remaining Pers Z operational personnel and some of the wives. This final security sweep brought in an additional 40 civilians, with seven of them important enough to be added to the air evacuation. Neff arranged to evacuate by road to Marbourg, in the American sector, all possible civilians with whom the team had been in contact.

The planes came in on the afternoon of Monday the 7th, the operation finally occurring smoothly, and all the important prisoners were able to leave as a single intact group. This finalized the major intelligence gathering phase of the mission. There were a few loose ends to tie up including a final quick search of tertiary targets of Halle/Nietleben, Muehlhausen, and Arnstadt.

The next day with the help of some Army engineers, the Hollerith equipment seized at Zschepplin was hauled out into the middle of a field and blown up with dynamite and thermite bombs; a fitting celebration for VE day. Neff found his own way to celebrate "… I called in the town mayor, the Burgermeister, and told him to produce some wine (because) we were going to celebrate…. He said, "There isn't any wine. It's all gone, been gone for years." I said, "Now look I've been very patient and I'd like to have by six o'clock a case of white wine. We'll even consider paying for it." So he finally broke down and said I'll see what I can do and at five o'clock or something he had someone deliver a case of white wine. So we felt good about the war being over."[52]

Three truck convoys over the next three days completed the evacuation of all remaining materials and civilians. The guard at Burgscheidungen was relieved and Nuff and the rest of Team 3 returned to Paris. Years later Nuff summarized the end of the operation: "We got a plane one day, escorted this crowd [Pers Z prisoners] down to the airfield, put them on the plane and

3. TICOM in Burgscheidungen

flew them over to London. The British picked them up over there and gave them a place to stay, fed them, and interrogated the hell out of them."[53]

4

Indeed, within two days of their arrival interrogations began. The seventeen male and four female cryptographers were held by CSDIC UK at two London locations, the Oratory School for the men and at 101 Nightingale Lane, Wandsworth for the women. A distinguished interrogation team from Bletchley Park chaired by Brigadier John Tiltman, deputy Director and chief Cryptographer of GC&CS met them. He was assisted by a core group of experts which included civilians Professor Eric Vincent, Italian specialist, and also Dr. Leonard Forster the Coordinator of Cryptologic Records. Also from the US Army 1st Lieutenant Alfred P. Fehl, a member of the TICOM committee who himself was to soon lead Team 5 into the field to conclude a vital mission, and Major John N. Seaman, the ASA liaison officer to Bletchley Park.

The initial field interrogations had gathered the basic information; names, organizational structure and historical overview. These more detailed interviews were designed to get to the business at hand, the specifics of Pers ZS's cryptanalytic activities. First up was Dr. Rohrback who clarified his role in the organization and the relationship of ZS to the cryptographic branch Pers Chi, along with background on the three section heads Kunze, Paschke, and Schauffler. Questioned that afternoon, the three described Pers ZS work on a variety of diplomatic systems, including French, Polish, Russian, Italian, British and American along with a variety of minor powers. In all they had read the codes or ciphers of 34 different nations.[54]

The next day, now with Professor Vincent in the chair, they interviewed the four female Pers ZS cryptologists. Fraulein Asta Friedrichs, who originally met with Lieutenant Fenn at Burgscheidungen, acted as the group's chief spokesperson. Described by her interrogators as an

"Able woman of strong character who would come to the top in any organization", with the curious caveat "Probably not too scrupulous." After describing her work she complained about the position of women in her organization, that they were not recognized in terms of rank or the pay that their talents and responsibilities deserved. Not unusual for their era, Friedrichs, despite being the deputy in the Slavonic languages department, held the rank of Technical Assistant, essentially a clerical title. The same was true for Hildegarde Sohltade the deputy head of the French, Dutch, Belgium, and Swiss group, and for Doctors Erika Pannwitz and Anelise Hühnkc of the Mathematics group. Even Ursula Hagen, the chief of the vital England, Ireland, Spain, Portugal and Latin American code breaking section was only a TA.

In fact, the chief purpose of the meeting was to try to find out about the whereabouts of Fraulein Hagen. Taken ill shortly before the arrival of the American Army with Erysipelas, a skin disease, she was last seen at the military hospital at Zschepplin. Inquires made by TICOM through the occupation authorities soon located her in Marburg where, evacuated with the rest of the area's civilians, she was in hospital. The four women were also concerned about the fate of their families left behind in Germany, and Friedrichs even expressed concern about how her male colleagues, most of them in middle age, would ever be able to start over and make a living.

Other information gleaned from the group was the opinion that Pers Z was a small, self-contained group with little liaison to other codebreaking agencies. The missing head of the organization, Selchow, was considered a competent manager, but understood little of cryptology. There was little feedback or acknowledgement from the Auswärtlges Amt, and Pers ZS did no intelligence analysis but just passed the intercepts up to Ribbentrop.

In the collection of prisoners from Burg was a group of OKW/*Chi* employees sent to Pers ZS for further training and experience in diplomatic systems. Kurt Rave, Edgar Hierer, and

3. TICOM in Burgscheidungen

Arthur Grosse all came to Pers ZS in December 1943, after OKW/*Chi* quarters in Berlin were bombed out. Rave was a student before the war, had a good knowledge of written Japanese, and while visiting his father in China picked up a good grasp of the language. He joined the OKW in 1941 and ended up working in Fenner's oriental language department along with his friend Hierer, hired on Rave's recommendation. Grosse worked on Italian problems at OKW but had been transferred to the Chinese desk despite having no knowledge of Chinese. Pers ZS did not welcome their efforts; Rohebach described the three as lower grade and spoke about them with obvious distaste.[55]

Four more interrogations held over the next few days with subordinate personnel who filled in the details provided by their managers. Pers ZS had one small intercept station, in Dahlem, Berlin. Its purpose was to cover some high priority diplomatic links such as those between Berlin and Turkey or Portugal. However, OKW/*Chi*, the Forschrungsamt or the Post Office provided the vast bulk of their traffic. In 1942, Pers ZS began acquiring machinery due to the initiative of Hans – Georg Krug of the mathematics section who had a personal contact with the manager of the German branch of the Hollerith concern. Eventually the collection consisted of 20 punchers, 10 sorting machines, and a small number of collators, reproducers, and tabulators.

5

However, of course TICOM's primary interest in these interrogations was the German's success with diplomatic codes and ciphers. Their questioning resulted in a summary:

Pers ZS's greatest pre-war technical feat was against the Japanese. Japan had used a considerable number of hand ciphers between the wars, including a variety of 2 and 4 letter, 2 and 4 figure codes, transposition systems, and eventually an additive reciphering system. Pers

ZS was successful in reading most of these starting as early as 1925 and continuing throughout the war. By 1930, perhaps alarmed by Herbert Yardly's 'American Black Chamber' revelations, the Japanese developed an encryption machine, the Angōki Taipu-A (Type A Cipher Machine), codenamed the "Red" machine by US intelligence. The Red machine was reverse engineered from an old Hagelin design, it utilized two rotors to encipher the six vowels (including 'y') separately from the twenty consonants to produce a cipher text that mimicked plain text.[56] This was for sending the encrypted message via commercial cable, which was cheaper for pronounceable text. This 'sixes and twenty' design was of course a major weakness. Introduced into service in 1930 – 31, it was broken by the British in 1934 and the Americans a year later.

The introduction of the Red machine (dubbed JB 48 by the Germans) appeared to be a shock to Pers ZS. "The moral effect of the machine on [us]… had been considerable and it was some time before they discovered that it could be theoretically read." Dr. Kunze later testified to TICOM.[57] By 1935 Kunze had broken it, and with the assistance of OKW/*Chi*, Pers ZS began reading it currently in addition to solving all the back traffic.[58] This effort continued until 1939 when the Japanese traffic suddenly changed and became unreadable. German cryptanalysts assumed that the Red machine was modified somehow, rather than realizing that the Japanese had switched over to a new device (the Purple machine). After an initial period of effort, Pers ZS gave up. "It cannot be said that this failing vas necessarily due to inability or ignorance. Perhaps, Japan being Germany's ally Germany felt it was not worthwhile to expend the great energy necessary to solve the difficult Japanese 'purple' machine." TICOM later concluded.[59] Had the Germans persisted, they might have realized that Japanese Ambassador to Berlin Baron Oshima was sharing with Tokyo a wealth of strategic information derived from his personal interviews with Hitler and other top Nazis.[60]

3. TICOM in Burgscheidungen

As to the Russians, the prewar Pers ZS had read Russian diplomatic systems until their switch to one-time pads for all diplomatic traffic in 1927. Kunz stated that that their commitment to this effort was dropped at this time and was not renewed during the war. Their lack of effort was surprising in the light of two facts dug up in the TICOM investigation, largely overlooked at the time but in hindsight was to prove to be important. Paschke said his knowledge of a Russian diplomatic one-time pad system that was used by the Red Army "under conditions which did not permit the normal instructions for use to be observed and which was thus compromised." [61] In other words, the one-time pad had been reused and this allowed the cipher additives to be stripped off. This same discovery was later made independently by a secret analysis cell in the US Army's SIS studying Soviet diplomatic telegrams sent from New York. This program was to be later codenamed "Venona". Also, on or about 22 June 1941, during the opening phase of the German attack on the Soviet Union, Finnish Security Police entered the Soviet consulate at Petsamo, Finland and captured a partially burned codebook of the First Chief Directorate of the KGB, a five figure code book that was re-encoded with one- time pads.[62] A photocopy of this codebook, given to their German allies, ended up in the hands of Pers ZS. Scoped up in the troves of documents from Burgscheidungen, the codebook ended up in the archives of the Army's ASA and later, at the newly established NSA. Here, in 1952, it was discovered and proved to be of some value in decoding some of the early Venona intercepts.

Ironically, Pers ZS' greatest success in both quantity and quality was against the Italians. TICOM later concluded "Work on Italian diplomatic codes was an outstanding PersZS achievement." Paschke led the effort and between 1935 and 1943, every major Italian code was read. This success solidified Paschke's reputation within the organization. After the Italians surrender to the allies, the work became more difficult with the introduction of bigram substitution over the additive, but the basic codebook remained unchanged. A double transposition system adopted by the post-Mussolini Badoglia government was never broken but at least three of the rival neo-Fascist government systems were read in the latter stages of the war. The effort that the Auswärtlges Amt put toward reading Italian diplomatic codes is reflective of Hitler's mindset toward his closest ally.

France, Germany's traditional enemy, had always been a major target of Pers ZS, and their success was considerable, reading 75% of French diplomatic transmissions in 1941. However the effort was greatly simplified after the defeat of France in June 1940 which required them to turn over their codes to the Germans. Most of the Diplomatic systems were four-figure, two-part codes, enciphered either through an additive system, or by bigram substitution tables. However the effort did not end with the surrender, for with the organization of De Gaulle's Free French Forces there were new targets to pursue. In a later interrogation that month, Dr. Wilhelm Brandes, head of the France/Belgium/Switzerland desk since 1938 claimed that they were reading a De Gaulle system consisting of a subtraction table of five digits repeated to the end of the message enciphering a codebook last revised in 1937. The table changed daily. The traffic passed on this system was of high order and was sent worldwide including to Washington, London, Moscow, Stockholm, and other major capitals. Brandes felt that he was satisfied with the work of his desk but felt that they could have achieved more with more staff.

However, TICOM greatest concern was with Pers ZS's effort against British and American diplomatic systems.

3. TICOM in Burgscheidungen

Paschke, Schauffler, and Rohrbach were all asked about British Systems, but their knowledge was limited. British unenciphered 4- and 5-letter codebooks were read regularly, and could be reconstructed after a change to a new book in three to five months. As to enciphered figure systems, they had captured no books, but the capture of a British cipher table in Norway allowed Dr. Kunze to strip the traffic for a few months, but they were unable to read the underlying plain text. They knew that a five figure Interdepartmental cipher also captured in Norway had been worked on by OKW/*Chi* and the FA.

Pers ZS's British expert and head of the British Empire, Spain, Portugal and Latin-American section Fraulein Ursula Hagen, was absent, still in hospital in Marburg. She was finally interrogated from her bed on 23 June. Still woozy from her illness the meeting was brief, consisting of verifying some basic information on her knowledge of British codes and providing some biographical information. Born in 1901 in Berlin she joined the Foreign Office in October 1922. She had a good knowledge of English and her preliminary training consisted of studying already broken code messages and any available cryptographic material. She was promoted head of the English, Spanish and Portuguese section in 1939. Interrogated a second time in early September she provided many more details on the British Foreign Office Long Subtractor, the Interdepartmental Cipher book that had been captured in Bergen in 1940, their work on the South African Government Telegraph Code traffic, some unimportant India Office systems, and their solving of Irish Diplomatic Substitution tables that they used with the G.T.C. The most profitable British systems were the unenciphered low-grade codes B25 and B31 (possibly Foreign Office "R" codes). Some South American systems worked upon were those of Chili, Argentina and Mexico. She added at the end that she was not at any time a member of the Nazi party.[63] On the whole it appears that Pers ZS's penetration of British diplomatic systems was minor, and no vital diplomatic information seems to have been compromised.

They were more successful against the Americans. The American diplomatic codebooks Grey and Brown were notoriously insecure. The "Grey code" had been in continuous use since 1919 and known by American authorities to be so readable that President Franklin Roosevelt, upon sending instructions to his ambassador in Tokyo on December 6, 1941 noted - "I think it can go in grey code - saves time – I don't mind if it gets picked up."[64] The grey code was a one-part unenciphered book which given enough traffic, could be easily reconstructed, and was read by the Germans. Its successor, the "Brown code", introduced in 1938 and which at least had the advantage of being a two part code, had been compromised in 1941 by theft from the American consulate in Zagreb, but had already been reconstructed by Pers ZS after 2 ½ years of effort.[65] The state department code "A1", an enciphered codebook, was also known through physical compromise, possibly captured by the Japanese.[66]

Karl Zastrow, who led the American section, described in his interrogation the US diplomatic systems as "… mainly 5 letter books with 10 reciphering tables for mononalphabetic and bigram substitution to each book. The tables ran for two to six months. Later other substitution tables began to be used, with 5 indicator groups to each table. The tables were changed in the course of a message, the indicator for the new table being enciphered with the previous table."[67] Another interesting fact he revealed was that a transposition system of the 'Coordinator of Information' (precursor of the OSS) had been intercepted but not solved. Zastrow was a veteran book breaker who had worked on US codes for 27 years, and was also a specialist on the Scandinavian systems. For a while, he had been lent to OHW/*Chi* to work on

3. TICOM in Burgscheidungen

British and American systems. His interrogators commented on his difficult and sometimes indistinct speech, which made him difficult to understand, even in German.

6

But Pers ZS's greatest feat, and the greatest example of pure cryptanalysis in all the German services, was the breaking of the US State Department's strip cipher. As war loomed, the State Department began to move its most critical traffic to a new system. The American Strip Cipher was a manual polyalphabetic substitution cipher known as the M-138A by the military, the CSP-845 by the Navy, and as 0-2 by the state department. It consisted of a metal frame that folded in the middle like a book, with slots in each side for the placement of paper strips. Fifteen slots were on each side for a total placement of 30 strips. Each strip had all the alphabetic characters imprinted on it in a truly random order, with 50 unique strips provided with the set (in the state department version), of which 30 were selected for the daily key. Each strip had a unique strip number on the left end which corresponded to the key. The key consisted of the order of the strips from top to bottom, which changed every day, thereby providing a new encryption. Once the order was arranged, the user would move a slider to indicate a line, and all the strips would be moved back or forth in the holder to spell out the first 30 letters of the message. Another line was then selected at random and the letters in that line written onto the message that was sent. On the receiving end, the cipher clerks, having arranged their set according to the order provided in the daily key, adjusted the slides to the indicator line that matched the seemly random jumble of the cipher text. Scanning either right or left from the indicator line would reveal one line in plaintext, carrying the communication. Initially there were 50 available arrangements of the strips, but until 1942 the set of strips were replaced only every six months, that meant that that during the period some strip days would be repeated. In August of '42, the arrangement was modified to avoid the repeat days and the changeover period of the strips was changed to quarterly, and a year later, to monthly. This system provided the US State Department with much better security than provided by the Grey and Brown codes. Over 17,000 sets were produced between 1935 and 1944 for use by the military and state departments.[68]

However, it was not foolproof. By 1942 the Pers ZS had accumulated a considerable amount of American diplomatic traffic in an unknown cipher. They put Dr. Hans Rohrbach on the job and he formed a team of the leading mathematicians in the department, including Erika Pannwitz, Helmut Grunsky, and Hans-Georg Krug.[69] Dr. Hans-Kurt Mueller was later brought in for his linguistic skills with the English language. Armed with Krug's newly acquired Hollerith machines, the first 40 letters of the intercepted messages, along with some of their traffic data, were punched onto cards and sorted. Out of these thousands of cards those pairs of cards with at least five consecutive letters in corresponding places were selected. It was discovered that a large number of parallels appeared, some extending up to the 30th letter, however no parallels extended beyond the 30th letter. In addition, a high percentage of parallels broke off with the 15th letter, indicating that the cipher had a period of 30 and often used blocks of 15. Parallels occurring in messages of different days were never of the same month, indicating that the entire system was changed every several months. There were no parallels between messages intercepted before August 1, 1942 and messages after that date indicating a major change to the system.[70]

Rohrbach decided to focus on the traffic accumulated after that date, with the first 30 letters of the first two lines punched onto Hollerith cards, resulting initially in a sample of 50,000 cards, later growing to 80,000. These cards were again sorted to find parallels and probability theory was applied to estimate the number random coincidences. Those with a low probability of

3. TICOM in Burgscheidungen

coincidences (that is, not in the group because of random luck) were sorted into classes of messages enciphered with the same key. Repeated sorting and statistical analysis such as bigram and weighting methods allowed Rohrbach and his team to identify specific messages on specific days enciphered with the same key. Focusing on five days traffic that seemed to have this same depth, at this point the team brought in Mueller to apply crypto – linguistic techniques to tease out some of the plane language text. Studying previously solved messages in the Grey and Brown codes, they measured the frequency of prefixes and suffixes and noticed a peak in the use in- and –tion beyond that expected in a normal sample of English text. Further analysis began to identify in the cipher text bigram combinations such as –an –on, -un. Using this as an initial clue, logical assumptions could be made of the resulting words, which compared to other messages enciphered on the same day with the same key yielded their meaning. Slowly, the cipher sequence of the first 15 strips was built up. Since a day's key used 30 strips, a process of elimination and further comparisons revealed the remaining 15 strips. The remaining 20 strips were sorted, identified, and revealed; the process going much faster since 3/5 of the possibilities were all ready known. Once all 50 strips were revealed, the daily key for each day of the 40-day period could be reconstructed, and work could begin on the next period.[71]

Now that the system was understood analytically and reconstructed, Pers ZS now could go into production. However, the masses of material needed a large number of workers with a sufficient knowledge of English to recognize the deciphered text. Although most of Pers ZS's cryptographers had some knowledge of the language, they were too few and too busy with other critical targets to spend all their time on clerical tasks. The problem cried out for automation, and Krug, Pers ZS's Hollerith machine expert brought was in. The result was the 'Automation'. It was a machine designed to decode, rather than analyze the identified traffic, by adjusting the 30 strips according to the cipher text automatically after input by keyboard or by reading a punched Hollerith card. The most frequent letters of the English language were printed in a heavier font, so the correct line stands out visually from the rest. The clerk writes this line down and the machine automatically sorts the strips to the next line. A double line of cipher text was sorted and recorded in about half a minute, as opposed to seven minutes manually. In his TICOM interview, Kuenze thought that the machine was in a load sent to Zschepplin, but only one of the three wagons arrived.

It had taken over a year of intense effort, but by late 1943, Pers ZS could read the O-2 strip cipher, but with a considerable time lag, seriously limiting its effectiveness. This success was not to last long however, in the spring of 1944 the State Department switched their communications to the highly secure machine cipher SIGTOT.[72] Rohrbach had an interesting postscript to this story, in a post war article about the breaking of the O-2 he wrote:

"Before I had to leave the castle in Thuringia I packed all the material which [I collected about the O-2] in a steel box and I stored the box in a hiding place beneath the roof of the castle. In the summer of 1946 I tried to get the box back with the help of a reliable person. But when he was on the way to the railway station to convey it as freight to my living quarters Russians captured him. The transport was betrayed to the Russian Military Government by the custodian of the castle. And so the box went to Russia. I do not know what happened to it after that...."[73]

7

Before the interrogations were over it became obvious to TICOM that Pers ZS's greatest weakness was a lack of intelligence assessment of their product. Their archives and records group, the backbone of any intelligence agency's assessment function, appeared to be a collection of personalities and place names from decodes, amplified by newspaper clippings,

3. TICOM in Burgscheidungen

rather than the extensive crossed-indexed card files utilized by other agencies, such as at Bletchley Park. It and its custodian Dr. Horn disappeared at the end of the war and never captured. Friedrichs testified that no intelligence was extracted from the material produced, except such as was necessary to continue reading the traffic. The decodes that passed up to the foreign office was selected by Selchow, and usually went directly to Ribbentrop. Friedrichs said that from time to time copies of the telegrams they issued had been returned bearing the stamp of the Führer, otherwise no indication of the importance of their work had ever been communicated to them.

However, TICOM was to state in their 1946 report:
"Considering the relatively small staff which Pars Z S had; the conclusion must be drawn that its cryptanalytic successes were considerable. Work was done on systems from approximately 50 countries. Of these 50 countries, apparently only three used diplomatic systems which completely defied successful cryptanalysis - Russia, Czechoslovakia, and Poland after 1942-43. It is easy to scorn the Pars Z S inability to solve high grade machine systems, whether American SIGABA, English Type X, or Swedish Hagelin. Yet, with their small staff, they were able to read the Swiss Enigma for a short period of time, and to solve the Japanese "Red" machine. As a diplomatic cryptanalytic agency, the investigator is forced to conclude that in its primary field, the solution of foreign diplomatic codes, the agency evidenced an extraordinary degree of competence..."

In reviewing the case, TICOM provided some self-criticism about its investigation. "The interrogations it is felt were not extensive enough. So large was the field covered by the Pers ZS cryptanalytic effort ... that few interrogators were available who were competent to meet the

German cryptanalysts on their own ground.... Faced with the necessity of conducting complete interrogations on subjects with which they were unfamiliar or on which for security reasons, they could not openly appear to be well informed, there were inevitably areas, which were not completely covered. The interrogations therefore, cover little more than those highlights which the Germans most readily recalled." Furthermore "In May 1945 the TICOM principle of requiring prisoners to do extensive 'homework' that is write papers, as detailed as possible and, in their own words, was not fully developed."[74]

After three weeks, seven interrogations, and the questioning of twenty prisoners, the TICOM interrogation team felt that the Pers ZS well was drained dry of its cryptologic secrets. In addition to the prisoners, Team 3 had bagged some 73 file cabinets, containing some 300,000 pages of material.[75] After cooling their heels for a few more weeks, the group of twenty was returned to Germany to join up with the remaining employees and families at Marburg. Marburg, a small city 180 miles west of Burgscheidungen, had become a major medical evacuation center for German wounded during the war and had been spared from the heavy bombing. Now under the control of Detachment F102, 2nd European Civil Affairs Regiment, this collection of Foreign Office civilians had been dropped off on May 9th with the orders to be "held until ordered release or otherwise disposed of by Lieutenant Colonel Neff." Now six weeks later, the detachment commander, Commander Bull, of the Royal Naval Reserve, sent an unaddressed plea up the chain of command. "...no further instructions of any kind have been received concerning the disposition of these persons.... Are these persons to be kept under guard indefinitely? Can they be permitted to circulate beyond the immediate vicinity of Marburg?" Finally, in an attempt to find out who is in charge; "With what higher headquarters can this detachment communicate should an emergency arise?"[76] By July 11, the memo had made its way to Bletchley Park and TICOM decided to release all the Pers ZS personnel except for the most important six; Kunz, Paschke, Schauffler, Karstien, and Fräuleins Friedrichs and Hagen. Karstien had been head of the Bulgarian, Croatian, Polish and Slovakian group and was Friedrichs boss. For those six specific rules were laid out; they should be kept under guard, they were not to be permitted to leave the city, they were allowed to have personal belongings sent to them if possible, and they may be employed locally if so desired. Finally, they were under the charge of Colonel Bircher, as director S.I.D. ETOUSA.

Final interrogations were held, after which the final six were discharged back to their civilian lives to face their first cold and hungry post war German winter.

8

Two years later, there was a final postscript to the Pers ZS case. The missing director of Pers Z, Kurt Selchow, was located in Hamburg. An Army Security Agency officer, Captain Mary C. Lane interviewed him in Frankfort on September 2, 1947, and submitted the result as a TICOM report, which provided first hand biographical details. Selchow was born on May 28, 1886 in Oppeln, Upper Silesia. Described as 6'2" tall, 160 pounds and tall, thin with grey and thinning hair, he had a wife, Erma and a daughter, Gitta. Selchow explained that he had served in the First World War as a signal officer with the troops. He had realized that much of the work done by the army was diplomatic in nature and properly belonged to the Foreign Office. Directly after the war, he offered his services to the Ministry of Foreign Affairs and was hired to organize the crypto bureau. He brought into the service a number of colleagues from the Army, such as Schiauffler, Paschke, Zastrow, Branndes, Hoffmann and Kunze. He built up the bureau to a war time high of 500 personnel, and remained its head until the surrender in 1945. Why he was absent from Burgscheidungen in mid-April 1945 he did not adequately explain, just stating that the bombing forced the move from Berlin and that is why he ended up in Weiler/Vorarlberg, Swabia in the French zone. He lived there for almost two years without ever being interrogated by the French authorities, although they knew his identity. Recently he moved to Hamburg where he lived with his family in a house of a relative, and worked in a family business. Expressing a desire to move to the American sector, Selchow, like many former members of the German government, was on the make for a job, stating that he was willing to move to Marburg and work with his old colleagues to write a complete organizational and technical history of the bureau. Captain Lane politely deferred him. She declared on the cover page "The report is of historical interest, and Selchow claims to have no technical knowledge."[77]

4. Fruits of Victory

From the beginning, the primary target for TICOM was the German Armed Forces Cryptologic Agency, the *Oberkommando der Wehrmacht Chiffrierabteilung*, commonly known as OKW/*Chi*. The Allies knowledge of the agency was limited, but it was assumed that, as the highest echelon-level signal intelligence service, it would coordinate and possibly direct the work of the three subordinate agencies of the German Army, Navy and Air Force. It was also believed to have the ablest cryptographers and attacked the most difficult Allied systems, including the machine ciphers. Information on its function, address, names of major personalities was gleamed from ULTRA. Air photoreconnaissance coverage of its HQ was delivered to TICOM, and even a German prisoner of war was located and interviewed for descriptions of the grounds and sketches of its headquarters building layout. A detailed target folder was produced to brief the TROs on the assault teams.

By mid-February, it was known through ULTRA that most of the German intelligence centers were moving out of the Berlin area due to the Russian advance. OKW/*Chi*, which had been located at Wilmersdorf, then at Juterbog, was now assumed to be in movement, location unknown. All of TICOM's carefully considered plans were in limbo, now having to rely on the Allied advance to uncover clues as to OKW/*Chi's* whereabouts.

By 3 May, when the German collapse appeared to be imminent, TICOM reinforce Team 6 with three additional army TROs, a Briton and two Americans. These officers, Major Eric Morrison and Lieutenants Louis Laptook, and Oliver Kirby, arrived in Venlo two days later. Morrison and Laptook were intelligence analysts from Hut 3 while Kirby was on the watch in

Hut 6 breaking the incoming German messages.[78] They all could speak German, so this group was to concentrate on military targets, especially anyone who was with OKW/*Chi*.

However, the fortunes of war were kind to TICOM. At the time of the surrender at Reims, Generaloberst (Col. Gen.) Alfred Jodl brought along a number of senior communications staff, including the chief of signals General der Nachrichtentruppe (Lt. Gen.) Albert Praun, his chief of Telecommunication Oberst (Col.) Grube, and Oberstleutnant (Lt. Col.) Mettig, second in command at OKW/*Chi*. Upon the signing, these officers were taken into immediate custody and interrogated by SHAEF signal officers.

1

The Wehrmacht was formed in 1938 by Hitler to replace the government War Ministry, whose staff officers and career civil servants had a propensity towards independence and loyalty towards the institution of the Army, rather than the regime. Hitler transferred its responsibilities to a newly created military staff, the *Oberkommando der Wehrmacht* (OKW), the Supreme Command of the Armed Forces. This allowed Hitler to appoint loyal Nazis to the staff in order to bypass the Supreme Commands of the Army (OKH), the Navy (OKM) and the Air Force (OKL). The OKW, although predominantly manned with Army Staff officers, had little respect among their counterparts on the other armed forces staffs, as its two most senior officers, Field Marshal Wilhelm Keitel and Generaloberst Jodl, were considered Hitler's toadies. Hitler practiced a strategy of divide and conquer among his friends as well as his enemies, setting up rival staffs to compete for his attention and approval. The result was to turn his military from a three way into a four-way turf battle. As the war evolved after 1942, the OKH assumed the primary responsibility for running the war against Russia, while the OKW commanded the Norway, western and southern fronts. As a strategy for insuring loyalty, it failure was demonstrated when

4. Fruits of Victory

two high-ranking OKW staff officers, head of intelligence Admiral Wilhelm Canaris and Chief Signal Officer Erich Fellgiebel, were both executed for their roles in the July 20th assassination plot.

The OKW staff in general parallel that of the Army, with Operations, Intelligence, Logistics and Administration as it major functions. Both the OKW and the OKH had signal branches, but throughout the war one officer had a "duel-hat" appointment to command both of them. This convoluted command structure resulted in two separate cryptologic agencies serving the military, the *Oberkommando der Wehrmacht /Chiffrierabteilung* (OKW/*Chi*) and the *Oberkommando der Herr/General der Nachrichten Aufklaerung* (OKH/GdNA).

Oberstleutnant Mettig was a career signals officer, having commanded a number of signals companies and served on various staffs since 1933. In November 1941 he was brought to Berlin to command Inspectorate 7/VI, the central cryptologic agency in the OKH for non-Russian traffic. Later, after a six-month tour commanding a panzer corps signals battalion in the summer to winter of 1943, he was ordered to OKW/*Chi* as the officer in charge of intercept. After the reorganization of OKW/*Chi* in November, 1944 he became head of the cryptologic division. Although primarily an administrator, he had enough detailed knowledge of OKW/*Chi*'s operations to be later included in the small group sent to England for interrogation. He provided SHAEF with an organizational overview of OKW/*Chi*, explaining that it, like many of the German staff organizations it had broken into two parts, a northern section in Flensburg and a southern section enroute for Austria. The northern section was mainly composed of the more senior command staff and cryptologists, selected to provide support to the remnant of the central government, and were under the command of his immediate boss, Oberst Hugo Kettler, currently remaining behind in Flensburg. The Southern section, composed of the main working party, was merged into the Army's SIGINT service, the GdNA, under the command of Oberst Boetzel. Mettig was the second in command of the northern section and did most of the day-to-day direction. Mettig however, showed some initial reluctance, feeling that "his dignity as an officer would be compromised by over-eagerness to volunteer information." However, he provided to the SHAEF interrogators a key clue, the location of Kettler's HQ, in country pub between Flensburg and Schleswig, which was passed to TICOM.[79]

2

The TICOM military officers were occupied helping their naval counterparts in Flensburg during the busy week after the surrender. However, by the 19th, word had filtered down from the SHAEF interrogators in Reims identifying Kettler and giving his address. Laptook and Kirby were able to break away from their duties and found Kettler at a village "Wirtshaus" (Tavern) in Ausacker, 6 kilometers southeast of Flensburg. In their initial interrogation, Kettler impressed Kirby as an alert, intelligent officer who was willing to cooperate. Kirby later wrote that

> "Kettler proved to be a very capable administrator with no technical background in cryptanalysis. His greatest value was in his ability to provide details regarding personnel employed in the various sections of OKW/*Chi*, and the movements of the parts of the organization after it was split up.... It was he who told us that the archives had arrived in Bad Schliersee."[80]

Most importantly, he located three of their most important cryptographers, Doctors Erich Hüttenhain and Walther Fricke and Oberleutant Schubert all in the Flensburg area. All three were located the next day in nearby villages and were brought to Flensburg for preliminary interrogations.

4. Fruits of Victory

Regierungsrat (Specialist) Hüttenhain was a mathematician hired by OKW/*Chi* in 1937 to build up a research section that investigated the most difficult enemy systems that were beyond the capacity of the regular cryptanalysis section, and to investigate the security of the German's own systems.[81] As chief of the mathematical section, he could provide detailed technical knowledge of the work of OKW/*Chi*, including their work on breaking allied machine systems. Kirby later commented that he "…gave evidence of his technical background, and there was no doubt at all that he was one of the men TICOM was interested in."

Hüttenhain had been an astronomer by training and was working at the observatory at the University of Münster the mid-1930s when he contacted Wilhelm Fenner, senior cryptanalysts at the war Ministry, with some suggestions for cryptologic systems. These suggestions were unusable, but they demonstrated a highly analytical approached to the problem. The following year Fenner received additional funding to hire staff, and sent for Hüttenhain. Although Fenner came from the traditional linguistic approach to cryptanalysis, he was perceptive enough to realize the increasing use of superencriphered codes and the more recent appearance of machine ciphers called for a more mathematical approach. He soon became Fenner's chief assistant for the studying of new, more complex systems. Intellectually curious, a critical thinker, and self-motivated, he soon became Fenner's most valued cryptanalyst. By 1944 he was director in Fenner's Main Gruppe B of Gruppe IV, whose formal duties were listed as "Analytical solution or reencipherments. Testing of cryptologic inventions. Development of cryptanalytic aids. Training and Instruction" [*sic*].[82]

As chief of the mathematical section, he could provide detailed technical knowledge of the work of OKW/*Chi*, including their work on breaking allied machine systems. Kirby later commented that he "…gave evidence of his technical background, and there was no doubt at all that he was one of the men TICOM was interested in." Indeed, he was the chief prize of Team 6, who proved so valuable in England that he was later loaned to the Americans.[83]

Sonderführer (Senior Technician) Fricke, also a mathematician who had done extensive work on the security of the Enigma and other German machine systems, gave Kirby a much different perception, that "...he did not give the impression that he had as great an amount of technical information as later proved to be the fact. He answered questions readily but did not enlarge upon them.... later when Fricke became acquainted with us he became very communicative and proved that he had a great amount of interest and information in common with R.R. Hüttenhain."[84] Fricke, like Hüttenhain, was also an astronomer, having studied in Berlin, worked at the Hamburg observatory, and in 1939 took his doctorate at Göttingen observatory writing a dissertation on the dynamics of stellar systems. Appointed to a position at Hamburg University, he was instead drafted into the Army Signal Corps and was assigned to OKH/ Inspectorate 7/ VI signals intelligence headquarters, where he specialized in the development of the German Army's ciphers. Transferred to OKW/*Chi* in November 1944 when *Chi* took over this function, he was at first mistrusted by Fenner. However, Fenner eventually warmed up to him, later describing Fricke as "... (having) a decent character, is a good analyst, takes his work seriously and has the gift of being able to recognize precisely the weakness of our own systems." Probably because of their mutual backgrounds, Fricke and Hüttenhain were close and "in many of the interrogation reports it is impossible to distinguish between the contribution of Fricke and that of Hüttenhain" TICOM later commended.[85]

Oberleutant (1st Lieutenant) Schubert was an OKH signals officer who had commanded HSL Ost, the Army's Russian front signals intelligence bureau. He was probably the German's foremost expert on Soviet codes and ciphers and as such worth his weight in gold to TICOM. His

4. Fruits of Victory

brief interrogation on 24 May revealed that the Germans had received a captured 5- figure codebook from the Finns and that the Russians had reused a one-time pad, allowing the system to be read for a while.[86] They also had success with three and four figured codebooks re-enciphered with conversion tables. Later he questioned about Soviet military and agents systems, he gave details of the codes used by the NKVD and their counter intelligence SMERSH organization.[87]

Although these three were an excellent start for TICOM's inquiries, one key official was missing from the bag. William Fenner, Chief Cryptanalyst and a founding member of OKW/*Chi*, was not with the Flensburg group, but rather had led the OKW/*Chi* operational group south.

The early history of OKW/*Chi* is reflected in the career of its senior cryptanalysts who almost single handidly preserved it during the lean years, and then built it into a major cryptologic force for Germany during the war.

Wilhelm Fenner was born in St. Petersburg, Russia in 1891 of German parents. Raised and educated in German schools to the primary level in St. Petersburg, he moved to Berlin in 1910 to study at the Royal Institute of Technology. After a short stint working as an engineer, he was called up to the Army in December, 1914 and spent the next year serving in infantry units in Russia, Tyrol, France, and Serbia. Because of his language skills, he was transferred to the 10th Army headquarters as a translator, and spent the rest of the war on various Army staffs. He remained in the Army for two years after the Armistice, taking his discharge in 1920. He tried his hand at working in the Public Affairs industry during which he met Professor Peter Novopaschenny, Russian emigrant and former Imperial Navy Captain who during the war commanded the crypto service targeting the German Baltic Fleet. With both men at career short shrifts, they teamed up. Novopaschenny taught Fenner cryptology and Fenner used his contacts to land a contract with Oberleutnant Buschenhagen, director of the War office Cipher Bureau, to break and translate intercepted Russian telegrams. Fenner was not only a talented cryptanalyst, he was also an able administrator and by 1922 he was in charge of the Russian section. He systematized their analysis, and picking Novopaschenny's brain documented improved techniques and formalized technical language. By the end of the year, this led to full time jobs for both Novopaschenny and Fenner, with Fenner hired as director of the cryptanalysis section, then comprising 11 employees. With energy and determination to professionalize the organization, he expanded coverage to include Poland and Rumania. Since the early 1920s, the Cipher Bureau had a strong interest in diplomatic communications. The conditions of Post WWI Europe resulted in a lack of foreign military communications for study, so Fenner believed that access to diplomatic traffic would provide the practice necessary to build the staff's skills and increase the influence of his bureau. The Cipher Bureau competed with the Auswärtiges Amt (Foreign Ministry) for access to diplomatic cables passed by the Post Office, successfully arguing that diplomatic communications would also contain information relevant to military matters. This stance caused a rift with the Foreign Office, which continued to be a point of contention between the two agencies up to the war.

But the pressure of events motivated closer cooperation between the two agencies, at least at the operational levels. OKW/*Chi* provided the Auswärtiges Amt with diplomatic traffic passed from its intercept sites, liaison officers were exchanged, and OKW/*Chi* detached some personnel to Per ZS. Both agencies worked on the American strip cipher, but as much in competition as with cooperation. When the quarters of OKW/*Chi* were bombed out in 1943, Auswärtiges Amt provided them with some borrowed office space.[88]

4. Fruits of Victory

Fenner continued to build his reputation, consulting with the Finns, writing papers and training manuals. Increased diplomatic activity in the late 20s led to more traffic and new systems to study, and led an increase of the Cipher Bureau's personnel levels. He suffered a blow in 1933 as a number of his employees bolted to join the Forschungeamt, a new rival, created when three Nazi sympathizers quit the Cipher Bureau and cut a deal with Herman Goering to form a new signal intelligence organization under his sponsorship and in the service of the Nazi party. Their ambition was to centralize all SIGINT within the FA, and they emphasized diplomatic communications along with domestic surveillance. Relations between these two agencies never recovered, Fenner complained about the FA sabotaging his reputation within the Nazi hierarchy, planting a spy in his office and tapping his phone line. Wendland, Fenner's second in command later characterized it: "The hostility between OKW and the Forschungeamt was especially political; the Forschungeamt people were all Nazis, whereas in OKW nobody ever said "Heil Hitler" and they were not slow to criticize the party".[89]

Other potential rivals appeared with the reorganization of the German armed forces after the Nazi's assumption of power with the creation of SIGINT organizations for the Army and the newly formed Air Force. However, the start of the war focused their attention on tactical SIGINT while OKW/*Chi* continued to focus on diplomatic communications.[90] This scattering of effort among competing intelligence organizations in strategic intelligence was a major German weakness.

By 1938 however, Fenner, now promoted to Ministerialrat (Undersecretary), was leading a department (Main Group B) that had grown to 200 personnel. This organization, now formally known as the *Oberkommando der Wehrmacht/Chiffrieerabteilung,* continued to grow throughout the war, and by 1944 it had 800 personnel.[91] Like many other headquarters, OKW/*Chi* was bombed out in the intense RAF attacks of November 1943. They were forced to work in damaged and unheated quarters, and under constant threat of further air attacks, their output declined by 25 – 30 percent. They finally evacuated Berlin in February 1945 to the Army Signal School in Halle, and then forced to leave again in less than two months as the American Army approached. OKW/Chi split into two parts, with Kettler, Mettig and some of the senior employees traveling north towards Flensburg; Fenner led the remaining operational sections south to Werfen, Austria, in the Burchtesgaden area. There, on 14 April, OKW/Chi was dissolved and all personnel were transferred to the Army's GdNA.

Although Wendland got on quite well with him, he later characterized his boss: "...nobody took him very seriously. Fenner was against everything, against the Party, against other forms of government. He was not very clever and most of his work was administrative. He was generally disliked, and people thought him hysterical. He was too quick in making decisions and passing judgments."[92]

3

A change in policy from interrogating enemy SIGINT personnel in England to interrogating them in the field however, created a problem for Team 6. The surrender had flooded the Combine Services Interrogation Centers (CSIC) in England, from now on only the most important prisoners, whose interrogations, expected to last for months, were to be sent back. Mackenzie was worried that his prisoners, now under house arrest, would be swept in the round up after the dissolution of the Flensburg government and be lost in the system. He had sent an urgent request on May 23, the day the Dönitz government was arrested, that this group of OKW/*Chi* prisoners be sent to the U.K. as soon as possible or that a field interrogation team be sent to Flensburg. The request seemed to disappear into the void, as Mackenzie received no

4. Fruits of Victory

reply. Two days later, he formally requested that the Military Control Commission keep Col. Kettler and his party out of the general POW pool. Informed that day by TICOM that the interrogation team was coming but would be delayed, Mackenzie decided to begin periodic checks of his charges.

On the 28th, the Control Commission decided to move the four OKW/*Chi* prisoners from their civilian quarters into custody at the Schloss Glücksburg, where high-priority prisoners were being concentrated. Finally, on June 8, a message was received that the interrogation team under Commander Dudley-Smith was on its way from BP and would be in Flensburg in a few days. Lieutenant Neulsen, now in charge of Team 6 after Mackenzie's recent return to the U.K., found out on the 10th that his prisoners had been removed from the Castle. Thus began one of those confused and chaotic journeys through the military bureaucracy.

Apparently the Kettler party had been shipped by VIII Corps with a large group of prisoners to a concentration area near Lansburg. Finding that camp full, they were forwarded to a 21 Army Group camp on the Kiel peninsula. The next day, Laptook and Kirby drove up to VIII Corps HQ and by flashing their high-priority "Eisenhower" SHAEF passes, managed to trace down their prisoners and arrange for them to be returned to Flensburg. Keller, Hüttenhain, Fricke and Schubert were back in Schloss Glücksburg two days later, in time to meet the interrogation team.

The same day the Dudley-Smith team arrived in Flensburg the 14th, an accidental massive explosion in the hills above the Signal School forced a temporary closure and evacuation. Oliver Kirby had a narrow escape from that event. He was heading in the direction of the dump to interview an enlisted sailor who claimed to have some firsthand experience with the Kurier device.

> "...I went there in a jeep, and at that time they were unloading sea mines from a German minelayer, and they dropped one and the entire dump blew up and killed the guy I was supposed to talk to and blew my jeep off the road into the ditch… and then it burned. And the "Patria," the ship we were staying on, was being shelled by exploding shells that were lobbing stuff. Oh, it was a beautiful fireworks display. So that was the major war damage that Flensburg suffered."[93]

Despite his close call, Kirby soldiered on, A week later he interrogated a Dr. Roeder, described as a member of the Foreign Office's Pers ZS at Schloss Glücksburg, and came away with further copies of the Russian codebook captured at Petsamo, Finland in 1941, known by the Americans as Code 26.[94]

Kirby also participated in a number of these early interrogations with the BP interrogation team, which also included such notables as Major Seaman, ASA liaison officer to GC&CS, Dr. R.C. Prichard, linguist in the Military Section, and Major G.W. Morgan, head of the BP research section, and his associate Captain A.G.R. Royffe, Interrogations were conducted at both Schloss Glücksburg or at the Signals school.

4

The most interest was on Hüttenhain and Fricke, the two cryptologists. Hüttenhain was questioned intently about his own role, and his knowledge of Russian systems. He identified at least four Soviet military book and substitution codes that had been read regularly and stated that the Russian additive systems had been easily broken until the last six months of the war when the traffic dried up. As for diplomatic systems, the Soviets used one-time pads and this traffic was

4. Fruits of Victory

always unreadable. He also described a Soviet cipher machine based upon the French Hagelin 211, which had been captured, but they had never intercepted any traffic generated by it. A second machine, for high-level encrypted radio teletype, had been introduced by the Russians and had become increasingly important the past year and a half.[95] Finally, he discussed a Russian scrambled radiotelephone system that the Germans were able to read in bits and pieces. As for American traffic, the strip system for both military and diplomatic communications was successfully read, but changes to the system in January 1944 made it more difficult and by the end of the war, it was barely readable. Operator mistakes such as encoding the same message in two different ciphers, the same message sent to various address with different strip settings (depths), stereotype beginnings, idiomatic phrases, and routine messages all aided the Germans in reading the system. The American Hagelin machine was only read when based on operator errors, and the British TypeX was known, but never broken. A TypeX machine was captured in Dunkirk but without drums, and the Germans weren't even sure if the machine had five or six of them. He was also asked about the security of their Enigma machine and stated

> "The security of the Enigma was never completely tested because the machine was thought to be secure. We concluded that further work on the machine was not necessary, because it is secure as it is."[96]

Dr. Walther Fricke was Hüttenhain's counterpart on the cryptologic end of the business; he was the head of Department A II, responsible for the production of codes and ciphers. He described to TICOM how OKW/*Chi* made up their cipher tables with the assistance of Hollerith machines, and Fricke's group was also responsible for making up the Enigma keys for the Army's three wheel Enigmas. Fricke was the developer of the Rasterschluessel 44 (RS44), a tactical field cipher that took so long to break that the resulting information was out of date and of no operational use. The RS44 was a stencil cipher in which a grid of columns and rows were given a different bigram identifier and every column given a random number. Random gaps were blacked out in every row, and the message was written out in the white spaces. in numbered order. Then the message was copied out vertically column-by-column in numbered order and then transmitted. A different cipher stencil printed for each day and bound in booklets for distribution to the field, was easy to use but difficult to break. [97] It was the most successful hand cipher of the war.

By now, a new idea had been implemented, requiring prisoners to do "homework"; write out accounts of their experiences and record their technical knowledge for later analysis by TICOM. Hüttenhain and Fricke were assigned to write a paper on "Development of OKW/*Chi*, sections A. III and B.V. Hüttenhain was given a further assignment to write on "Special Apparatus used as Aids to Cryptanalysis."[98] Homework soon became a standard requirement, and it became TICOM's best source of information.

5

On May 16th, a party from the Forschungsamt suddenly showed up at the Signals School with orders to join up with the B-Dienst. This was the remnants of the FA branch office in Berlin (Zweigstelle Berlin), largely an administrative unit it including security, correspondence, administrative detail, personnel matters and, in addition, technical maintenance of equipment and communications. It consisted of a number of department heads including: Dr. Martin Paetzel, head of the Research section, RR Hoeckley Oden, head of the communications branch, and Min. Rat. Walter Seifert, a senior manager in charge of the intelligence branch. They and a few other minor figures constituted what was informally known as the FA North. FA North's long retreat from Berlin began on 21 April when they moved to Eutin, Schleswig-Holstein where offices of

4. Fruits of Victory

the evacuated Third Reich were being set up. There, the old rivalry between Göring and Himmler resumed, with the Gestapo attempting to gain control of the FA. This was feigned off by the political astuteness of Seifert, and after the destruction of their technical facilities on May 2nd, they were ordered to Flensburg. En route, they were attacked by an allied fighter-bomber and the group took some casualties. Finally arriving after the surrender but with little notice from the allies, they destroyed their remaining cipher materials and went to work on 4 SKL/III's news service. They continued working there until the dissolution of Dönitz's Flensburg government when the group was arrested.[99]

It was another three weeks before TICOM interrogated FA North at Schloss Gluecksburg, where they were being held. By then information about the FA had been sent from SHAEF investigations and Team 1's exploitation of Kaufbuerden in the south. Seifert, the senior member, described the organization structure and functions of the FA, largely confirming information coming from Team 1's investigations. Paetzel described many of the different systems they worked, and Oden listed the intercept stations comprising FA's network. A second interrogation held a month later, added no new information.[100] Kirby, who participated in the interrogations, was not impressed:

> "… the answers given to the few questions which the Forschungsamt group were asked, indicates that this organization had accomplished nothing of importance in the field of German SIGINT, and our observation of the individuals during the interrogation led us to believe that this motley group were a very low type."[101]

About this time Kirby and Neulsen, along with Major Seaman and Captain Royffe of the interrogation team had the chance to interview a senior German signals officer, Oberst Mügge. The colonel was a career signals officer, having served on the staff of the Chief Signal Officer

General Fellgiebel early in the war, and then while serving in Russia as the chief of signals for a Panzer Corps, he was wounded, losing a leg. After recovery, transferred to command KONA 4 in Athens, and later KONA 7 in Italy, he supervised radio intelligence operations during the Tunisian, Sicilian and the early phases of Italian campaigns. Taking ill again in November of 1943, and sent home to recuperate, eventually reassigned as the signals officer for the 15th Army in France, retreating with them back to Holland and Germany. In April of '45 he became the chief of signals for Army Group Northwest under Field Marshal Busch. Although full of information about triumphs and difficulties of the signal organizations he ran, he, like Kettler, was an administrator and had no real knowledge of cryptology. He proved cooperative, almost too so, and provoked from Kirby the comment "…our greatest difficulty proved to be not to get him to talk, but to get him to stop talking." [102]

6

At the end of May Lieutenant Nuelsen was sent to locate and pick up the dumps of documents that Kupfer had admitted to. Nuelsen took along Ensign Phillips and easily found the dump near Neumuenster, consisting of three boxes of papers. On the way, he and Phillips took a detour to see the huge German Very Low Frequency transmitter that the Kriegsmarine had constructed at Kalbe an der Milde in Saxony-Anhalt, to communicate world-wide with its submarines.[103] The other dump on the Elbe, behind the lines in the Soviet zone, proved far more problematic. MacKenzie later reported:

"On the 31st, Lieutenant Nuelsen returned and reported that No.1 dump, as we called it, the one on the Elbe near Torgau, was definitely in Russian territory. He had contacted the nearest American authorities, who considered that when the final line between the Russian and American zones was drawn, it might be possible to get at this material. One

4. Fruits of Victory

of the difficulties about these dumps was that the friends of Captain Kupfer, who were holding them, were quite unaware that the contents of the boxes were anything but Captain Kupfert's personal effects; and so it was of the first importance that no attention should be drawn to their presence in the Russian zone. During the trip Lieutenant Nuelsen had been to Captain Kupfer's home and made contact with his wife, who had told him that she was under the impression that the holder of the Torgau dump had already been arrested by the Russians as the senior member of his community."[104]

Oliver Kirby had his own story about a dump. Based upon his reading of some ULTRA intercepts back at Bletchley Park, he had an idea about the location of another document dump. The message detailed the hiding of an archive of signal materials dealing with the German investigation of the "Rot Kapella" spy ring. The dump was in the Soviet zone in central Germany, and almost a half-century later Kirby recalled

"… they had put all this stuff in tins, sealed and wrapped, waterproofed and put down a well. Okay, well remember, we [TICOM] had the authority to do a whole bunch of things, and you never asked a question because you might not get the answer you wanted. So the [British lieutenant, possibly E. Morgan] and I decided we would go into the Russian zone. He spoke Russian. We had a driver, who was Polish, and he spoke enough Russian, and we'd be fine. We decided we would go into the Russian zone, and it wasn't too far down to this place, and we would go down there and see if we could pick that up. We understood the Russians were really not much in that area. [But] they were...and our intelligence was all wrong. They were all through there. The minute we crossed the border our friendly Russian allies greeted us, and man, they escorted us every foot of the way. So we very quickly decided we would go to another place where we would tell them that what we were wondering about - it was a place that had a small airbase - that we understood that they had some strange, new types of helicopters. I forget what the lie was. So we went there. We did not go to the place we intended. They were with us every inch of the way. They escorted us back to the border. When we got back to the border, they liked to take our weapons carrier apart. At that point, I decided these are not really very friendly guys. They took it apart, and they had been with us every inch of the way. But they were convinced somehow or other we must have picked something up, and we were hiding something. They made us layout everything in our duffle bags; everything. They searched everything." [105]

7

The additional interrogations by Dudley-Smith's group, conducted over a three-week period from the middle of June to July 5th, allowed TICOM to piece together a profile of the organization.

By 1945 OKW/*Chi* had been reorganized into four principal groups concerned with liaison, cryptanalysis and translation, interception, and intelligence. Hauptgruppe A developed the German's own code and ciphers, prepared crypto manuals, and concerned itself with Communications security in general. Fricke was head of its Referat IIb, which did the actual development of new systems. Hauptgruppe B, lead by Fenner, was the cryptanalytic section. The interception group was Gruppe I and controlled the agency's main stations at Lauf (near Nurnberg) and Treuenbrietzen (Berlin). These stations employed about 420 people in total and comprised military, civil servants, and Women signal auxiliaries. Gruppe IV under Hüttenhain's was the dedicated mathematical section, which concentrated on the more challenging ciphers. Gruppe V was composed mainly of linguists, comprising some 22 desks concerned with the

4. Fruits of Victory

crypto systems of various counties, allies as well as enemies and neutrals. Min. Rat. Wendland, Fenenr's second in command, was in charge of this section. Gruppe VI monitored and evaluated foreign news broadcasts, press services, and inter-state W/T calls. It had a monitoring outstation at Ludwigsfelds, and prepared a daily foreign news summary. OKW/*Chi* also received intercepts from the other German SIGINT organizations, and received raw traffic from Germany's allies. The intelligence section, Gruppe VII, was responsible for evaluating and distributing broken and translated messages, and controlled the agency's archives. It periodically issued VN (Verlässliche Nachricht, i.e. 'reliable reports'). It was also known as *Chi*-X.[106]

Towards the end of the war, there was a shift in emphasis away from intelligence and towards cipher security, as represented in the November 1944 reorganization of OKW/*Chi* into a cryptology division and a cryptanalysis division. However, they never achieved a strong centralized authority over cipher security and were limited to the military and a few minor government agencies.[107] This lack of a centralized authority over cipher security was a contributing factor to the insecurity of many German systems, including the ENIGMA. During the war the Germans developed a number of new machines, such as the SG-41, a more secure device utilizing interactive wheel motions and a potential replacement for the ENIGMA, and prototyped advanced versions of secure teleprinters, the T-52 *Geheimschreiber* D and E models. These systems were much more secure, and had they been adopted earlier, could have had a major impact on the Allies ULTRA program. However, engineering disagreements, inter-service rivalry, and manufacturing difficulties from all the bombing delayed their efforts.[108]

In terms of cryptanalysis, the agency did achieve a series of minor success. Reporting on diplomatic intelligence was a function of the linguistic section, under the supervision of Fenner.

OKW/*Chi* maintained a large section, up to 40 to 50 people, dedicated to attacking Anglo-American communications. Breaks made into the diplomatic American strip system made in conjunction with Per ZS, and some breaks into military attaché M-209 traffic keep a steady flow of intelligence to the high command, and represented OKW/*Chi's* greatest success.[109] They had a role in the successful break into the cipher of the American military attaché in Cairo. In the winter of 1941-42 they received a copy of the US Military Intelligence code from the Japanese (probably captured in the Pacific). About the same time, the encipherment tables were stolen from a US diplomat in the Balkans. Study of this system allowed OKW/*Chi* to continue to read the traffic from Colonel Fellers in Cairo even after the encipherment tables ran out. It dried up when the Americans, tipped off by BP, changed to a strip cipher system. Other US diplomatic systems were attacked including the well-worn Gray code (unenciphered and in use since 1918 and read by most of the world's cryptologic agencies) and the more recent Brown code, largely reconstructed with help from Per ZS and completed when the Japanese provided a copy of the codebook. The A-1 code was compromised by the Japanese and the C-1 codebook was recovered by Pers ZS and the enciphering tables solved by OKW/Chi.[110]

As to British systems, the R Code, an unenciphered four-letter code introduced in 1935, was broken and OKW/*Chi* was able to read the new version of this code when it changed every four years. This, along with the American Gray code provided the bulk of the Anglo-American section's work prior to the war. There was successful work done against the British Interdepartmental Cipher, when the book was captured in Norway. OKW/*Chi* cooperated with the Luftwaffe Chi-Stelle in solving the encipherment tables. However, the material was dated and did not provide much value. However, no attacks were successful against high-level American or British machine ciphers and even though a Type X machine was captured at

4. Fruits of Victory

Dunkirk minus its rotors, OKW/*Chi* soon gave up its attempts. Attacks were made against many other systems of both Germany's enemies and allies, totaling at least 29 nations.[111]

However, the Russian section of OKW/*Chi* was small and seems to have accomplished little against Soviet diplomatic traffic. This traffic, encoded with one-time pads, OKW/*Chi* found impossible to break. In the 1944 reorganization, Novopaschenny's Russian desk was transformed into a research section to evaluate newly discovered codes and ciphers. As to military traffic, the Soviet OK–5 through OK-8 series of codes was read; these were four digit codes with partial encipherment by two digit substitution tables. However, the code was largely reconstituted by captures from the field rather than by pure cryptanalysis. Other German SIGINT organizations had much greater success against Soviet military and administrative traffic than the OKW/*Chi* had against Russian diplomatic systems.[112]

Just as the interrogations were to begin, MacKenzie was ordered home to the U.K. He paid a final visit to the Allied Control Commission, who was threatening to close down the Signal School, and successfully argued that 4 SKL/III should be kept intact and not mixed into the regular PW population. It was imperative that the B-Dienst cryptologists continued to be available until every drop of intelligence was drained from them. The group was kept in Flensburg for a few more weeks until most of them were transferred to DUSTBIN, the recently established interrogation center at Kransberg Castle, 25 miles north of Frankfurt.

MacKenzie left Lieutenant Nuelsen in charge to wrap up the interrogation party, to pack the remaining material for shipment to BP, and to doublecheck the prisoners. Nuelsen decided to send the rest of Team 6 home as soon as possible, leaving behind a small holding party. On the last day of the month, Hüttenhain and Fricke were flown to England in the custody of a BP officer, soon to be followed by Mettig. The next day Nuelsen shut down their communications unit, SCU "Barney", and sent Kirby and Laptook home by air. He, Lorton, and their W/T operator left by ground, crossed the channel by LST on 4 July, arriving back at BP by 2200. Next day Nuelsen made his final verbal report to TICOM and the mission of Team 6 was complete.[113]

8

TICOM's first two outings proved to be outstanding, yielding not only important information, equipment and personnel, but allowed the allies to capture intact two of Germany's signals intelligence organizations. However, the rest of the enemy agencies were to prove to be more challenging, scattered as they were across southern Germany and Austria, in bits and pieces.

One of those bit and pieces was Wilhelm Fenner, whose fate was to be unknown to TICOM for a full year. By mid-April, Fenner with the remnants of his Hauptgruppe B had been evacuated to Werfen, Austria, just a few miles east of Berchtesgaden. On April 14 OKW/*Chi* was dissolved, with all of its personnel transferred to the Army's GdNA's South command. With the approach of the American Seventh Army, all of their papers were burned and the remaining equipment thrown into the Salzach river. After the surrender, the Americans transferred the group to Heufeld, upper Bavaria, where Fenner spent his time processing the discharges of his people and writing letters of recommendations. His turn came on 18 June when he was officially discharged from German government service with nothing but a letter of recommendation to show for 25 years service. With his wife and daughter living in the Russian zone, and his son dead from wounds suffered in the war, and barred from professional employment due to his status as an official of OKW, he eventually made his way to Straubing, Bavaria, where he found a job repairing bicycles and cars at a local firm.

4. Fruits of Victory

Fenner's disappearance was neither deliberate nor planned. The American appointed local officials knew of his presence; it appears that he merely became lost in the shuffle of postwar Germany. The following July his name appeared on a potential witness list for the Nuremberg trials and he was found and arrested by the US Army Counterintelligence Corps. This time he was held at the Haus Alaska, on the grounds of the 7707 European Command Intelligence Center in Oberursel, which housed high-ranking prisoners. Interrogated thoroughly over next four months he provided a lengthy series of written reports to the Army Security Agency about his knowledge and experiences with OKW/*Chi*.[114]

The truth was that OKW/*Chi* wasn't what the Allies were expecting. The German approach to SIGINT wasn't centralized or coordinated; rather it was riddled with redundancies and internal rivalries. Although it had developed some high level expertise, especially in mathematical cryptanalysis, its continued focus on diplomatic ciphers in competition with both the foreign office and the FA limited its effectiveness. Its energies and brainpower should have been expended on breaking the Allies' strategic communications systems such as TypeX or SIGABA. Its sparse success did little to attract Hitler's attention, and thus limited the amount of resources the Third Reich would commit to SIGINT.

Rather than the all powerful inclusive agency, like Bletchley Park became, OKW/*Chi* was just another intelligence organization jockeying for position, its failure revealed by the outcome.

5. Success

The allied armies on the western front broke out of their Rhine bridgeheads in late March. On the right General Patch's 7th Army made a great arch along 12 Army Group's flank and then turned south to capture first Munich and then Nuremberg after a fierce week of fighting. On its right, the French 1st Army captured Stuttgart and cleared the remainder of southern Bavaria. On their northern flank Patton's 3rd Army swept across northern Bavaria before sending task forces into Czechoslovakia and Austria. By the first week of May surrender appeared imminent, however large German units were scattered across the area, having retreated from both the western and eastern fronts to the hoped for sanctuary in the Tyrol. This provided TICOM the opportunity to insert their teams into the area and begin searching for the remnants of the German intelligence agencies reported retreating into the Alpine Redoubt.

1

TICOM Team 1 was originally set up to capture the OKW/*Chi* targets in Wilmersdorf and Juterbog. After cancelation of the Operation Eclipse airborne drop on Berlin, Team 1, like the other teams, was modified but kept its OKW focus, with most of its officers drawn from Huts 3 and 6, and having experience with Germany's highest-grade communications.

The team was under the command of Wing Commander Oscar Oeser RAFVR, a veteran BP'er who had been a duty officer and senior Air Advisor and had co-ordinated Hut 3's Fish processing requirements. Originally, from South Africa, Oeser had studied physics there before switching to experimental psychology at Trinity College Cambridge and University of Marburg, Germany, receiving doctorates from both universities. Prior to the war, he was a lecturer at University of St Andrews, Scotland.[115]

As intended, the team's second in command was an American, Lieutenant Commander Howard Compaigne, USNR, who prior to his transfer to Bletchley Park, had become OP-20-G's leading automation expert; having helped designed the navy's Duenna machine to test the assumptions necessary to identify the Enigma reflector wiring. He had been sent to GCCS to learn from the British their techniques for breaking FISH, and had worked in the Newmanry, the unit that was responsible for the Colossus machine utilized in breaking the SZ-42 teleprinter "Tunny" cipher.[116]

Probably the most distinguished member of the team was Major Ralph Tester, head of the BP crypto unit named after him, the "Testery". Set up in October 1942 to exploit the recent break into the Tunny, it used hand methods to decrypt the messages which enabled further research into automating the process with electronic systems, such as the 'Colossus' proto computer. Despite having worked on 'Tunny' for almost three years, nobody at Bletchley Park had ever actually seen an SZ-42 machine. This was Tester's major goal of the trip.

Junior officers on the team included Americans, Captain Louis Stone, who also worked in the Testery, and 1st Lieutenants Paul Whitaker and Selmer Norland, both German linguists who worked in Hut 3. Among the British officers were Majors Angus McIntosh, another machine expert and Edward Rushworth, a fusion expert in Hut 3, both of the Intelligence Corps. Another dozen or so officers from TIOCM Team 2, Bletchley Park or local G-2 staffs were detached for various periods to help.

5. Success

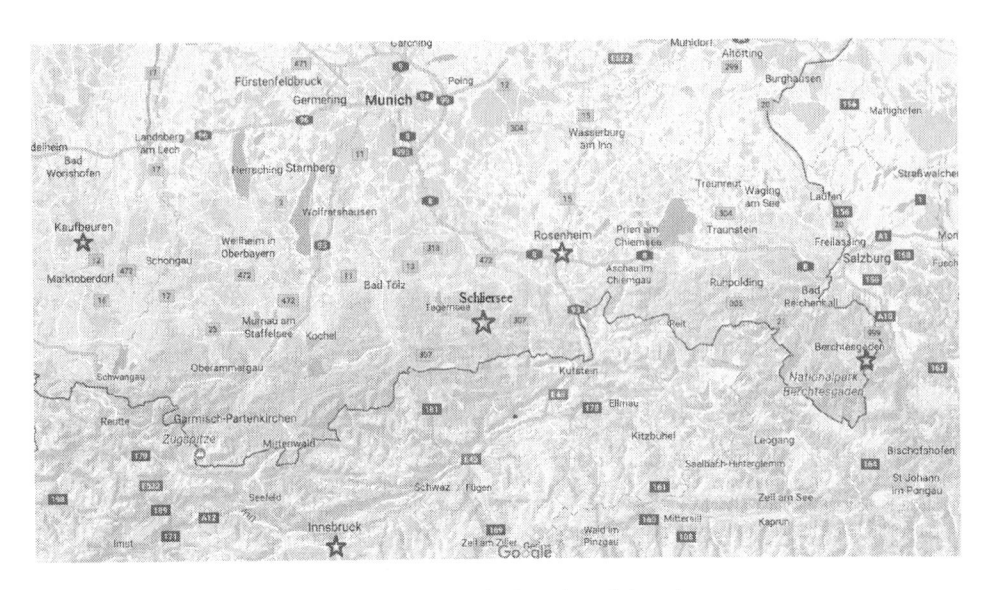

TICOM targets in Bavaria and Austria

TICOM Team 1 on a rest stop in Germany, (Left to right) PFC William E. Hoin (US Army) driver; LAC L.H. Howells (RAF) radio operator; F/Lt. Gerorge H. Sayers (RAFVR) Hut 3; Lt./Comdr. Howard H. Compaige (USNR) Block H Newmanry and deputy chief of the team; Sgt. H.G. Anderson (Royal Signals) radio operator; Capt. Louis T. Stone (US Army) Block F Testery; 1sr Lt. Selmer S. Norland (US Army) Hut 3; Major Angus McIntosh (Intelligence Corps) Bock F Testery ; Major Ralph P. Tester (Intelligence Corps) Block F Testery; Capt.Edward Rushworth (Intelligence Corps) Hut 3 ; W/Comdr. Oscar A, Oeser, (RAFVR) Hut 3 and Team 1 commander, Sgt. Clarence L. Ray (US Army) driver. (Photo by 1st Lt. P. K. Whitaker)

Oeser and his team left for Paris on 4 May for the usual rounds of briefings from Bicher's SID, clearances and arrangements for vehicles. En route they stopped for the night to do some sightseeing at the castle ruins at Heidelberg, and the next day the 7th, the first stop with operational interest was made at Augsburg, where Oeser conferred with 7th Army HQ. At the conference, 7th Army agreed to screen any prisoners selected by Team 1, and to provide a special "freezing" camp for their detention. Later, outside the CP, he by chance met Lieutenant (JG) Coolidge USNR, and Major Eldridge, sent earlier by Bicher to investigate the reports of an electronic research laboratory at Ebermannstadt, and Oeser invited them to join the effort. That afternoon when the team received a message from TICOM they first learned that a previously unknown German SIGINT agency had been identified and was in their path.

THOUGHT TO HAVE GONE TO KAUFBEUREN IS CHI DEPT OF LUFTFAHRT MINISTERIUM. THIS FORMERLY SCHILLERSTRASSE BERLIN THEN MOVED TO BRESLAU HARTLIEB BARRACKS; JUETERBOG; FINALLY KAUFBEUREN. MVN RAT SCHROEDER RPT SCHROEDER IS HEAD; FOUR DEPARTMENT HEADS ARE OBERRAT WAECHTER RPT WAECHTER COVERING PORTUGAL SPAIN EIRE CHINA JAPAN TURKEY UL ENGLAND, WITH AUSTER RPT SAXEX RPT AUSTER, THONAK RPT THONAK ND KISCHNER RPT KIRSCHNER WORKING FOR HIM; ORR SCHULTX RPT SCHULTX DEPUTY HAUMEG RPT HAUMER COVERING GREN ITAL RLUMAN VAPLS, MBWITT REGRAT EOGELKET RPT ENGELKE WORKING IN DEPT; ORR WENXEL RPT WENXEL ALL GREEK ND SLAV WITH TONDORF RPT TONDORF ND LEHR HELPING; DR. PAETXEL RPT PAETXEL COVERS ALL SORTS MAT PRBLEMS

This information about the Reich Air Ministry's 'Research Bureau' RLM/Forschungsamt (FA) was based upon the interrogations of the Pers Z cryptographers by Neff's team at

5. Success

Burgscheidungen, which in turn confirmed earlier information derived from POWs, Private. Lothar Guenther, a former member of the FA captured in Jan 45, and the more recent interrogation of Generalleutnant Friedrich Kersten, a retired Army Signal officer, detained in the Ruhr pocket a few weeks earlier.

The next day the rest of the team investigated the abandoned remains of Luftgau VII, a German Air Force communications station. The only item of interest was a plain language message on a teleprinter tape that confirmed that the RLM/Forschungsamt had been at Kaufbeuren, an airfield 40 miles south of Augsburg. According to Whitaker the Germans had departed so suddenly that a dangling teletype tape warning of the appearance of American units was left in the machine, "My God, here they are now", it suddenly ended.[117] There were a number of locked safes found in the center and Norland, given the responsibility of opening them, had them blown by a US Army engineer. The danger of the safes were that you couldn't tell if they were booby trapped, and Norland, out of a sense of noblesse oblige stood by the engineer as he set the charges off. The safes opened but were empty. "That's how I spent VE day", Norland later recounted. That evening the team drove down to Kaufbeuren.[118]

This Luftwaffe airbase had been under constant air attacks and it was abandoned upon the approach of the American Army. Now occupied by some POWs and displaced persons, the FA had occupied six blocks of barracks directly opposite the main gate. The team searched the site on the morning of the 9th, discovering a few documents among the empty offices, including a directive signed by the director Gottfried Schapper, which included a table of organization which provided clues as to the existence of its code breaking section. This was the first hard documentation Allied intelligence had pertaining to the Forschungsamt. Cards removed from the doors of the various offices helped indicated the locations of the various subsections, remains of a card index of monitored phone calls gave TICOM evidence of the nature of the work. Equipment was found in Block 10, telephones, teleprinters, radio receivers, T-52 Sturgeon machines, tape recorders and at least 5 Hollerith machines, all evidence of a sophisticated signals intelligence operation. In the next building was a large amount of photographic equipment. A few remaining low level employees were rounded up in the town the next day and they revealed that that Hauptabteilung (department) IV at least included cryptographers, of whom ORR Paetzel was the chief, and that Abteilung (section) 8 dealt with France, Italy, the Vatican, Rumania, Belgium, Switzerland, and that that a large number of the messages translated were commercial in content. The informants also stated that the FA was disbanded prior to the arrival of the Americans, and that all documents were burned.

2

After packing the equipment and documents for immediate shipment to the U.K, and a final inspection, the team drove to Munich to bunk with T-Force for the night. The next step was to investigate the heart of what was left of the German High Command in the Berehtesgaden area. Here the party split up into different groups to explore more territory as they moved in to the area. Oeser accompanied by a 6th Army Group air liaison officer Lieutenant Colonel L. L. Rood, took one route to Berehtesgaden, while Eldridge and Coolidge shortly later started for it via Salzburg. The next morning, after drawing rations for the team, Campaigne also went down to Berehtesgaden and ran into Tester and Rushworth in the main street. They had just arrived after a futile trip across the Tirol in search of a rumored signals dump.

With most of the team assembled again, a concentrated search of the Berchtesgaden area began. First stop was at the OKL headquarters in the BDM building at Strub, a two-story whitewashed former sport school built for the League of German Girls (Hitler youth). Here

5. Success

Oeser, Rood, Eldridge and Coolidge inspected the signals room in the basement, with its telephone exchange and teleprinter rooms intact. There sat six T52 *Sturgeon* machines with their rotor wheels removed. Major Rawisch, a Luftwaffe signals officer, appeared on the scene in time to prevent Oester from "liberating" three Mercedes-Benz staff cars, by presenting his written authorization for his possession of them stamped by the 101 Airborne Division. The telephone exchange still had good communications with Kesselring, Martini, von Winter, and other high staff officers in the Berchtesgaden area. The building was empty of documentation, and while Eldridge and Coleridge went off to inspect other buildings on the compound, Rood and Oeser were intercepted by General Karl Koller himself. The Luftwaffe Chief of Staff was in the process of trying to reoccupying the building, with the aim of rebuilding his shattered signals organization. Koller, who had celebrated Hitler's last birthday in the bunker, had flown out of Berlin on April 23, and had surrendered to the Americans with Göring at Zell am See on May 7th. Now back in Berchtesgaden, he was trying to reassemble his staff to get back to work again. "How can I work without a staff?" he pleaded. He was eager to cooperate and gave Oeser and Rood the last known locations of Oberstleutnant Kienitz (Intelligence) and Oberstleutnant Friedrich (Y-Service). He also telephoned GAF Chief Signals Officer General Wolfgang Martini trying to discover what had happened to the T-52 cipher drums, finding out that they had been in the possession of a Hauptmann Krause, last seen standing forlornly on the road in the path of the American advance. As an additional item, Koller gave them the location of Hitler's mobile headquarters, the BRANDENBURG Fuehrer HQ train.

The next day Major Eldridge and Lieutenant Coolidge made a trip to Hitler's home and compound, the Berghof, in search of crypto gear or documents. The house had been gutted by bombing, with a storeroom filled with furniture, books and papers, most pertaining to medicine and architecture, but no classified documents. Behind it dug into a hill was an air raid shelter with a large telephone exchange, and again a library of fine books reflecting Hitler's passion for architecture and art, but nothing of military interest. Göring's house, offices, and air raid shelter were also inspected, with even less results than Hitler's; no communications instillations were found. A bit more luck was had at Borman's which at least had the appearance of a working office. A handful of commercial Siemens T 37 teletype machines, along with one T 52c *Geheimschreiber*. Miscellaneous unclassified papers found detailing such mundane matters as real estate holding and staff personnel records and news digests, in all a disappointing haul from the mighty rulers of the Reich. The next morning Coolidge returned alone to search the *Reichskanzlei*, the alternative Reich Chancellery built by Hitler in 1937 in Stanggass, just northwest of Berchtesgaden, and used by Field Marshal Keitel as a headquarters during the war. Now occupied as the headquarters of 101st Airborne Division, results here were just as disappointing as the day before. No papers and been found by the division G-2, and the air raid shelter found down the hill from the building had already been looted. On his way in Coolidge met a Lieutenant Colonel burdened with a large armload of books and documents who commented "I consider everything down there legitimate loot". Inside the cellar were three or four apartments and a suite of communications gear including a T 52c *Sturgeon* machine with badly damaged wheels. Books, personal belongings, stationary files and papers, including some highly classified were found. The documents pertained to administrative matters and had no apparent value from a SIGINT viewpoint.

5. Success

The following day, the 14th, having collected its various wandering members, the team established headquarters at the Hotel Deutsches Haus. That morning TICOM Team 2, under the command of Major Charles J. Donahue, and accompanied by Captains Carter and Barringer, showed up in a jeep, soon followed by the rest of the team consisting of 5 BP officers along with 2 radio operators and 2 drivers. They had been dispatched to reinforce Oeser's team in the search of the Obersalzberg region. While the reunion was occurring, Oeser took Rood south to Zell am See to follow up on General Koller's tips. Forced to take the back roads through the mountains to circumnavigate a blown bridge they unknowably violated the 101 Airborne's orders banning allied personnel from the area. The whole region was still under the control of the German Army and was only thinly supervised by one US regiment. Despite their ignorance, they managed to make contact with the OKL headquarters, which obviously had been notified through the grapevine that they were to be visited by Allied intelligence officers. No documents other than a few reports pertaining to Russian order of battle were found. After this initial contact, Oeser and Rood left for the small town of Saalfelden to search for Hitler's command train. There located in the ruins of the BRANDENBURG headquarters train they found two cars containing new and fully intact T 52s, which were put into the custody of the occupying airborne troops. From there the trail led the pair to the nearby village of Alm, the location of OB West, headquarters of the German Commander in Chief West, where they received from their Chief Signal Officer the location of a convoy of communications trucks in Doefheim, just a few hundred yards up the road from the BRANDENBURG train location.

Oeser and Rood realized that this mobile communications unit, officially known FuFe Trupp 19 to the Germans, was better known to Bletchley Park as "Jellyfish". It was OB West's Tunny link to Hitler's high command. This Fish circuit, between OB West headquarters in Paris and Berlin, had been broken and read by Tester's unit. It yielded vast amount of high-grade intelligence to SHAEF during the Normandy invasion, including confirming the Germans continued deception that the "real" invasion would take place at Pas de Calais, and revealing Hitler's plans for the counterattack at Mortain. When the Wehrmacht withdrew from Paris, the unit now motorized, followed the headquarters of OB West to its various locations as it retreated. When Oester and Rood quickly backtracked, they found six 5-ton diesels trucks intact with all of their communications equipment, including a dozen of fully functional SZ 42 Tunny machines. After carefully photographing the machines, to the dismay and objections of the German officer in charge, the pair withdrew to consider their options.

One of the captured FISH trucks parked in a field in Germany.

The next day Oeser and Rood drove back to Augsburg. While Oester was busy drafting and sending a report back to TICOM about the find, Rood, using his authority as a member of 6th Army Group staff, persuaded the command at 101st Airborne to allow him to remove the trucks, now referred to as the "Kesselring Fish Train" by TICOM, as far as Berchtesgaden. Tester and Rushworth, returning from a side trip to the German 19 Army HQ at Tösens where they had

5. Success

liberated some SZ 42s and decimeter sets and shipped them back to the UK, were informed of the find. This had proved to be a red-letter day for Tester in his roving search of Austria in pursuit of the elusive Tunny. That same day orders from SHAEF came down to all forces in the area to freeze all enemy personnel, material and documents and for all German officers to leave and relocate to the barracks at Strub. "There they celebrated their reunion so well that two officers had to be sent to hospital with broken legs, and others remained blotto for 36 hours and could not be interrogated", Oeser later reported.

3

The next morning after Oeser and Rood secured safe conduct passes from the 506th PIR at Zell am See, the trucks were moved up to Berchtesgaden and put into the charge of Major Tester, with Lieutenant Arthur Levenson, detached from Team 2, accompanying him. Levenson, having worked in both the Testery and the Newmanry, and with talents in both mathematics and languages, was considered the American with the best overall grasp of the Fish problem.[119] The convoy, consisting of six trucks, eleven enlisted PWs and their officer, moved out that afternoon, with Tester in the lead truck and Levenson bringing up the rear. They got to Munich that evening and spent the night in a requisitioned house, the PWs in the attic and the TICOM officers downstairs. The next day they made it to Augsburg only to be told by Seventh Army that they could not continue until they had written orders. This took four days, the prisoners, held at the Kaiserhof Hotel under the protective eye of the Seventh Army Interrogation Center, spent their time servicing and making minor repairs to the trucks. "We got to know them a little better and it became fairly obvious that they were cooperative and unlikely to make any trouble." Tester later wrote in his official report. Finally written orders from SHAEF came through and the party continued on through Germany via Heidelberg, Wiesbaden, Rheinbach and then onto Brussels. The group attracted the attention of curious civilians at every stop. Levenson later said "When we got to Belgium... these trucks had no cap numbers and we looked like German troops. And the people were very mad at the Germans and they were throwing things at the truck. I got hit once when they threw a tin can or something.... That was quite interesting because when we got there (the PWs) said, "Where are we?", and I said, 'Litisch?', which is the German name for Liege. They said, "No, it can't be," and I said 'What do you mean?' well, they said they were told it was destroyed by the V bombs. Then they said, 'You can't go to London because London was destroyed by the V bombs.' I said, 'Well, you'll see it when we get there.' Where we were there was no evidence of that. They said they didn't really believe everything they were told. Now they knew that wasn't the case but, they were really scared. Then I would leave them and go off and they pleaded with me that they were being threatened. That I should stay there because without me they were in danger. But, these guys...they would do anything we asked. Partly it was that they felt they were better off with us than any alternative. But in Belgium they got really scared. They really thought they'd be lynched or something. Because there were hard feelings, and it was so obvious. We never bothered to write capture numbers on the trucks or give any identification. We did put a big star, big white star, but for all purposes it looked just like the German trucks that the natives had seen during the war. (The locals) thought, 'well, if the Wehrmacht is back, what's going on here?'...When I walked off, (the prisoners) got scared to death, they said, "No, no, stay around." The trust between the prisoners and Levenson grew strong. "...We became very friendly. These were not combat troops they were communicators. I had a gun. Finally I told them I'd let them carry it. They were obviously not going to run anywhere. In fact, they felt much better off with us than anywhere

5. Success

else, including escape. Because they'd only be picked up and terrible things would happen. We were giving them pretty good food." [120]

Driving from Brussels to Ostend, the convoy was loaded onto a LCT that sailed to the Thames Estuary that night. Next day, a Sunday they came ashore at Tilbury where British MPs escorted the prisoners to Kempton Park, and six drivers arrived from BP to take the trucks back up to Beaconsfield, 25 miles outside London, near High Wycombe. There engineers from GCCS (including H.C. Kenworthy, the director of the Fish intercept site at Knockholt) inspected the gear. Two trucks were used for each end of the link, a transmitter (the Senderwagen) and an operations truck (the Betreibswagen) equipped with two Tunny crypto machines, two telex terminals, a voice frequency modulator, a teleprinter and a paper tape reader.

The operators first set up the daily wheel patterns and settings, and contact between stations was initiated in the clear by hand, exchanging Q codes to test the strength and tone of the circuit. The operator then shifted from manual to automatic operation by activating the tape reader with its pre-punched message, which was XORed with the key sequence coming off one of the Tunny machines,§ then sent through the telex terminal and the frequency modulator to the transmitter in the other truck. At the receiving end the process was reversed, the encryption removed, and the output printed in the clear on the teleprinter on a sticky tape that was cut and pasted onto a message form. It was also possible to use duplex mode, in which both ends of the circuit could send and receive simultaneously, but this could only be done under favorable atmospheric conditions.[121]

4

---

§ See Chapter 8 for an in-depth explanation of this process.

While Tester and Levenson were on their scenic tour of Europe, the rest of the TICOM team was keeping extremely busy. The same day that they left, McIntosh borrowed a jeep and two sergeants from 101 Airborne to scout the location of two rumored sites at the Haus Hienlein and the Hotel Vierjahreszeiten in Berchtesgaden. There he discovered in a large house next to the hotel, a telephone center that had belonged to LV 1000, a Luftwaffe Signals Unit. This well equipped center, besides the extensive switchboard, had a large multi-channel carrier frequency room for the landlines, and half a dozen T52d-es with strip reading machines, in addition to a number of unsecured teleprinters for general use. The secret teleprinters were removed for transportation back to BP, but the bulk of the other equipment was left in place, with McIntosh recommending that it be used by the occupation. Close by in the Hotel Vierjahreszeiten was LV 1000's High Speed Morse station. KWEA Short wave receivers and LWEA long wave receivers were found, along with power supplies and keying apparatus. From the rack panels, two remote transmitting locations were identified, Schloss Klessheim and Fridolfing. Few documents were found but pair of Enigma Uhrs were in the room, with a collection of other Uhrs piled up in the cipher room. [122] The next day Campaigne and Carter visited Schloss Klessheim, finding in the stable the transmitting room, consisting of 11 transmitters of varying power and frequencies. The office was in disorder. The few remaining documents consisted of award recommendations and records, the site was probably stripped due to a T-Force party occupying the it for four days prior to TICOM's arrival. A few days later Fridolfing was visited. This was the receiving station of LV 1000 and, in addition to Rhombic antennas still standing, the receivers had special multicouplers for combining the outputs of up to three transmissions at the same time.

5. Success

On 17 May Dr. Fredrick Pickering, a German linguist and GCCS specialist on enemy SIGINT organizations showed up, followed shortly after by Group Captain Humphries, the senior air intelligence liaison officer at Bletchley Park.

Stone, Hugh Cockerell, one of the team 2 officers, and McIntosh were sent over to Bad Gastein, a spa town near south of Salzburg where 127 Japanese had been discovered at the Hotel Astoria. This was the diplomatic party evacuated from Berlin, and it included the Ambassador himself, Baron Ōshima.[123] He claimed diplomatic immunity for all but six of his party and stated that he had no archives with him. The local American military government unit was without instructions and was somewhat mystified as to how to handle the situation, but was persuaded to at least strengthen the guard. The rest of the team fanned out across the area investigating some SS barracks and Army headquarters, a few documents were found but nothing relevant to TICOM.

Having learned the locations of various German Army SIGINT officers from interrogations, Donahue, Rushworth and Captain Lawrance, bringing along Pickering, drove over the mountains to Luggau to contact the commander of the *General der Nachrichten Aufklaerung (GdNA),* Colonel Fritz Boetzel. They located him in his "office", a borrowed bedroom in a farmhouse, reached through the kitchen. Boetzel was a career signal officer having headed the War Office Code and Cipher section (which evolved into OKW/*Chi*) from 1934 to 1939, and later served as commander of KONA 4 in Athens before being named as the Chief Signal Officer of the 6th Army and retreated with it from Russia. In October 1944, the German Army SIGINT forces were reorganized by the amalgamation of three separate agencies, Inspectorate 7/VI, LNA, and HSL Ost into the GdNA, and Boetzel was named as commander.[124] The official interrogation report characterized him as:

"Oberst BOEZEL is a slim grey-haired man of about 60. Cheery and fully cooperative. We had the impression…that BOETZEL is little more than figurehead; he knows little about his organization.... Other interrogations show that BOETZEL was considered a ludicrous figure. When he made an inspection of all his units in the field there was much sweeping of quarters, picking up of cigarette ends with imprecations to 'be more tidy, the boss is coming."[125]

Despite his reputation to his men as a marionette, and unknown to TICOM, Boetzel had been a member of the "Lucy" spy ring passing information to the Soviets.[126] This of course, was not mentioned in his interrogation; instead, he described the outline of his organization and provided a few details about what type of traffic they handled and what traffic was passed to OKW/*Chi*. As to cryptanalytic success, he claimed that SLIDEX had been easy to break, that the American M-209 machine had been read, but the 'Grosse Englaender' machine (probably TYPEX) had not.

However, the greatest value Boetzel provided to TICOM was when he called in two of his associates, Leutnant Alex Dettmann and Oberinspektor Otto Kuehn. Dettmann was GdNA's Soviet cipher expert, having spent a large part of the war 'forward of division'. At this initial session, this young, bespectacled, studious cryptographer explained the fine points of breaking the 10 X 10 PT code and described some of the tactics employed against Russian communications. Kuehn was Boetzel's head of training and apparently well informed on cryptologic matters, but he did not impress Pickering, "…oval sallow face, shifty, fond of flattery, etc. Definitely a nasty piece of work" he wrote.

Also produced this day was Oberstleutnant Rudolf Friedrich, the senior Signals Intelligence officer of the Luftwaffe. He was on General Martini's staff and was the direct

5. Success

supervisor of the Chi-Stelle, the headquarters' SIGINT organization, now known formally as Luftnachrichten (Air Signal) Battalion 350. On request, Friedrich produced a chart of the order of battle of all his now scattered units, and reported that he thought that LN 350 was in the Innsbruck-Imst area of Austria. When asked directly about his chief cryptanalyst he had to be reminded of Voegel's name, "He blushed and said that it had been hoped to keep him out of enemy hands; since you know him already, however, Voegele accompanied Battalion 350 into the Innsbruck area and has been reported in Murnau." Pickering later reported. He complained that he had gotten little results from his cryptographers for the past two years and passed along the gossip that Voegele had recently taken to drink.[127]

The next day Pickering hunted down Colonel Kopp, the senior commander of signals intelligence for the OB West staff, which included direction of KONAs 5 and 6 on the western front. Kopp had not been listed in the muster received from OB West, but when Pickering showed up in Alm and pressed the matter, he was produced. It took a bit of time since he bothered to dress formally, but when he showed up, he was characterized as a "barrelly cheerful" person, smelling of brandy. Retreating to the village school for some privacy, the ice was broken with some gossip about various German SIGINT officers that they had encountered, "It is amazing to see what good can be done by a casual reference to the wooden leg carried by Oberst Muegge" of KONA 7. Getting down to business, Kopp was of the opinion that American signals had caused little difficulty to the German intercept service, content of tactical signals forward of division were easily broken and traffic analysis had kept track of higher echelons. However, tracking VHF transmissions were more difficult due to equipment limitations of the Germans. The British had been more elusive in their signals security, with the Air Liaison nets being the only reliable source for the Germans. Kopp knew little about cryptology, being more of a 'Y' service type, but he called in Major Dr. Hentze, head of GdNA's Groupe IV. Hentze proved to be quite shy and modest, not what you would expect from the GdNA's head of cryptanalysis. He confirmed that SLIDEX was easily broken and CODEX could be gotten out with a bit more effort, but the American machine SIGABA could not be broken, and he did not mention TYPEX. Pickering warned future interrogators that "Hentze need careful but probably not rough interrogation…. Hentze is a dear old man who will probably not respond favorably to bullying."[128]

5

At this time TICOM Team 2, with some personnel shuffling, broke away to pursue their own mission. They departed Berchtesgaden for Innsbruck to search for the Luftwaffe Signal Intelligence Regiment 350. Oeser returned once again to Augsburg to coordinate with 7th Army and draft command directives about the handling of enemy 'Y' service personnel. An order had just come in from SHAEF freezing all enemy personnel, occupants and equipment in the south area, preserving it for intelligence investigations. Group Captain G. Rowley Scott-Farnie, a veteran RAF 'Y' Service officer now assigned to SHAEF intelligence, showed up to survey the scene for the Air staff. After a brief conference, Oester left again by air to Reims to arrange with the Supreme Commander for priority air transportation to the U.K. for their prisoners wanted by TICOM and the Air Ministry, and also to arrange clearances for the Jellyfish convoy. He took the opportunity to brief the Chief Signals officer about the communications situation in the redoubt, and then left for the U.K to report in to TICOM at BP.

Back at Berchtesgaden McIntosh was busy blowing a safe in Herman Göring's adjutant's house. Reverting to acetylene blow-torch to cut into the stubborn container, they set fire to the asbestos material in the door which produced clouds of white dust. Finally reaching in the hole, they withdrew a packet of shampoo powder. Unfortunately, nothing else of interest was found.

5. Success

However, the afternoon brought better luck. McIntosh brought along Norland, Carter, Campaigne, Whitaker and Coolidge from Team 1 to Straub to sort through a large collection of documents, mainly Abwehr, that had been found in a local barracks, the Jäger Kaserne. The cellar contained a variety of signals equipment, including a Tunny machine, a number of badly damaged T 52s, a large amount of switchboard equipment, two tons of maps, and several boxes of already fused stick grenades. Upstairs they found a locked room, which upon break-in was discovered to contain some private baggage of some of the staff officers. Among the baggage were the personal effects of a Major Neilsen, Operations Officer for the Chief Signal Officer of the Wehrmacht, which upon inspection, yielded a number of highly classified documents, including an activity report for OKW/*Chi*, for the first half of 1944. This report, signed by Kettler, was the first hard documentary evidence that TICOM had on the organization; it spelled out tasks, identified intercept stations, statistics of monthly radio coverage, and numbers of finished reports submitted.[129] The team barely had time to start celebrating their lucky find when they received a telephone call from Major Dunn, 7th Army SIGINT officer, who asked them to investigate a tip about some German PWs at Bad Aibling who claimed that they had buried some signals equipment at Rosenheim. Unbeknown to the team, they were about to embark on TICOM's greatest success.

6

The morning of the 21st May, while the rest of the team fanned out to again follow up on a number of unproductive targets, Campaigne, Rushworth and Carter were detailed to drive up north to the large POW cage at Bad Aibling in Bavaria. There they were introduced to Unteroffizier Dietrich Suschowk, who claimed he had knowledge of certain signals intelligence equipment and documentation pertaining to the interception and decoding of Russian traffic.

Suschowk explained to the TICOM team that he worked for GdNA Gruppe VI, a platoon size unit responsible for intercepting high level Soviet Radio Teleprinter traffic. The last location of this unit was at the Pionier-Kaserne, a barracks at nearby Rosenheim. Suschowk described, as "the natural leader" of this group of twenty or so prisoners, was eager to cooperate with the Allies. This was quite a coup because Anglo-American intelligence knew very little about Soviet communication, and was not aware of Russian teleprinter traffic. If true, it would give the western allies an enormous gain in the already budding cold war.

Next day the TICOM officers, now augmented with Collidge and Whitaker, returned to Bad Aibling and escorted the Groupe VI prisoners back to their quarters at Rosenheim, now occupied by a US Army ration dump, and were put to work digging up the equipment buried under the cobblestones and in the yard. The prisoners recovered a dozen large chests, 53 smaller chests and another 53 boxes totaling about 7 ½ tons.[130] Suschowk and his team then volunteered to put one of the machines together to demonstrate that it was in good working order. Paul Whitaker later reported "They were intercepting Russian traffic right while we were there. And pretty soon they had shown us all we needed to see."[131]

5. Success

German POWs digging up and unpacking their gear at Rosenheim. (Whitaker)

Pickering, who dropped by on his way to Munich, had a chance to chat with some of the prisoners.

"Twenty-one NCOs and men had just completed digging up from bomb craters the vital parts of the 'Fish' intercept machines," he later wrote, "...(I) buttonholed in the corridor of the cellar, to which the dug-up parts were being carried, amidst much din and vituperation, Uff'z KARRENBERG,

It was immediately obvious that here were the people who talked the same language as the experts of G.G. & C.S. "Wheel Lengths, 'turn overs', and 'depths'.

This Army intercept unit has been covering since practically the beginning of the German- Russian war Russian non-Morse teleprinter traffic of the BAUDOT system. The Germans have successfully followed the Russians in various modifications of the nine-channel system, and used for the purposes machinery which, in dispersed form, seems to equal in bulk that of three or four Knockholt receivers....

The traffics picked up and broken carried what would probably, taking our standard from German 'Fish', call medium grade intelligence.

The team consists of technicians who claimed they would be able to reconstruct their machinery and have it in working order in a day. When they saw their machinery they specified a longer time; the security scavengers had been in after them, further dispersed the parts of the machinery, and done a certain amount of unearthing of what had been buried.

The team includes operators, breakers, and evaluators.

We have not; in our TICOM field experience met a more intelligent batch of Germans. The highest rank they could muster was one Wachtmeister. The reason is that, in the time of emergency Oberst BOETZEL has turned all the civilian experts in his organization (some of them with high civil service rank) into soldiers, privates, We must be grateful to Oberst BOETZEL (Soldiers are easier to handle as prisoners. People with a grievance interrogate easily). The sum total of remarks passed on Oberst BOETZEL (whom we had judged harmless) was illuminating. It seems that we can dispense with interrogating many of the higher-ups whom we had on our lists: 'they sign our reports, nothing more'.

Detailed interrogation of these NCOs and men is essential particularly of Unteroffizier KARRENBERG, the man who is working on 'wheel lengths' and 'turn-overs'". Pickering concluded.[132]

The equipment was a special receiver that the Germans called the "HMFS" (Hartmehrfachfernschreiter), i.e. Multichannel intercept teletype.[133] Designed to intercept the Soviet equivalent of the "Fish" traffic, these encrypted radio teletype signals had a twist. The

5. Success

Russians had devised a method to multiplexed these messages on up to nine separate channels.[134] Without knowledge of the signal characteristics and the proper equipment, interception was very difficult.

The HMFS "Russian Fish" captured at Rosenheim. (Whitaker)

The German prisoners and their gear was then taken to Seventh Army HQ in Augsburg and held awaiting transportation to the UK This provided both TICOM and Seventh Army G-2 an opportunity to initially interrogate the prisoners. Twenty-one prisoners, a senior NCO, three mechanics, eleven operators, two decoders and four evaluators, formed this group. Three in particular were found to be most helpful. The aforementioned Suschowk was described as "unquestionably the natural leader", an intelligent man with a firm grasp of the "Russian Fish" apparatus and its operating procedures. Unteroffizier Werner Hempel, an engineer by profession, was not only responsible for maintaining the equipment but had also helped the Lorenz Company build it. TICOM commented, "…he is not a leader like Suschowk, preferring as he does to get on with his job in a quiet and apparently efficient way." However, the most useful prisoner for TICOM eventually proved to be Unteroffizier Erich Karrenberg. He was born in Poltava, Russia in 1911, the son of a German manufacturer. After being educated in Russia, he returned to Germany in 1930 to study music and was later employed as a lecturer in the History of Art and Music at Berlin University. He either joined the Army in 1939, or was called up in 1941 (sources vary), but nevertheless he ended up utilizing his Russian language skills in a wire-tapping detachment at the front. After a stint teaching Russian to trainees at an Army school, he took a cryptanalysis course at Jüterbog and was attached to GdNA Groupe VI where he specialized in working out the daily letter-scramble that the Russians used. He was described as "…very intelligent, extremely cooperative and has a multiplicity of interests." Over a series of interrogations, he was probably the single best source for TICOM on the details of the Russian Fish.

After loading the truck with the gear, the entire party traveled to Augsburg to be hosted by Seventh Army for the rest of May, awaiting interrogations and transportation.

7

Now the roots of the Kaufbeuren planting began to take bloom. On the 21st word passed to TICOM that the director of the FA, Gottfried Schapper, had been apprehended in Rosenheim by Counter Intelligence Corps, and was being held in Augsburg. Rushworth, in town attending to the Bardot gear and crew, had the opportunity to interrogate him on the 29th. One of Schapper's department heads, Regierungsrat Erwin Reitschler, also was picked up, and Norland interrogated him the following day. These two, in addition to the information soon flowing from the FA North party in Flensburg, provided TICOM with a detailed picture of the organization.

5. Success

The most unusual fact about the FA was that the existence of this agency was unknown to Allied intelligence until TICOM's interrogations of Per ZS personnel at Burgscheidungen.[135] The FA has been described as '…the richest, most secret, the most Nazi, and the most influential of the …agencies….'[136] Created in 1933 when Gottfried Schapper, a dissatisfied employee of the Defense Ministry cipher bureau approached Reichsmarschal Herman Goering with the idea of creating a new centralized civilian signals intelligence agency free of the influences of the traditional government ministries. Goering saw this as an opportunity to centralize his own power and approved the creation of a 'Research Bureau' under the cover of the German Air ministry.[137]

Rushworth described Schapper as "a small, rather pleasant, with rather ingenuous blue eyes. He had a short beard during his residence in Augsburg; this may, however, be due to the fact that CIC pulled him in without giving him time to bring a razor with him." Appearances aside, he seemed eager to cooperate, "the reason for this was, he explained, a sincere desire to cooperate with the Allies for the promotion of world peace", the sincerity of this attitude should be judged in light of his long history in the Nazi party.[138]

Schapper had been an officer in the German Army from 1910 to the end of the First World War. From 1916 he served in the German High Command collecting, decoding, and evaluating communications intelligence. An ardent Anti-communist, Schapper joined the Nazi party in 1920, but was kicked out a few years later for his failure to take part in the Putsch. After a variety of jobs as a business manager of national organizations, clubs, businesses, and newspapers, he secured a job with the Cryptographic bureau of the Reichswehr War Ministry. After Hitler came to power in 1933, he and his companions Corvette Captain Hans Schifupf, a naval liaison officer to the Crypto Bureau, and Prince Christoph Von Hess, approached Herman

Göring, whom Sahapper had known from the war, to propose the formation of a new signals intelligence agency under the sponsorship of the Nazi party. Rejecting what Sahapper claimed to be the thoroughly incompetent methods of the cryptographic bureau, they aimed to provide the Nazi leadership with "reliable and objective" information (i.e, not tainted with the professionalism of the War and Foreign Ministries). Göring, seeing an opportunity to expand his power within the Nazi hierarchy, approved the formation of the "Forschungsamt" (Research Bureau), reporting to him under his personal sponsorship. This shadowy organization, financed by Prussian state funds and later by money from the Five Year Plan, was hidden administratively within the Reichsluftfahrtministerium (RLM) but in fact was largely independendt. Hitler probably tolerated it because it p him a check on Himmler and other Nazi leaders.

Despite Sahapper's claim to be the brains behind the idea, Schifupf was appointed as the first director. The FA began an aggressive move to recruit members of the War department Cipher Bureau, promising better pay and more opportunity, causing a serious rift between it and what would soon to be known as OKW/*Chi*.[139] Located on the Behrend Strasse in Berlin, it soon outgrew its quarters and moved to Schiller Strass in Berlin/Charlottenberg where it eventually grew to 3600 personnel. Schifupf, an unstable character, committed suicide in 1935, allegedly over a love affair. His successor Von Hess, a member of one of Germany's oldest and noblest families, was a great-grandson of Queen Victoria and younger brother of a crony of Göring's. Sahapper, who had rejoined the Nazi party in 1931, was made the deputy director. Von Hess was an able administrator but he requested leave from the FA to go on active duty with the Luftwaffe after the beginning of the war. Sahapper, was made acting director but after Von Hess's death in a plane crash in Italy in 1943, he was promoted to its permanent director.

5. Success

The FA organization consisted of a main office in Berlin and various liaison offices, regional offices and intercept stations. The Berlin office had six main sections dealing with Administration, Personnel, Intercept, Codes and Ciphers, Evaluation, and Technical matters. Each of the main sections contained a number of specialized subsections; for instance, the Technical section had subsections dealing with development of IBM type machinery and another to evaluate captured enemy machinery.

The FA's original focus was on telephone monitoring within Germany, and was reportedly involved in various Nazi political operations, including the 1934 'blood purge' and the Anschluss (March 1938).[140] The diplomatic crisis of the late 30s turned the FA's attention to foreign policy by intercepting all diplomatic cables passing through Berlin, and expanding its cryptanalytic capabilities to work on diplomatic and commercial communications along with a broadcasting monitoring service. After the start of the war, cable and landline communications with the outside world largely dried up, and the FA became more active in radio intercepts.

The FA employed five different types of intercept stations, 'A' stations dealt with telephone intercept, 'B' with wireless intercept, 'C' with radio broadcasting monitoring, of which there was only one station, 'D' intercepted teletype and telegraph, and 'F' stations did mail censorship. Traffic from Type B stations at Breslau and Lebben along with traffic passed from other German SIGINT agencies were the prime source of material for the FA's cryptanalysts.

The code and cipher section (Main Section IV) did this work and among its successes was the interception and reading of Chamberlain's messages to London during the Munich negotiations, the solving of a Russian teletype machine, and some commercial systems, including the Swiss Interbank code. The FA had the rather unique mission of monitoring foreign commercial communications, especially Soviet, to assist German intelligence in estimating the economic potential of its enemies. They were the first ones to intercept Russian Baudot teletype messages, and their analysis of the encrypted traffic was handed off to the Army, resulting in the activity of the Karrenberg party and the 'Russian Fish'.

The FA also attacked a number of foreign diplomatic systems, often with the cooperation of the other German SIGINT agencies. TICOM concluded that the FA possessed copies of a surprising number of foreign codebooks, although there was no information in the documentation as to how the FA acquired them.[141] FA informants stated that some low-grade US systems were read, including a plain five-figure system, the American State Department system, and a Joint American-British system concerned mainly with ship movements. Some British Diplomatic systems were read when captured books were available early in the war, and they managed to break the Bank of England code in 1941, in addition to the previously mentioned Interbank code. Most of its work against commercial codes concerned the traffic of German firms to foreign countries prior to the war. The diplomatic systems of many other minor powers were attacked, including Bulgarian, French, and Italian, Chinese, Finnish, Danish, Japanese and various Latin American systems. Overall, cryptanalysis supplied less than 20% of the information delivered by the FA, and there was a shift from telephone monitoring to commercial and press traffic as the war progressed.[142]

The Evaluation section produced the finished intelligence product of the FA, the 'brown reports', which, filtered through Göring, were sent to the highest officials such as Keitel, Doenitz, and Ribbentrop.[143] The main office intercept section had two units, one to supervise and administer the FA's intercept efforts, the other a message center to sort and distribute the incoming traffic, employing about 200 people, and operated a large number of small intercept

5. Success

stations throughout Germany. They were of various types, including wireless intercept, teletype and telegraph, telephone intercept, radio broadcasting monitoring, and mail censorship. Much effort pre-war was put into telephone interception; they maintained approximately 1000 telephone taps, half of them in Berlin.[144]

Like all the other intelligence agencies, the bombing of Berlin in November 1943 interrupted operations, forcing the agency to move to Breslau, later to Jueterbog, and finally to Kaufbeuren, with only about 450 personnel left when it was dissolved in late April. There was little hard documentation found on the FA; probably because of its Nazi nature, its leadership was more through in destroying its paper trail than the other German crypto agencies. The bulk of TICOM's information came from interrogations of FA and its rival agencies personnel. In the intelligence developed by TICOM on the FA there is a serious lack of information on the FA's role in Hitler's consolidation of power pre-war, and of Hitler's relations with foreign banks and business entities. Modern historians must regret what treasure trove of information could have been found in those lost files.

A year later, TICOM was able to conclude:

"The FA undoubtedly had many faults as an intelligence agency but they seem to have been faults inherent its history (the personalities involved, the Nazi taint, etc.) and also occurring in other German intelligence agencies.... In the light of all the evidence available the FA must be recognized as a highly successful source of intelligence in the fullest sense of the word. So important was the intelligence produced that careful arrangements were made for furnishing it throughout the final stages of the war."[145]

TICOM Team 1 spent the final days of May scouring the Tyrol and southern Bavaria in search of any loose ends. Signals dumps, offices, residents, and PW camps were checked once again, mostly with no results. Carter and Coolidge returned to Bad Aibling to interview a member of the SS, Martin Grobe, who claimed to have had experience with secret inks. Grobe was an unemployed chemist when he joined the SS in 1935, apparently for employment opportunities, and had worked in the chemical industry in the Protectorate of Bohemia. His interest in cryptology was mainly a hobby, and he was of no interest to TICOM.

On May 27th, the team finally had a rest day, after working continuously without a break for over three weeks. Three days later Oeser, returned from the U.K. where he had reported on progress and results of the team, and had begun to make arrangement for the air transport of the Baudot equipment, still in Rushworth's custody in Augsburg, and the remaining documents. Oeser had a team meeting and they agreed that, unless something dramatic turned up in the next few days, the mission was largely complete. The next day it rained, so the team drank their last bottle of wine from Kaufbeuren.

Oeser departed for the U.K again via Frankfort, Campaigne, Stone, and Witaker made a last, unsuccessful check for remnants of the Chi Stelle at Marnau, and then the team began filtering by road back to Paris, for airlift back home. Rushworth and Carter finally arrived by air with the Baudot equipment on June 5th.

Probably unbeknownst to the team at the time, they had accomplished a remarkable success. The capture of the 'Kesselring Fish Train' with its suite of SZ-42 crypto machines put a close to one of BP's greatest cipher breaking efforts. The collection of various personnel, documents and equipment from the German headquarters in the Burgscheidungen area added

5. Success

considerably to TICOM's knowledge base. But most importantly, the exploitation of the 'Russian Fish' was to have long term consequences to the budding cold war.

6. Captured Intact

When Donahue and his Team 2 left the main group in mid March, it was to go south in search of units of the Luftwaffe's Signal Intelligence Service. This was a result of Oberstleutnant Friedrich's interrogation where he stated that Luftnachrichten Regiment** 351, the intercept unit covering western traffic, was in the Innsbruck area and that Regiment 350, the Chi-Stelle, had been ordered to Imst. This turned into wild goose chase. The Innsbruck–Imst area, a 30-mile valley stretched between mountains in the Tyrol, turned out largely empty of German troops, even lacking POW cages in the immediate vicinity. A check at VI Corps headquarters revealed that they had no information pertaining to the GAF regiments. After wasting three fruitless days in searching, Donahue gave up and concluded in his report that:

"A unit overtaken near the Imst area would have to be either in one of the PW cages in the area or in the valley to the south in the vicinity of Pfunds where a considerable number of German troops were living under their officers.... The valley was methodically combed including the upland villages where many of the Germans were living. In Pfunds, Oberleutnant Lehwald, who had acted as liaison officer between intercept units and the IC [Intelligence Officer] of *AOK* 19 (19th Army) was interviewed. In Kreidt, we talked to Oberst von Knau, air liaison officer with AOK 19; in Toesens to the Feldkommandant, an Oberst, and a lieutenant of the Nachrichtenkompanie ZBV 8; at Fiss to a Lieutenant of Luftnachrichtencompanie 200. All these officers seemed willing to give information, but all denied that they had ever heard of any personnel of GAF Signal

---
** An air signals regiment, abbreviated LN.

6. Captured Intact

Regiments 350 or 351 in the area. It was ascertained that there were no Germans in the Pilz or Oetz valleys farther to the east.

The general conclusion from these investigations plus the information on the actual fighting in the area we got from American officers was that GAF Regiment 350 had never got to the Imst area at all or that they had been able to put on civilian clothes and disappear."[146]

What Donahue did not know was that TICOM had a rival. In late April, the U.S. Army Air Force (USAAF) ordered to Europe an intelligence officer, Col. J. G. Seabourne, and assigned him to the Headquarters of the Ninth Air Force, located at that time in Wiesbaden, Germany. He was appointed as the head of a Air Technical Intelligence Team, and joined by two recently arrived junior USAAF SIGINT officers, was tasked with making a detailed study covering the operations of the German Air Force (Luftwaffe) Signal Intelligence Service. It is unclear from the existing documentation whether this operation was approved or coordinated with other allied intelligence agencies, but Donahue and his team seemed unaware of the Seabourne mission.

The Seabourne Report

The Colonel had the advantage of quick access to the Munich area once the surrender took place, and was able to locate a single GAF Signal Intelligence Service prisoner at the cage at Fuertenteldbruck, a Feldwebel (Technical Sergent) Karl Jering. Jering was an educated, fluent English speaker with six years of experience in the SIS, including the central Chi-Stelle and with various field units. He was willing to cooperated and proved to be instrumental in Searbourne mission. He provided the mission with a list of names of leading personalities in the Luftwaffe SIS, which was circulated through the various PW cages in Bavaria. However after three weeks of waiting, Seabourne, with Jering in tow, began touring these camps on his own, and at a Luftwaffe Concentration Area near Aechbach, Bavaria, they discovered the SIS LN Regiment 353, East, less one battalion; one battalion of the LN Regiment 352, South, and assorted personnel of the 351st Regiment, West.[147] Thus, in a single stroke, Seabourne corner a considerable cross section of the Luftwaffe SIS.

On June 18, 22 selected officers and non-commissioned officers from this pool were evacuated to the new US Ninth AF HQ in Bad Kissingen, where they were housed comfortably for long-term interrogations. Among Seaborne's prisoners were the commanding officer and two battalion commanders of the 353rd Regiment, East, the commanding officer of the 352nd Regiment, South, the chief of the SIS for the defense of the Reich, and eventually, Ferdinand Voegele, chief cryptanalysis. When Donahue gave up the search at Imst, he was within 100 miles of Kressbronne on the Bodensee (Lake Constance) where Voegele and his crypto unit, Referat E of the Chi-Stelle, were cooling their heels after the surrender. The Referat, ordered to retreat from Berlin in February and proceed south to the Bodensee, soon found themselves cut off from new radio traffic and their operations ground to a halt. That part of southern Germany was in the French occupation area and since the French were not part of the ULTRA partnership and knew nothing of the TICOM mission, were ignorant of the priority that Anglo-American intelligence was putting on enemy crypto personnel. It took weeks before Voegele's name, processed through normal channels, came up on the PW lists circulated among the allies.

Seabourne's team, now augmented by three USAAF SIGINT officers detailed from the field, settled down to work. Knowing that the type of detailed information the team was seeking required the active cooperation of their prisoners; effort was made to develop relationships. The quarters at Bad Kissingen were in a comfortable villa, a drastic change from the often open air conditions of the PW cages scattered across Bavaria. The guard was withdrawn after the first two days, prisoners were granted a large amount of freedom, issued permanent passes permitting them to move about the town at will until curfew. This strategy seemed to work, no untoward incidents occurred, and the prisoners became cooperative. Although a few of the Luftwaffe officers were Nazis, as members of the regular armed forces they were not active in the party. Attempts were made to enable the prisoners to contact their families and day trips were arranged for those whose homes were in the vicinity. Overall, conditions were better in Bad Kissingen for the prisoners than what could be expected outside on their own, and the prisoners were promised quick discharge as soon as their tasks were completed.

Based upon the preliminary interrogations, the work was organized geographically with accounts to be written about activities in the Eastern, Western and Southern fronts, and by technical approaches, such as cryptanalysis and air defense warning networks. The prisoners were divided into groups based upon their background, and the group senior officer was given responsibility in organizing the effort and submitting a plan. Once approved, each individual in the group was assigned to write an account of their experience and knowledge (in TICOM parlance, 'homework') and be available for follow on interrogations. Although many of the officers and non-coms had knowledge of English, few of them were fluent; therefore, all accounts were written in German. This required a challenging task of translation, particularly since much of the information was highly technical in nature and exceeded the vocabularies of the average G.I. interpreter. In this effort, Feldwebel Dr. Karl Jering, the team's first prisoner, proved invaluable. His fluency in English enabled him to accuracy retranslate many of the accounts, his writing and editing skills pulled together in coherent form the resulting reports. Jering became a de facto member of the team, acting as editor in chief.

This work ground on for three months, and as promised, most prisoners were discharged as soon as their homework was determined to be completed. An exception was made for prisoners wanted by other intelligence agencies, including TICOM, seven of whom were shipped to the U.K. for further interrogations.[148] The result was a 13-volume report covering the full spectrum of GAF SIGINT activities.[149]

The Luftwaffe had the newest, and largest, of the Wehrmacht Signal Intelligence services. The newly established Luftwaffe had relied on the Army for its signal intelligence needs for the first few years, but then established its own service on January 1, 1937, known as the Chi Stelle, OB d L. Starting with one officer and twenty civilians, it grew into an intelligence force of 13,000 by 1945. Its outstanding achievement during the war was what TICOM described as '....signal intelligence without cryptanalysts'. Its skill in interception and traffic analysis enabled the Chi Stelle to exploit all sorts of Allied radio emissions; radar, navigation beacons and radiotelephone chatter, which created a reputation for yielding valuable tactical and strategic intelligence. For instance, as early as December, 1939 Chi Stelle units detected a large formation of British Wellington bombers over Northern Germany and were able to provide the location, height, speed and size of the formation to the defending Luftwaffe fighters. This taught the Germans that signal intelligence could play a critical role in air raid defenses.

The Air Force SIGINT service paralleled the army service in that it had a central analysis and administrative center, the Chi Stelle, located in Potsdam. At the start of the war, it had 10 mobile intercept companies and 14 fixed intercept stations under the cover name of "weather stations". As the war progressed, the Luftwaffe organized radio reconnaissance battalions for each air fleet supported by a fixed station back in Germany. Eventually the field service was organized into three radio reconnaissance regiments; the 351st covering the western front, the

6. Captured Intact

352nd in the Mediterranean and the 353rd in Russia. The Chi Stelle, headquartered at the Marstall, the royal stables of the Prussian kings in Postdam, was designated the 350th Battalion. It was primarily an evaluation agency with three geographic evaluation sections for the Western, Eastern and Southern fronts. Along with its administrative department, it had two specialized sections, a cryptanalyst unit known as Referat E, and a dedicated unit for studying Direction Finding results, Referat F.

Referat E was very much the creation of its chief, Ferdinand Voegele, a linguist and Philologist with international business experience who was hired by the Air Ministry as an interpreter in 1935. His background led to him being assigned to the Chi Stelle upon its creation in 1937 to head up the cryptanalytic effort. At this point, the entire Chi Stelle consisted of about a dozen people, and Voegele had but a single assistant. Czech, Polish and Russian traffic was tackled, soon followed by attacks on the French Air Force 4 letter alphabet code, with Referent E expanding to about 10 employees. After the outbreak of the war 50 enlisted signal operators were assigned to Voegele for training, many of them later detailed out to the field LN regiments. The referent continued to expand, peaking at about 400 personnel by late 1942, including an added Hollerith (IBM) machine section. Women auxiliaries were recruited mid-war to replace men drafted for the front. Despite the growth, Voegele remained a hands on director, twice personally breaking the 4 figure RAF code.

Following the German decentralized philosophy, the Chi Stelle sent a number of detachments forward to support the field forces, and TICOM concluded '…it was considered more effective to have the long-term evaluation center close to the intercept units rather than close to the staffs which they have to feed. However, as the war drew on, all of these detachments eventually merged into evaluation companies for the Air Signal regiments and battalions they served.

The cryptanalytic effort on the Russian front was almost entirely field based, with 85% of the low and medium grade Russian systems read.. Despite this level of cryptanalytic success with the Russians, the Chi Stelle failed to solve other enemy high-grade systems such as SIGABA or Russian one-time pads. The nature of air warfare required a rapid response, with intelligence results needed in a matter of hours rather than days or weeks as with the ground forces Facing the much more difficult cryptanalytic challenge in the West, the Chi Stelle relied heavily on interception and traffic analysis for this type of response. The Chi Stelle and its field tactical units became the prime source of intelligence for the Air Raid Warning Agency of the Reich, a function that became critically important as the Anglo-American bombing campaign developed in 1943-45. They developed sophisticated techniques for intercepting Anglo-American radar and navigation systems. Eventually the Germans were able to track the exact strength, composition and probable targets of enemy bomber raids in near real time. David Kahn concludes:

"German air force radio reconnaissance gave advance notice of many Allied raids, and indeed provided 70 percent of the most valuable intelligence about the enemy that the Luftwaffe received. However, German flak and fighters were often too weak to do much against the broad and endless stream of Allied bombers. In the end, air radio intelligence did little more than to prove once again that knowledge without power is worthless."[150]

Lieutenant Colonel Friedrich, the GAF senior SIGINT officer, was a proponent of this "signals intelligence without cryptanalysis" approach, which in the postwar world would be labeled ELINT. He complained to his TICOM interrogators that "He had had practically nothing from his cryptographers for the past years and he concentrated on much more profitable lines:

6. Captured Intact

route tracking etc." He also gossiped that Voegele had recently taken to drink.[151] Voegele, for his part, complained "Cryptography was considered of secondary importance and consequently he was never allowed any say in the allocation of tasks for the intercept units."[152] This difference in approach can be explained by the changing nature of air warfare. By 1943, the GAF was on the defense in the west, the critical task was to determine the launch of an allied bomber attack, tracking its route, and identifying its target. This could be done in near real time via "signals intelligence without cryptanalysis", i.e. traffic analysis, direction finding, interception of navigation beams and radar tracking. By the time a cryptanalyst broke the content of a message, the raid would be over.

Nevertheless, not all signals intelligence success was due to these methods. As Voegele testified a few months later during his TICOM interrogations at "Inkspot" in England, the Chi Stelle did attack a number of allied air crypto systems successfully. They assisted in the breaking of the M-209 machine cipher and by spring of 1944, the GAF was reading 6-8 days of encrypted traffic per month. Their reading of M-209 traffic from the US XXIX Tactical Air Command tipped off the Germans to a planned ground offensive in the Aachen area. However, the delay in reading the traffic was 8 to 10 days, far too long to be of much value to them, so the problem was left to the Army. In addition, many low-level systems of both the USAAF and the RAF were read, including aircraft movement codes and bomber codes, such as the RAF Syko[153] and 2 and 3 letter codes. Of the 140,000 five letter groups of The US Telegraph Code, the Chi Stelle had recovered 12,000 by May 1944 and was able to read the traffic currently by February of the following year. Some US strip cipher was read from the summer of 1942 to late in 1943, when the introduction of the strip elimination procedure made it unreadable to the Germans. However, the high-grade Anglo-American machine systems, TypeX and SIGABA proved unreadable.[154]

Conversely, on the eastern front, Air Force SIGINT could be of great help to the Army. The Russians had a practice of imposing radio silence prior to a major offensive, but their attached air armies had to continue to communicate in order to both move their forces and operate their aircraft. This allowed the Luftwaffe signals intelligence service to tip off their ground colleagues to be prepared.

Decentralization however created problems for the Chi Stelle. Although it permitted flexibility and an emphasis on tactical intelligence, it diluted any coordinated approach to attacking the high-grade strategic systems of the enemy and the cryptanalysts resented their lack of ability to control intercept targets, which denied them the amount of traffic they needed to work on specific systems. The Luftwaffe signals intelligence effort was under the control of the Chief Signals Officer rather than the intelligence chief, and this created some problems in coordination and emphasis.

After a number of reorganizations, by late 1944, the Air Force SIGINT service was placed under a Senior Signal Intelligence Officer, Generalmajor Willy Klemme, a veteran signals officer. His operations officer, Lieutenant Colonel Friedrich, who had direct supervision of the 350th Battalion, the Chi Stelle, aided him. Friedrich was a general staff officer and had no background in signals, a fact that later created problems as he struggled to keep up with a fast changing, highly technical field. The British captured Klemme and Friedrich separately in May 1945. Friedrich was flown to the UK to be interrogated and Klemme ended up working for the British until 1948.

Seaborne completed is work and was able to submit his report, all 13 volumes of it, to the Commanding General of the USAAF on 15 November 1945. Its extensive breath of subject matter, written when memories were still fresh, resulted in the most comprehensive report on any

6. Captured Intact

of the German SIGINT services. TIOCM (augmented by their later interrogations) relied on it for the bulk of its report on the GAF in "European Axis Signal Intelligence...."[155] Longer term, the Seabourne report and TICOM's follow on interrogations revealed how the Germans developed the techniques of utilizing ELINT for air defense, lessons that would influence the next generation of air strategists as they struggled with the challenges of the cold war.

The KONA from the East

Although ignorant of Seabourne's efforts in Bad Kissingen, TICOM pulled Donahue's team off the search for the Chi Stelle after three fruitless days, and based upon reports from 3rd Army intelligence officers, sent them east to Czechoslovakia. On the way they stopped in Innsbruck for a day to investigate, at the address at Innrain 9 the Marineoberkommando Sued Druck-vorschriftverwalltug, a German Navy document storage and distribution center, which during the war issued code and cipher materials. Occupying part of the third floor of a convent school, it was badly damaged by departing Hitler Youth and looted by arriving American troops. A fire had been set that damaged one of the rooms on the third floor and ash heaps from burned documents were found in the courtyard. The whole building including cellars and air raid shelter was searched, and five unopened safes were blown with the help of some local safecrackers hired for the occasion. Copies of two types of codebooks, a number of water soaked one-time pads, and as many as 50 Enigma machines were discovered. Although of interest, nothing new was discovered at the site, and its contents were quickly packed and shipped to Berchtesgaden for forwarding to TICOM at Bletchley Park.

In the final days of the war Patton's troops, continuing the momentum of their drive across central Germany crossed the border into Czechoslovakia, penetrating as far as Pilsen.

Tens of thousands of German troops, retreating from the eastern front, suddenly, happily, found themselves behind American lines. Among them, sitting in the 16th Armored Division cage at the village of Konstantinovy Lazne, was an intact Signals Intelligent Regiment, KONA 1.

The KONAs (*Kommandeur der Nachrichten Aufklärung*)[156] was the German Army's field SIGINT regiment. Experience in the Polish and French campaigns show shortcomings in the Army's practice of providing intercept platoons at the division level, which were uncoordinated, and of relying on the Central cryptanalytic bureau in Berlin to provide timely tactical intelligence to the field armies. The solution to this problem was the establishment of KONAs to implement the German doctrine of establishing intelligence functions as far forward as practicable. They not only provided tactical intelligence by the classic means of traffic analysis and direction finding, but also had organic cryptanalysis sections. In 1941-42 five KONAs were established and assigned to Army Groups or regional commands. KONAs 1, 2, and 3 were assigned to the eastern front, KONA 4 to the Balkans, and KONA 5 to the western front. Later three additional KONAs were created to bulk up additional coverage in the western and eastern fronts. These organizations provided a full gamut of SIGINT services, interception, direction finding, traffic analysis and decryption to their assigned Army Group commanders.

Major Ernst Hertzer, a regular officer with long experience in Signals Intelligence, commanded the regiment. He commanded an intercept unit during the Spanish Civil War, and during the Polish Invasion, he was in charge of the evaluation and fusion of information from Polish Army signals. He spent the next two years on regular signals duties, but in the spring of 1943 he was appointed the head of NAAS 7, the evaluation center for KONA 7 in Italy, where he provided evaluations of the Sicilian, Salerno and Anzio landings. He was made acting commander in the latter part of the year, but some apparently some political troubles in OKH (he

6. Captured Intact

claimed) blocked his permanent appointment. Nevertheless, he was appointed commander of KONA 1 in the summer of 1944 and was posted to the Russian front. His interrogators, Dr. Pickering and Lieutenant Colonel Pritchard, were not impressed:

"He makes up by bark and monotonous loudness what he lacks in stature and bulk. He gives the impression of great Efficiency. It is reported that HERTZER is a fanatical Nazi – so eager to denounce his men for wavering sympathies that his accusations were in the end no longer heeded by the party…. [But] of his efficiency as an organizer there can be little doubt."[157]

KONA 1's five companies were divided into two battalions, Abteilung 3 and 4, created mainly to coordinate the companies' activities at the Army level. They were small administrative staffs added to the KONAs in 1944, and usually headed by an elderly Hauptmann, they were not considered an improvement.[158]

Four different types of company-sized units conducted the operations of the regiment. A close range SIGINT company, NAK,[††] operated closest to the front, at the army Corps level, and as its name implied, intercepted the shorter range transmissions of the enemy, both W/T and voice. In addition, its platoons operated D/F lines, intercepted enemy field telephones using ground loops, and provided initial evaluation services. Each NAK was composed of a single officer commanding about 250 enlisted men.

FAKs,[‡‡] the long range intercept companies, had a headquarters section, a monitoring platoon, an evaluation section, a cryptanalytic section and a communications line platoon. FAKs were mobile and also operated at the Corps level but provided cryptanalytic services, responsible for translation of plane text transmissions, breaking of known 2, 3, and 4-figure codes and ciphers, and to search for and identify new traffic.

[††] Nachrichten Nahaufklaerung Kompanie
[‡‡] Nachrichten Fernautklaerung Kompanie

TICOM: The Hunt for Hitler's Codebreakers

Continuing this idea of 'specialization by distance', Fixed Intercept Stations (FESTE)[159] were semi-mobile stations that were set up in an Army Group area and provided coverage deep into enemy territory. Their responsibilities included searching for new signals in the 3500 -5500 Khz band, coverage of specialized nets, such as those of the NKGB or mobile commands, and cryptanalysis of new systems and identification of keys. They did analysis of new traffic and prepared advance reports and technical reports for passing up to the NAAS.

All this data from NAKS, FAKs and the FESTE were passed up to the Signal Evaluation Center at the regimental HQ, the *Nachrichten Aufklaerung Auswertestelle* (NAAS). The KONA and its NAAS were usually co-located with the Army Group headquarters in order to quickly pass the finished intelligence to the command. Finished intelligence reports, weekly technical reports and for unsolvable systems, raw traffic, was passed up to the Army's central bureau, the GdNA.

KONA 1 falling in to the hands of TICOM was fortuitous for Anglo-American intelligence, for KONA 1 had spent its entire career on the Russian front, attached to Army Group Northern Ukraine.[160] It had, by now, the largest intact body of knowledge of Soviet signals in the west.

When Donahue and his team reached Konstantinovy Lazne they discovered that 16th AD intelligence officers had already begun the interrogations to establish the basic facts. KONA 1 was under the command of Hertzer, and was composed of the evaluation center NAAS 1, FESTE 10, two long range companies FAK 617 and 623, and a close-ranged company NAK 954[161]. At the surrender, the regiment consisted of 28 officers, 932 enlisted men, and 132 women auxiliaries. PWs whose homes were in the American sector were sorted out and quickly released. The regiment had destroyed the bulk of their records prior to surrender except for three brief

6. Captured Intact

cases and a book of the most essential papers. However, after making contact with American forces on May 9, rumors began to spread that the Russians were to soon move into the area and take over the PW enclosures, and the remaining records were burned. The initial interrogations revealed that the regiment used a variety of receivers, mainly of the HE series covering a range of frequencies from 85 KHz to 200 MHz, in addition to a Tornister Empfaenger b as the main intercept receiver. In addition, the regiment had been experimenting with a new way of locating and identifying enemy radio stations by recording their individual wave characteristics (radio fingerprinting). The technician working on this system was Corporal Arno Graul, who was to later attract much attention from TICOM.

With this foundation of information, Donahue went to work sorting out the prisoners. All were initially interviewed and 41 were carefully selected to provide sample of experience, and a cross check of memories since TICOM, like Seabourne, would have to rely completely on interrogations rather than documentation for their report. In general, the prisoners were anxious to cooperate, given their close escape from the Russians, and a few even expressed disappointment that they were not selected for further interrogations.

Donahue got an early start on the homework assignments, having Leutnant Harry Loeffer, of FESTE 10 draft a report on Russian cryptographic systems. Leutnants Woellner and Soess of the NAAS section wrote an account of the regiment's activities during the final phase of the war.

Donahue however was facing a situation similar to Neff's in Burgscheidungen, the area was to be soon turned over to the Soviets. In addition, the Czechs were in full revolt against their late occupiers, resulting in one of the KONA prisoners in the cage being randomly shot by a

Czech civilian. Quickly, arrangements were made for their transportation back to Germany and 39 prisoners left for Oberursel on May 29.

The stay at Oberursel was temporary while TICOM sought more permanent arrangements. They were housed in an unused barracks with Team 2 responsible for guarding them 24 hours a day and procuring them their rations. Fortunately, it was comfortable enough and Donahue kept them busy drafting their reports. Over a dozen reports, the basis for the later interrogations, were written in the brief three-day layover. On June 3, the KONA PWs and Team 2 were transported in the trucks of the 124th Radio Intelligence Company to Revin, France.

Revin was the site of the 6824th Detailed Interrogation Center, the main site for ETOUSA's PW intelligence gathering. DICs were used to interrogate high value prisoners; the 6824th had already hosted such notables as Franz von Papen and Generals Von Kleist and Von Knobelsdorff. Once set up, Revin became the interrogation center for a number of TICOM prisoners, in addition to those in KONA 1. Passing through its gates during the following month were Oberstleutnant Friedrich, the Luftwaffe's senior SIGINT officer, Dr. Liebknecht of the German Army's signals development center WaPruf 7 who had been working on a secret phone scrambling system, GdNA's expert on Russian Ciphony Dr. Otto Buggisch, and Col. Willi Graube, OKW's head of telecommunications.

To help deal with this load, Team 2 was reinforced with TICOM's now experienced interrogation team of Major Owen, Lieutenant Colonel Neff, and Captain MacIntyre, and released from their duties corralling the Burgscheidungen prisoners, linguists Lieutenant Colonel Pritchard and Dr. Pickering. Starting with the documents produced at Oberursel, the team crossed checked accounts, probed deeper for details and fleshed out the knowledge about German army SIGINT operations.

6. Captured Intact

KONA 1 like all the KONAs, was a tactical intelligence unit, it prime responsibility to provide timely accurate information to the commander of their Army Group. For this, it relied heavily on Traffic Analysis. The primary task of TA was the diagramming of enemy communication networks. The study of traffic patterns, call signs, frequencies, preambles, message numbers, often combined with direction finding, could provide the commander with immediate information without the delay of cryptanalysis. TICOM estimated that the value of traffic analysis verses cryptanalysis on the Russian front was at least three to one. KONA 1, operating on the central part of the Russian Front, intercepted and studied the traffic of the Soviet Army, Air and secret police (NKVD). From this data there were able to compile an accurate picture of the opposing order of battle, predict build-ups and attacks in sufficient time for the German commanders to react [162]

The whole process started with intercept, the primary mission of the FAKs, NAKs, and the FESTE. The bulk of the day-to-day intercept was accomplished by the Long Range intercept company, which had an interception platoon of approximately 90 W/T operators, organized into three shifts for known nets, and two additional search shifts for new nets. The company operated for 16-hours each day of the week. The NAKs, the close range companies, also heavily manned for intercept operation, were organized into intercept platoons assigned to each Corps that they supported. Approximately twelve men were engaged in radiotelephone intercept, two in W/T intercept and five in direction finding. The FESTE engaged in intercepting specialized targets. All intercept information was recorded on standardized forms and forwarded daily to the evaluation center, the NAAS.

From before the beginning of the war, the KONAs kept an elaborate card index file of Russian cal signs and their associated stations and nets. These cards traced whether and in what connection a call sign had previously appeared. Russian call signs were changed daily by use of call sign books, which enciphered the stations permanent identity number. Each day the ten basic digits (0-9) had an associated simple substitution, which yielded a new three-digit number, with the digits referring to a page, column and row of the code sign book, which gave the unique call sign for the day. Each book had a list of 1,100 – 1,200 unique call signs composed of letters and figures, beginning with 32 different characters 3-letter call signs per character, and four call signs were two letter call signs beginning with the remaining two letters of the Russian alphabet. The simple substitution table was changed daily, and periodic reshuffling of the call sign book pages added additional security. Thus, up to a thousand stations using this codebook could make daily changes by changing the simple substitution. Compiling and studying the daily changes, along with occasional captures of the books themselves, soon gave the German cryptanalysts the ability to predict the daily call signs, which when matched to the daily communication patterns identified the nets. Combined with direction finding techniques, which physically locate the transmitters, the basic mission of the KONAs, determining the order of battle of opposing forces, was accomplished.

Russian frequencies usually changed daily. Each radio link had two different frequencies during the day and two for the night. Daytime frequencies were in the 5,000 to 8,000 kHz range, night frequencies lower in the 3,400 – 4,500 kHz range. Units below division level used low frequencies. KONA 1's study of Soviet frequency changes was not productive; apparently, the Russians did not use systematic patterns for changes. The German intercept operators had to rely on their experience to search within the known bounds of frequencies, relying on call signs and externals to identify the net. In addition to the monitoring of known nets, KONA 1 put a considerable level of effort into discovering and identifying unknown traffic. Their experience

6. Captured Intact

showed that unidentified traffic could include that of new formations in addition to that of mobile formations back on the air after a period of radio silence, both critical pieces of information for the Army Group intelligence officers. This, carried out by the intercept platoon of the fixed intercept station, FESTE 10, also had the mission of intercepting special targets such as mobile formations and NKVD units.

A critical aspect of the whole process of tactical intelligence was direction finding, which became more important as the war continued and Russian radio discipline improved. KONAs were equipped with both long range and short-range direction finding sets. The Long Range Companies operated their D/F line approximately 120 to 200 miles behind the front, with the short-range sets assigned to the intercept platoons of the close range companies, closer to the front at Corps headquarters. The FAK had an average of eight D/F outstations, spaced five to ten kilometers from each other parallel to the front creating a baseline of at least one to several hundred kilometers. The intercept duty officer at the FAK, would send requests for bearings to the outstations who reported via W/T or if available landline. The long-range D/F stations could fix the targeted station to within 15 kilometers, where as the close range sets could narrow it down to two. The whole process could be accomplished within 60 seconds. This data then passed to the NAAS for fusion into its analysis and daily reports.[163]

Shifting order of battle provided basic intelligence to the German Army Group commanders, predicting build-ups, or changes in Soviet tactics. Even the sudden lack of radio activity could be used to predict an imminent attack. At the beginning of July 1944, Soviet radio nets maintained radio silence for seven weeks preceding their large summer offensive. When they came back on the air their call sign system had changed, and the Germans spent the rest of the war trying to recover them.

The intercept operators of the KONAs also kept close tract of the Soviet Air Force nets. The Red Air Force was mainly a tactical air force, working closely with the front armies. During a build up when the front armies went into radio silence their supporting air groups, by necessity, had to stay on the air to conduct operations. Thus, buildups could be monitored through the Red Air Force, and identification of the air divisions could reveal the locations of their supported ground units.

Although the bulk of intelligence might be derived from traffic analysis, cryptanalysis had a critical role to play on the Russian front. The codebreaker's efforts were frustrated at the highest levels by the Soviet's routine use of one-time pads, but there was plenty of tactical intelligence to be gleamed from more easily broken two, three and four figure ciphers. These codes were useful in confirming order of battle information, and provided place names, coordinates, and commander's names for the extensive card index built up by the KONA's evaluation center.

Dozens of different 2-3-and 4-figure ciphers from the Russian Army, Air Force and NKVD were identified by KONA1. Two figure codes were common in the early years of the war but had largely disappeared by the end of 1943. The most common was the PT-39, a code based upon a 10 X 10 square giving 100 groups. The alphabet lay in three partial columns with the rest of the cells composed of standardized commands, names, and phrases. The message encoded by a bigram reference to the appropriate cell, and then enciphered by reference to a 10 X 10 Latin square of random numbers, added to the code using non-carrying addition. The appropriate line (or column) of the Latin Square was the key to the encipherment, changed daily, but repeated periodically. The large amount of traffic generated by the PT-39, aided by captures, allowed the

6. Captured Intact

Germans to easily read it. Versions of the code were used by Soviet Army Groups, Armies, Corps, along with their supporting divisions. Versions of this code was used all along the Russian front until superseded by the PT-42 in May 1942, a system similar in construction to its predecessor. A smaller version, the PT-42N was used from division forwards. The Germans easily solved both codes.

Three-figure codes had first appeared in February 1941, originally used most often by the Soviet Air Force, but the army began to use 3-figure systems in the Caucasus in 1942, and it had become almost universal for field armies by the time of Stalingrad. Three figure codes allowed up to 1000 elements to be encoded, although this many were never used in a single code. The original three letter codes were simple in form consisting of at most, 10 pages of phrases, hatted or semi-hatted, in addition to the numbers 0-9 and punctuation marks.[164] A Latin Square was often used for the encipherment of the indicator, with the starting point of the additive was referred by its coordinates, and was read in three directions, defined in the instruction for the specific cipher. The resulting three pairs were divided into two three-figure groups placed at either the beginning or end of the message, thus telling the decipher where to start the subtraction of the additive to revert the message back to the plain text code. Army Groups down to Regiments used these three figure systems, for strategic and tactical reports along with supply and personnel matters. These ciphers were current for approximately a month and were changed after each big operation. The Russian Air Force units also used this type of ciphers but were current for much longer periods, sometimes as long as a year. These types of ciphers were superseded in 1943 and were replaced by three figure Signal Codes, which contained no individual letters but only word and phrases of tactical import. Instead, they contained a "read initial letter" code group that told the cipher clerk to use the initial letter of each successive group to spell out a letter until encountering the "read the word" group. Non alphabetic but grouped under associated headings, each meaning had two or three figure groups allotted to it, and anything not in the code was sent "en claire", which of course was exploited by the German cryptanalysts. Every unit from Army downwards had its own Signal Code, which was used by its subordinate units, and generated a large amount of codes, which were constructed in a variety of ways. It also generated a large amount of traffic, which with its associated depths augmented by captures, allowed the Germans to read most of these codes throughout the war.

Four figure codes, known as 'General Commander's Codes' were used to communicate from Corps to Armies and from Armies to Army Groups, and therefore contained vital information and operational orders. Four-figure codes were construction similarly to three-figure codes but the codebook could contain up to a possible 10,000 groups. Cryptanalysts of KONA 1 described codebooks containing anything from five to 100 pages. Air Force codes had about 10,000 groups but various Army codes had about 5,000 or less. Indicators of the codebook pages were enciphered and the code text itself could be further enciphered with an additive.

The first four-figure codes intercepted had 4,600 groups enciphered with diagraphic substitution, and a general commander's code known as 'OKK 5' which was captured in the Russo-Finnish War. This code, used from Army Group down to regiment, and by Air Divisions, was protected by use of unique encipherment tables for each large formation. Although the Russians knew of the loss of this code, only the compromised encipherment tables were replaced and the system itself remained operational for many months. German forces also captured its successors, OKK 6, 7, and 8 during the war; although Leutnant Dettmann, the GdNA's Russian

6. Captured Intact

expert, claimed that all these codes had been solved cryptanalytically prior to their capture. The OKK 5 code, consisting of 50 pages of 100 groups each, was so well composed that its successors only varied slightly in changes. This facilitated the Germans success with these codes; so much that the Red Army gave up on the OKK series in late in 1942 and withdrew them.[165] However, other four-figure codes continued in use throughout the war by other Soviet organizations, particularly the NKVD, the Air Force and some mechanized units. Four figure codes could give the give the German cryptanalysts trouble, and they required a considerable amount of traffic in order to be broken. Luckily four figure enciphered codes were changed less frequently than the others, but still, veteran cryptanalyst Dr. Wilhelm Gerlich warned that "a more frequent change of encipherment would have made decipherment impossible."[166] In addition, some four letter codes of the revolving stencil or transposition types were used, usually to communicate technical signal matters but also occasionally for coordinates.[167]

Routinely these 2- 3- and 4-figure codes were broken at various level of the KONA. The close range companies, the NAKs, had a small evaluation staff, decoders more than cryptanalysts, who broke known 2, 3, and some 4-figure traffic, before passing it on up to the FAK long range company. The FAKs, 617 and 623, had cryptanalytic platoons of 15 – 20 men organized into separate sections for 2, 3, 4 figure traffic, and a general section to maintain records and build card indexes. Moreover, it had a clear text section for translating all the voice and unencrypted traffic picked up by the NAK. Leutnant August Schroeder, an officer at a NAK stationed further north on the Russian front, stated that the Russians "regarded R/T as an ordinary telephone and spoke very freely....Very many private conversations were heard and these gave useful indications of enemy morale."[168] The FESTE had a small cryptanalytic section of one officer and 15 men specializing in solution of new ciphers, identification of old keys reoccurring in new unknown traffic, and P/L translation. The codebreaking function was part of the evaluation platoon for these three types of companies, however, for the evaluation center, the NAAS, there were separate platoons for evaluation and cryptanalysis. Thus, the various organizational level of the KONA acted as a filtering mechanism, separating out and solving the more easily broken traffic and passing the more complicated systems upward. At each level the companies also passed results laterally to their supported formations, Corps, Armies and Army Group to provide those commanders with intelligence in the timeliest manner possible.

The culmination of all this activity was at the NAAS, which had the responsibility of sorting out the details and building the intelligence picture. The cryptanalytic section double checked the solutions provided by the companies, worked on the traffic that could not be broken by the lower formations, identified the keys, solved new keys and passed them back down to the companies, and worked on NKVD signals. Subsections were organized to work on the full range of crypto problems, 2-, 3- , 4- figure ciphers, P/L transmissions, book building and new developments, which did the cryptanalysis of all unsolved systems passed upwards by the companies. Although authorized a compliment of 60 cryptologists, it never reached this full strength according to Oberwachtmeister (Staff Sergeant) Klaus Eickhoff, the NAAS's senior cryptanalyst.

The evaluation platoon wove all the detailed information from the companies into useful intelligence. The heart of its operation was the collection and recording of the smallest details into an extensive card file, which was constantly crossed-checked during its work. Recorded details included names and cover names, map coordinates, D/F bearings, key characteristics, technical characteristics of the signals, and a complete library of all decoded content. A detailed reporting system developed for the companies, was compiled into daily situation reports

6. Captured Intact

covering traffic analysis, message content and technical reports. "By and large, SIGINT gave an almost most complete picture of the grouping of Russian forces... (However) the part played by decoded messages in the total success of SIGINT diminished steadily towards the end of the war." NAAS 1's OIC Hauptmann Roman Roessler reported to TICOM.[169] The NAAS reported directly to the intelligence officer of the Army Group and to the central cryptanalytic bureau (IN 7/VI, later the GdNA) in Berlin.[170]

Five-letter ciphers were beyond the capability of the KONAs and were routinely passed to the GdNA for analysis. This traffic carried the communications of the Soviet high command in Moscow to the Army Fronts and Air Armies. This traffic was enciphered with an additive, centrally controlled by Moscow, called Blocknots. Five different types of Blocknots were used; two for two way communications between parties, one for one way communication, one for emergency use, and one utilized as a one-time pad and therefore unbreakable. Five-figure messages address to individuals were usually enciphered with the one-time pad, in which the table of random additives was used only once and then discarded. More general messages, address to more than one recipient, used a table for only one day, with an indicator of the starting point of the additive sequence. However rarely, the Soviets, through either carelessness or because of low supplies of the pads, would reuse a pad, thus generating a depth for enemy cryptanalysts to exploit.

"Occasionally the same Blocknot was distributed to two units on different parts of the front with the result that a depth was established. Records of all Blocknots used were kept in BERLIN and when a repeat was noticed a "BLOCKNOT ANGEBOT" was sent out to all German SI units. It seems that depths of up to 8 were established at the beginning of the Russian

Campaign but that no 5-figure was broken after May 1943." Leutnant Harry Loeffer of FESTE 10 explained.[171]

For a few months in 1943, KONA 1 attacked five-figure traffic as an experiment but the effort was soon given up. This traffic could only be broken if a depth of at least three messages was found, and that the underlying codebook was readable. In Berlin, the GdNA, with the assistance of some personnel from OKW/*Chi*, made persistent attempts to break the traffic with occasional success. Even if the additive could be stripped off, the underlying codebooks needed to be read. This only occurred in the case of captures. In June 1941, the Finns captured a Soviet five-figure codebook, during a counterattack at Petsamo. A copy of the book was sent to the Germans, and although the Russians changed it shortly afterward, the changeover was bungled and the Germans were able to reconstruct 2,000 groups of the new code within a week.

"The 5-figure code books contained about 25,000 out of the possible 100,000 groups, the pages being numbered 000999 with a hundred lines on each page. Code books were changed semi-annually, but the Germans never broke a book and any examples they had were captures." Loeffer added.[172] However, captures occurred frequently allowing the Germans to stay caught up with the code, which were found to contain groups signifying specific units of the Red army, full stops and commas on every page, all designations of types tanks, ammunition and other equipment.[173]

These five-figure codes, used by the Army, Air Force and the NKVD were worked exclusively by a unit lead by Leutnant Alex Dettmann, head of cryptanalysis at HSL Ost in Zossen, and later after the reorganization, of GdNA's Russian desk in Group IV. He had considerable initial success on five-figure traffic until a change in the code in spring 1942 delayed further progress. At this point he was augmented by a special party from OKW/*Chi*, led

6. Captured Intact

by Fenner's mentor, Professor Novopaschenny. The professor returned to Berlin the following year but left most of his personnel behind, to be absorbed into Dettmann's unit, which eventually numbered as many as 40 – 50 men. Dettmann made heavy use of Holireth machines for his attack on five-figure encipherments.[174]

The NKVD, (predecessor to the KGB) was the Soviet Union's huge security service. Among its vast scope of duties was the control and security of Soviet territory immediately behind the fighting fronts, which in addition to its policing duties, also included a counter-intelligence effort. The NKVD also controlled the border police and railway troops. The study of NKVD traffic was a critical mission of the NAAS; it was intercepted by the FAK, but evaluation and cryptanalysis done by a specialized section the NAAS under the leadership of Leutnant Edward Woeliner. This section worked on NKVD signals originating in KONA area of responsibility, signals from outside its area were sent to GdNA in Berlin.

NKVD was the first Soviet agency to use radio communications for a large part of its internal traffic, and before the war, 70% of intercepted Russian radiograms was from them. Two primary networks were identified, a network controlled by the NKVD central authority in Moscow, and networks utilized by the security troops behind the front lines. The Central Authority network carried the high-level communications between Moscow and the Security troop HQs and certain lower formations, the Border troops and the railways units. The traffic, consisting largely of 4 or 5-figure codebooks enciphered with Bloknot, was not readable by the NAAS and was passed to Berlin. The formation networks communicated between the Front security staff Headquarters and their subordinate regiments and battalions, utilizing 2-, 3-, 4-figure substitution systems, could usually be read by the NAAS. Despite the large number of

NKVD departments only a small number of codes were used and these for long periods of time (often more than two years).[175] Four- and five-figure traffic from the NKVD central authority could be easily distinguished from Army traffic by it unique use of discriminates, and by the tuning practices of its operators. Call signs camouflaged with daily changes made up from a substitution square, soon yielded to German cryptanalysis. Even though the traffic was unreadable, analysis of it could indicate major strategic movements. Furthermore, D/F of the traffic addressed to the regiments of the Border Troops would indicate the extent of the Front, and D/F of the commander of the supporting security troops could be used to locate the Front HQ.

Two-, 3-, and 4- figure codes used by the security troop's formations behind the front lines could be read by the KONA. This traffic often revealed the names of the Army formations they were covering, therefore providing important order of battle information, and lines of advance and boundaries of battalions were often mentioned. During buildups for a major attack when the Russian army networks went silent, the NKVD networks kept chatting away, filling in the gaps for the Germans. A plethora of information revealed during the war from these lower level codes included not only tactical intelligence, but also information on the moral, desertions, and the political attitudes of the troops. Dettmann stated, "… the NKVD cipher messages were usually more interesting…" than the Army traffic.[176]

Two different code systems were used by these security troops. One, used forward of the NKVD regiment, which covered an Army Group sector, was alphabetical and contained 100 pages of 25 or 50 groups per page. It was enciphered by means of a substitution table, and both the code and the tables ran for long periods of time. One specific example, exploited by KONA 1, was known as R4CZ4, a prewar code whose 100 pages contained 100 lines each reciphered by

6. Captured Intact

31 bigram tables. The Germans broke this code in 1940. Its successor was R4CZ 1800, known to the Russian as the "ZERNO" code, consisting of 50 pages with two column lines of 25 items, totaling 2500 groups. This was the only codebook known to be used by the NKVD from October 1943 to late 1944. It used a 'chiffrant' (enciphered indicator) and bigram substitution tables. Each table was 10 x 10 to allow each bigram to be reciphered in two different ways and each table was designated by a figure from 0 – 9. The series of substitution tables were replaced every 2 to 6 months. This code became very familiar to the Germans, both at GdNA and at the KONAs,

A second code, introduced in the latter part of the war by NKVD for use rearwards of regiment, was enciphered by a figure subtraction taken from a table then enciphered again by another table. This rather complicated to use system provided no great security since the subtractors were used quite frequently and generated a great number of depths, along with code clerk errors, allowing the Germans to solve it by February 1945.[177]

The interrogations continued at Revin throughout June. The prisoners were set to the task of revising their work. All the resulting reports were group efforts, credited to the leader officer of the group. Major Owen and Captain MacIntyre, recently returned from his duties in Burgscheidungen, began working with the PWs to flesh out details.

One PW created a brief flurry of excitement for TICOM. Unteroffizier (Corporal) Arno Graul was a technician assigned to the NAAS. He claimed to have invented a device for radio finger printing, and described it in more detail at Oberursel:

"The method: to register the incoming telegraphic traffic in the form of an image on a cathode ray tube … and analyze the image. Analysis consists of a number of steps, so that all details and peculiarities of the transmitter are comprised. The apparatus is attached to a normal intercept set. The individual characteristics of the transmitter can be recorded graphically by means of tracings, or in the form of photostats in a card index."

GC&CS had developed RFP into a high art during the war and the news that the Germans may have also been on the same track was greeted with excitement at Bletchley Park. Major McIntosh, who questioned him, reported that Graul claimed that the method of analyzing the resulting patterns were fully worked out and that it was even possible to determine if a transmitter was working over land or water. TICOM sent a signal to the team telling them to continue to hold Graul while they negotiated with MI 9 about bringing him to the U.K. for further interrogations. However a few days later Pickering sent his own signal to TICOM doubting the veracity of his claims, noting that he had no notes on him and has difficulty recounting details. He recommended that Graul be processed and released with the rest of his party. This seems to have damped B.P.'s enthusiasm but they did continue to hold Graul for another month, sending an American specialist officer, Lieutenant. G. B. Tompkins, to talk to him in more detail in July. He reported:

"The equipment was never finished; Graul claims that it was destroyed one and a half days from its probable completion date to prevent its capture by the Russians, which seemed imminent. It had been tested, on only one transmitter.

Graul furnished circuits and a brief description. The man is a technician only, with great persistence and ambition. His equipment for this problem is childish in many ways, He has shown no conception of RFP as it is understood by us, and rakes no use of transient phenomena, relay breaks, etc,

6. Captured Intact

Graul is an obvious liar in many respects. No evidence is available to lead to a belief that he has or will accomplish anything of value. His chief characteristics are a love of telling trivial lies and an optimism concerning his inventions which seems wholly unwarranted. It is recommended that he be released." [178]

BP had no reason to be concerned. Graul's effort was idiocentric, based upon his own initiative, and had no support beyond his own superiors. He was probably trying to impress his captors with his abilities, as many prisoners did, to lay the foundations for future employment with the occupation authorities.

Once settled in Donahue started sending redundant members of his team home; Major McIntosh, detached from Team 1 to act as special interrogator, left first, followed a few days later by Captains Barringer and Lawrence, Pilot Officer Maxwell, and their radio operators and drivers. By June 13 Lively had been relieved by Team 1's Selmer Norland., and the interrogation team spent six days studying the documents and conducting follow up interviews to clarify details. Pritchard and Pickering were left behind to polish up the drafts and submit them as official reports.[179] As the KONA 1 teams completed their work and had a final debrief, they were released into civilian life, with most of them discharged by July.

Revin had proven to be a comfortable and efficient interrogation center, and TICOM continued to use it for a number of months as other German cryptographers, identified and located, went through its gates.

Wachtmeister Dr. Otto Buggisch, was a mathematical cryptologist and speech encipherment expert with Wa. Pruef 7, the Army's signals Research and Development bureau.[180]

During his busy wartime career, he studied the French C36 machne, worked on Russian 5 figure codes, and later studied the security of the Wehrmacht's T 52 models a-c (Sturgeon) and the SZ 40 (Tunny) cipher teleprinters, and later worked on development of cipher machines models 39 and 41, and consulted on the teleprinter T-43.[181] In the last year of the war, he became a ciphony expert by first analyzing the Russian voice scrambler system X^2, and later visited the Feuerstein laboratory to view their developments on encrypted speech. He passed along an interesting story about studying a captured ciphony R/T apparatus from a shot-down P-51. It was salvaged and lay at a German airfield for six months until indentified and forwarded to OKW/*Chi* in the spring of 1945.[182] Assigned to analyze it, Bugisch, concluded that it was possible to reconstruct the key settings by studying the oscillograms, however, this solution was too slow to be of any tactical use in air combat. Interrogated by Major Bundy in July and August, he eventually was the source for half a dozen TICOM reports.[183]

Dr. Werner Liebknecht, a civilian colleague of Buggisch in Wa. Pruef 7 was an engineer working on many of the same machines, including voice scrambler systems. The Germans tried four basic approaches to enciphering speech, a time scrambler, a carrier variation, noise masking, and an inverter.

Time scrambling recorded the speech, divided into an equal number of parts of approximately 60 milliseconds, and then transmitted in a different order according to a key sequence, where it was reconstructed at the receiver. It never scrambled thoroughly enough and implemented a delay in the speech.

The carrier variation employed a frequency shifting technique known as 'wobbling'. One band of speech shifted up over the other and modulated together on the carrier frequency. A further refinement known as 'triple wobbling', where one of the wobble frequencies was

6. Captured Intact

controlled by the cipher output of an SZ-42, thus requiring the receiving station to have the daily key for the cipher attachment to reconstruct the speech pattern. Although holding promise, this complicated method was still undergoing further development when the war ended.

Noise masking was a system where a band of random noise masked the band carrying the voice. At the receiving end, a noise band exactly equal to the transmitter, but at 180 degrees out of phase, canceled out the noise, leaving the speech band intelligible. Speech quality was poor due to faulty compensation of the noise channel and problems introduced by fading and distortion of the signal during transmissions.

A type of inversion scrambler known as the 'Baustein' was developed, utilizing two bands, the speech band and a noise band that wobbled at a rate of 100 to 200 milliseconds, creating an echo effect that masked the speech. This technology too, had problems in the synchronization and control of the receiving station, still being worked out at the surrender. Although seven different electronic firms worked on these projects before and during the war, by 1944 only the Feurestein Laboratory under Dr. Vierling was continuing development. Liebknecht was transferred by TICOM to Ebermannstadt shortly afterwards to help with the exploitation of the Feurestein Laboratory.

The capture and exploitation of KONA 1 proved to be a gold mine of information, Not only did it provide a model of how the Germans provided tactical intelligence in the field, it also provided Allied intelligence with its first in-depth knowledge of Soviet communications, ciphers and codes. Russian communications, for reasons of distance, priorities, and political policy had been largely off limits to Allied intelligence. Now, with the cold war fast approaching, Anglo-American military leaders needed all the help they could get.

7. Mopping Up

Although both TICOM Teams had met with spectacular success in the south, another team was formed to provide a final sweep through Bavaria and Austria in search of any overlooked odds and ends.

Lieutenant Commander Howard Campaigne, the senior American officer of team 1, had barely returned from the month long trip before he was returned to the field as the OIC of a small, newly formed TICOM Team 4. Joining him were Lieutenant Christopher Hungington USN and Lieutenant Evelyn Talbot-Ponsonby of the Royal Navy.

Campaigne and his team left the UK on 14 June and crossed the channel on an LST en route to Paris, for the by now usual briefing at Bicher's office. Since their orders had not explicitly authorized this stop, Campaigne had to beg for accommodations for the weekend.

In Paris, they learned that the main purpose of this trip was to return to southern Germany to double check on a number of targets the Team 1 search had passed over quickly. Specifically, they were to meet with an American liaison officer with the French Navy at Landau. Then join up with a small team from 30AU and accompany them on their sweep of naval targets in Bavaria and Austria checking on the coverage at Vierling's Lab in Ebermannstadt to insure it was being properly exploited. Finally the team was to revisit the burned out ruins of the building at Innrain 9 at Innsbruck, to reassure TICOM that it had been fully searched.

On Monday, after picking up their radio operator Corporal A.G. Able, Royal Signals, with his set "Valet" from the SCU, and a Dodge 6 x 6 1 ½ ton truck, the team drove to

7. Mopping Up

Wiesbaden, Germany. There they were joined by Captain M.A.G. Howgate, from SIXTA, who had been dispatched from BP to accompany the group of Pers Z prisoners being returned from England to Marburg. Typically, there was a foul-up, with the authorities at Frankfurt Aerodrome uncertain as to where the prisoners were supposed to go. Howgate followed his verbal orders and got a ride for the group to Marburg, only to find out their arrival was a surprise to their liaison officer Captain Lokwood, who had no idea what to do with them. It was finally decided to put the civilian PWs up in a local hotel with a security guard. Howgate had Lockwood sign a receipt for them, and undoubtedly relieved, went on to Wiesbaden.

Once the team had gathered in Wiesbaden, Campaigne took them east to Frankfurt to meet up with their escorts from 30 AU consisting of two officers and five enlisted marines, in a jeep and two light trucks. The 30 AU team had brought along a list of targets they were to inspect, mainly a score or so of miscellaneous naval targets in Bavaria; the most interesting included a variety of sites working on V-2 components.

Next day the convoy proceeded to Lindau, on the Bodensee (Lake Constance), for clearance by the French, who occupied the area. Here they met up with the liaison officer Lieutenant Drayton Phillips, who had arranged a house for temporary quarters. Phillips also brought a box of his documents, which turned out to be from Innsbruck, indicating that there was still material remaining at Innrain 9. Setting up housekeeping, they made radio contact with TICOM via "Valet" that evening and among the first items of business was an instruction to cancel their visit to the Vierling Lab, "situation at EBERMANNSTADT now in hand. Ignore this target." [184]

On Friday, having received their clearances, the team began their searching. Talbot-Ponsonby had a bizarre experience when he accompanied 30 AU to the Island of Mainau, over the causeway from Konstanz, to follow up a tip about a supposedly evacuated experimental station from Peenemuende. At the gate to the compound, they were refused admittance because the island was neutral territory, the property of Prince Bernadotte of Sweden, despite the fact that the French were currently using it as a Displaced Persons center. Further inquiries with the Chief Medical Officer brought forth the claim that two British intelligence officers had already visited the island. The team, sent back to Konstanz to get passes, found that all official offices in the town had been closed in honor of a visit by the Sultan of Morocco. Talbot-Ponsonby had to give up, an example of the confused situation, poor communications, and competitive interests that were to plague TICOM throughout its searches. Most of the targets investigated by the 30 AU team were unproductive from a SIGINT viewpoint, having been previously thoroughly picked over by other Allied Intel teams.

The team fanned out for the next few days searching the Bodensee area. Campaigne, Talbot-Ponsonby and Howgate wasted a day chasing down rumors about a possible Wehrmacht radio station in the area. It turned out to be a civilian broadcasting station. While following a tip from SHAEF G-2, Hungtington and the Marines made their way to the small village of Grafenhauson in search of Alois Gautert, reported to be the inventor of a one-man torpedo. "We found no one in the village of the name of Gautert, but several people named Gautert were mentioned by the villagers who had, however, never heard of Alois. The Gauterts are all simple peasants. It seems very unlikely that the man in question should be one of them."[185]

A more productive visit further west to Tunau turned up a small naval acoustical research station run by a Herr Boettger. This laboratory once employed 60 people, but was now reduced to 10 researchers. They were developing a device that could determine the bearing and distance

7. Mopping Up

of depth charge explosions by measuring the wave front form detected by a cathode ray oscillograph; a sort of underwater direction finder. Ten had been built but none were installed.

Leaving the area for the Schliersee, the team made a brief stop in Innsbruck to check on the condition of Innsrain 9. The building itself was back in the possession of the nuns, and numerous Austrian civilians had been on the premises. The area of interest, the third floor, was in bad shape, as reported by TICOM Team 2. In the meantime, a number of specialists from both the US and Royal Navy had been picking over the site with some materials being held by T-Force, including code books, various editions of cipher tables, water soluble pink sheets, and a box of one-time pads in poor condition.

Campaigne and his team finally arrived at the Schliersee that afternoon to follow up on the tip Colonel Kettler had given Team 6 in Flensburg. They met up with a Hauptmann Kunz, a former Vienna police officer, now affiliated with the Freiheitsaktion Bayern (FAB), an anti-Nazi militia group now eager to ingratiate itself with the Allied military government. He led them on a careful search of various buildings in the town, including three hospitals, the railway station, the school and adjacent book deposit, the post office and telephone exchange, a hotel, and the site of a nearby landslide on the railway. Except for a number of abandoned teleprinters and telephone sets, they found no other items of interest. However, they heard an interesting rumor from more than one source; Campaigne later recounted the story:

> "On May 1st or 2nd, there was a train that came into the town and parked on a siding on the far side of the lake, across the lake from town, and had stood there for a day or so. And there were some soldiers around it and they thought that they had unloaded the stuff and threw it in the lake. Well, we did a little searching. The lake's kind of deep and we couldn't do anything. But we recommended that it should be dragged.[186]"

The next day Kunz led the team up the mountain to search the surrounding countryside. Some debris from the German army was found in some of the local farms, but nothing unusual or important. They also visited Himmler's hunting lodge and followed up on a rumor about a German Army radio station that had been active in the area, but again, found nothing.

On the 28th, while getting the unit's radio repaired at a nearby US Army artillery unit, Captain Howgate was told by the unit signal's officer of a large cache of wireless equipment found in a canyon above the Municipality of Bayrischzell. The sergeant in charge of the original search party led them to a few remaining boxes further up the ravine, but they contained only food. After a couple of fruitless hours trying to track down the original source of the information, a local bathing pool attendant, they abandoned the search. Nor did they find any trace of the mysterious Dr. Schaedel, the archivist for OKW/*Chi*.

In the final report of the Schliersee search, Campaigne concluded that the OKW/*Chi* archives might have been dumped into the lake from the railway tracks near the landslide; buried up in the mountains; or evacuated further to the south.[187] He recommended that TICOM request a dive team for further explorations of the lake.

Team 4 left the area on 30 June and for the next week investigated a number of miscellaneous targets. Often, tips from local intelligence officers led to dead ends. As Campaigne later explained:

> "…we heard there was a research establishment up in the Tyrolean Mountains on a lake way up there…. There was … a guard, a US guard at the door…And so we went up to the guard and identified ourselves and said, "What went on here?" … apparently, it had to do with seaplanes, because they had been running experiments with pontoons… but nothing (was there) that was … cryptanalytic.[188]"

7. Mopping Up

This was a small lake named the Toeplitzsee, and was a field site for the Chemisch-Physikalische Versuchanstalt, a research institute associated with the Kriegsmarine. A great amount of material had been dumped into the lake, which was already being searched by divers.

Two more days were spent in a return to Innsbruck for a final check of Innrain 9. This cryptanalytic distribution center for OKM was not to be passed over lightly, and although they found some miscellaneous materials of minor importance, they were finally convinced that the possibilities were exhausted. Upon leaving Innsbruck, they received a signal from TICOM recalling them back to England.

Although largely a bust, Campaigne and his team did dig up some important clues as to the whereabouts of OKW/*Chi* archives.

* * *

When Campaigne and his team had their trip to the Vierling lab at Ebermannstadt called off, they missed out on a chance to see one of the greatest treasure troves of electronics in Germany. TICOM first heard of this lab from Colonel Willy Graube, the OKW Chief of Telecommunications, during his interrogation about German developments in secure voice systems. After describing a system relying on splitting the speech into sidebands that were scrambled with oscillators during transmission, he named Professor Vierling and his lab as the developers of this system. He also identified Dr. Werner Leibknecht of Wa Pruf 7[§§] as having helped developed this system, which he believed was in Southern Germany. Both these names were added to the TICOM Brown list, and the teams were signaled to keep a lookout for them.

Meanwhile, Third Army had overrun the Ebermannstadt area, and its Signals Intelligence officer, Major Flint, sent a report to Colonel Bicher in Paris about a possible TICOM target in

---

[§§] German Army Development and Testing Group, Signal Branch

the area, a communications lab ran by a certain Dr. Vierling. Bicher dispatched one of his staff officers, Major Jonathan Eldridge, and one of Ely's officers, Lieutenant JG Coolidge, who was also temporally at the Paris headquarters. The pair arrived at Forscheim, HQ of Signal Security Detachment 'D' on May 5, and the next day they drove the few miles toward Ebermannstadt, stopping first at a commercial electric testing lab, where the manager, confirming Vierling's presence, directed the party to the mountain top location of his lab. There they found the laboratory occupied by a German hospital, with Dr. Vierling still in his house nearby.

Vierling proved cooperative, and he explained that the week before the American army showed up, the Wehrmacht ordered that the critical projects be evacuated further into the Alps, and the rest of the lab equipment be destroyed. Vierling took advantage of this by sending his assistant, a fervent Nazi named Dr. Wilhelm Göing, to a site at Kirchental near Lofer, Austria. Göing and his handful of fellow SS technicians had been assigned to the Lab more to keep an eye on Vierling than to assist, and he was glad to be rid of them. After their departure, Vierling hid his most important scientific gear nearby, and put the rest of his employees on leave, continuing the pay of fifteen of his most critical men and requesting that they stay in the area.

7. Mopping Up

Dr. Oskar Vierling

Born in 1904 to poor parents and raised in the Ebermannstadt area, Vierling attended a school for mechanics in Nuremberg under a scholarship, where he filed his first patent, and was bright and ambitious enough to land a job as a laboratory assistant at the National Office of Telegraph Technology in Berlin. After three years there, he joined the Heinrich Hertz Institute in1928 to do oscillator research, and studied at the University of Berlin where he received his doctorate in 1938 after publishing a number of papers on acoustics. He became a pioneer in the development of electronic music, inventing an electro-acoustic piano designed and built in collaboration with Benjamin Franklin Mießner in the 1930s.[189] He taught for a year in a graduate school for technology in Hannover, but feeling chances for advancement were slim he approached the Siemens Corporation in search of employment. They advised him to form a private research laboratory instead, to work under contract on projects that the military was demanding but had little peace time applications, and offered to help support it in return for options to any of his inventions. He therefore became a prototype for a figure that was to become familiar in the post-war electronics industry, the military-industrial entrepreneur conducting government sponsored research and development. After his original laboratory was bombed out in 1942, he moved his operations to a new lab in Ebermannstadt, named the Laboratorium Feuerstein after the mountain it was perched upon, where he built a modern facility with its own machine shops for metal fabrication and well equipped with instruments and meters for radio frequency research. Employing about 150 men including 20 high frequency research scientists, he conducted research on a variety of critical projects including speech scramblers, cipher teleprinters, and electronic calculators.

The TICOM representatives toured the lab, consisting of a main building, two small special laboratories, a house and some small outbuildings. It was well constructed, and was disguised as a medieval castle with Red Crosses painted on the roof in an attempt to protect it from Allied bombing. Vierling claimed that it cost over 1.25 million marks to build (over $6 million dollars in current terms). Vierling also volunteered that with some assistance he could reconstruct his lab and resume work on his projects. Eldridge and Coolidge sent a signal to Bircher in Paris reporting on their discoveries and recommending that Vierling and 15 of his key men be placed under arrest awaiting interrogations. Debating on what to do next, Eldridge decided that they should return to Augsburg and report into Seventh Army HQ where they ended up meeting Oester and joining his Team 1.

7. Mopping Up

Contemporary view of Berg Feuestein (Janericloebe, Wikimedia Commons)

There the matter sat for a month. Uncertainty about the exact nature of the research conducted at the lab, combined with the rush of events occurring at the surrender, delayed TICOM's response until mid-June. Major H.C. Barlow, one of Bicher's officers, and Major Mark F. Heller, a British SIGINT officer on the staff of G-2 SHAEF, were then sent out to take a closer, more detailed look. Stopping first at the evacuated lab site in Kirchental, they found it closed down and the undesirable elements, i.e. Göing and his SS technicians, had been arrested by the 101st Airborne CIC detachment when a search revealed six hidden weapons. Also found was Dr. Werner Liebknecht, the Wa Pruf 7 speech scrambling expert. Liebknecht was arrested and sent to Third Army HQ where, quickly shipped off to Revin, he was interrogated by Major Bill Bundy. By August, Liebknecht found himself back at Ebermannstadt, working this time under TICOM supervision.

The Kirchental lab was found to house three uncompleted projects, "Gleichlauf", "Baustein" and an unnamed high-grade voice scrambler, which were deemed by the Wehrmacht to be the highest priority items worth salvaging. Gleichlauf was a synchronized teletype machine, which used a crystal-controlled frequency generator at both the receiving and transmitting sites. This eliminated the need for start-stop signals and solved the frequent problem of line noise or atmospheric propagation knocking teleprinters out of synch. The Germans were planning to combine this with an improved version of the Tunny machine, the SZ-42c. This machine also used an electro-mechanical drive motor replacing the motor wheels with a magnetic device providing greater irregularity. Proposed improvement to the machine would have allowed the SZ42c to produce a key stream with a period long enough to provide for continuous transmission over a 24-hour time frame. In between messages, the system would transmit a stream of pure key without any break in the traffic, preventing enemy traffic analysts with any distinguishing characteristics. An experimental link utilizing the Gleichlauf device had been set up between Ebermannstadt and Vierling's subsidiary near Hannover. However, during evacuation of the subsidiary to Ebermannstadt, the convoy was caught in an air attack and the device and all of its documentation was destroyed, preventing its completion before the surrender.[190]

Baustein turned out to be a medium grade speech scrambler designed for landline use only. This "Little Building Block" combined noise addition/suppression with frequency inversion to make the signals secure to the human ear. A band pass filter passed signals from 300 Hz to 1,300 Hz and then split it into a lower band between 400 and 1,400 Hz and a higher band between 1,400 and 2,400 Hz. The alternating band then superimposed noise to the unused channel to mask it. These two bands were inverted by two carrier bands at a rate of three to six times a second depending on the volume level of the speech. Vierling had built a single one-way circuit for tests, but switching imperfections and problems with the filters also prevented its completion before the end of the war.[191]

The high-grade voice scrambler used the principle of synthetic speech. This idea was rooted in the American research of H. Dudley of the Bell Telephone Laboratories in the 1930s. Vierling developed a band filter to split speech into eight frequency bands of between 180 – 3060 Hz. The channels, amplified and rectified, were modulated into eight direct voltages and passed to the line. A ninth channel used to balance out the melodic tone of the voice and pure noise, became the ninth carrier frequency. These nine carriers were rapidly transposed through a threefold "wobbling" process, created by varying four condensers controlling four master oscillators. The resulting beat frequencies could be produced via a key tape generated by an SZ-42c. The project was only 50 % complete by the end of the war but had been producing good results in initial testing.

After reviewing the projects at Kirchental, Barlow and Heller then moved up to Ebermannstadt to interview Dr. Vierling in greater depth. In addition to the three projects mentioned above, the Laboratorium Feuerstein was working on additional speech devices, a speech spectrum analyzer and a speech stretcher, designed to double or halve the speech frequency while doubling the time base, to be used for interception purposes as a means of cutting out interference and distortion. In addition, a speech writer had been worked out in principle, it was to have resolved speech into 25 representative symbols that could then be transmitted by a teletype and be reconstituted at the receiver. An agent's transmitter was developed to compress the signal for burst transmissions and provided 80 KW of power on up to 80 selected, preset frequencies. The heart of this capability was based upon a multiple frequency generator from a single crystal. In addition, work was being conducted on an acoustic torpedo, anti-radar submarine coating, and a night fighter control system based on phased displacement, called the "Nachfee". And most intriguingly, an electronic calculator was being developed that would instantly solve equations to the sixth power. It was almost completed and was meant to be used in designing the wings of high-speed aircraft and in the design of projectiles. Vierling claimed it could quickly solve problems that would take 14 days to solve manually.

These and a few additional miscellaneous projects represented the cutting edge of German electronics research, and paralleled Allied developments. The high-grade voice scrambler was based upon the same principles as the recently developed American SIGSALY system, the electronic calculator was similar in function to the still under development ENIAC computer, and the Nachfee could be compared to the LORAN or GEE navigation systems. The greatest strength of the Lab was in advance filter design with one of Vierling employees, Dr. Glubrecht, being Germany's foremost expert.

As soon as Major Heller reported back to Bletchley Park, he recommended that the target be immediately frozen and exploited. Although in the Third Army occupation zone, the site was unguarded and open to visitors, including curious intelligence officers or others just looking for souvenirs, and still occupied by the German hospital. The equipment from the Kirchental lab was on its way back to Ebermannstadt; the remaining gear was still in various hiding places around the site, including behind a false wall built into a bombproof vault, and Vierling was still in residence, prepared to recall his essential employees and get back to work. Bicher, signaled about these developments, sent a formal request through command channels that the laboratory be frozen for TICOM exploitation. The next day he flew back to the UK to confer with the

7. Mopping Up

TICOM committee and they decided to gather a team of electronic engineers and technicians to spend six to eight weeks doing detailed analysis and documentation. Security was a problem, and the issue of the hospital had to be addresses sensibly. Sick and wounded German soldiers and civilians could not be chucked out suddenly without alternatives, for if nothing else it would draw attention. Now that it was frozen, the site could at least be controlled by TICOM.[192]

The technical team began to arrive on scene by mid-July. The hospital was in the final stages of removal; Vierling had put his people to work cleaning out the buildings and conducting repairs and electrical work. Lieutenants Charles Tomkins and John Howard, both of the US Navy were now in charge of leading the effort, and they had to prod Vierling to stop tiding up and clear out some floor space to organize the equipment, which was still in disarray. Eighteen of the lab's employees were at work with another eighteen expected back soon. Three full days were spent in in-depth discussions with Vierling on organizing the work and reconstituting the projects. Physically and psychologically, Vierling was in bad shape. Described as 'a very sick man' by Heller, he was estranged from his wife and was worried about money matters, with just enough funds to pay his workers for two more weeks. Vierling was also on the military government's wanted list, as he was a member of the party, although he claimed reluctantly, but also held an appointment in the SS. It was not known how much time he had before he was arrested.

Over the next two months, the TICOM engineers, working closely with the Feuerstein workers, rebuilt and then thoroughly documented each of the projects. Time caught up with Vierling when he was arrested on August 16, but the exploitation continued with the team issuing over a dozen detailed technical reports by September. After the arrest of Vierling and the completion of the exploitation, the lab officially closed down and the staff dispersed.[193]

TICOM: The Hunt for Hitler's Codebreakers

There was a postscript to this story. In the spring of 1948, Dr. Vierling, now de-Nazified and rehabilitated, submitted a claim to the Chief of the Monuments, Fine Art and Archives branch of the Bavarian military government for the return of the technical library sized by TICOM from his laboratory, which he claimed, was personal property. This collection consisted of pre-war technical volumes and journals that he had acquired over the years to support his research. Items included almost 50 volumes, most of which were now out of print and some quite rare, and the multi-year volumes of some 20 technical journals. A search was launched through Army channels to find out what had happened to this collection. Review of documentation revealed that the collection, which had been inventoried by TICOM at Ebermannstadt, ended up in the custody of the physics library at the nearby University of Erlangen. In July 1946, at the request of the R&D branch of the Army Security Agency in Washington, Captain Mary C. Lane, assigned as assistant TICOM representative to ASA Europe, was sent to Erlangen to retrieve the books, only to find that they had already been transferred to Washington and incorporated into the ASA library. All inventoried items were found with the exception of two volumes, one on electro acoustic transducers and the other on subject of decimeter and centimeter waves, believed to be lost to student theft in Erlangen. Memos flew between the various offices in Europe and the US debating the various merits of returning the books to Dr. Vierling, with a major concern that the books, many of which had been stamped "PROPERTY OF THE UNITED STATES ARMY SECURITY AGENCY LIBRARY" would pose a security risk by revealing that the agency had an interest in electronics. Captain Lane, in her report on the matter, cautioned that:

"A further point that merits consideration is the fact that the collection is of considerable value and may represent in certain instances the only copy of a periodical or book readily

7. Mopping Up

available to the Army Security Agency or the Armed Forces Security Agency. Although the usefulness of the books has largely been curtailed by the fact that few persons readily read scientific German, and by the fact that articles contained in the volumes have not been translated, these books may in the future be a valuable asset to the research division of ASA and AFSA." On the other hand she concluded: "The fact that the books have not been used to any extent during the past five years, and that because of the rapid advancement of contemporary science, the matter contained in the books is largely of historic interest."[194]

Apparently reassured that the national security would not be unduly endangered, the books were eventually returned to Dr. Vierling. Vierling went back to Ebermannstadt and reestablished the Feuerstein laboratory, where it is still in business in its original location, now known as the Vierling Group, it specializes in electronic manufacturing services. Oskar Vierling, continued his cooperation with the allies, he also worked for the Gehlen Organization, and later became professor of physics at the Philosophical-Theological College in Bamberg while continuing to run his business. Dr. Vierling died in 1986, but his legacy, the Vierling Group is still family owned, and recently welcomed its third generation, Martin Vierling, into its management ranks.[195]

* * *

By late July, the field work of the TICOM teams was largely complete, with the exception of the mystery of the OKW/*Chi* archives. Oberst Kettler, the head of the northern branch of the agency, had revealed back in May that the archives had been transported south, to the Schliersee area in the custody of the senior archivist, Dr. Schaedel. Team 1 TROs Pickering, Cockerell, and Whitaker visited the lake on May 21 for a brief inquiry which turned up nothing.

Campaigne's multi-day investigation in late June developed the theory that the archives had been dumped into the lake, but the team was pulled out of the field before any firm evidence could be found to prove it.

But for a stroke of luck the archives of OKW/*Chi*, may have remained lost. In the last week of July, at Lake Schliersee, a soldier from the Third US Army drowned. While dragging for the body, officials snagged a box from the north end of the lake.[196] Upon inspection, it turned out to be a waterproof box containing a number of translations of decoded messages and a file of correspondence addressed to OKW/*Chi*.[197] TICOM, having already submitted Campaigne's request for a dive team for Schliersee, paired the recently returned Lieutenant Talbot-Ponsonby with US Army Lieutenant Alfred P. Fehl and quickly dispatched them as Team 5[198]. Stopping in Paris for the usual round of clearances and discussions, they proceeded overland to Schliersee, arriving on 8 August.

Starting at the north end of the lake near the Schloss Freudenberg where the box was recovered, the team did an initial survey, finding the beach still littered with abandoned radios and teleprinters. Talbot-Ponsonby and Fehl then attempted dragging the lake near the landslide on the west side and nearly snagged an object several times, but it was too heavy to recover. While this was ongoing, a further inquiry launched into the whereabouts of Dr. Schaedel by the local Counter Intelligence Corps detachment again produced no results.

7. Mopping Up

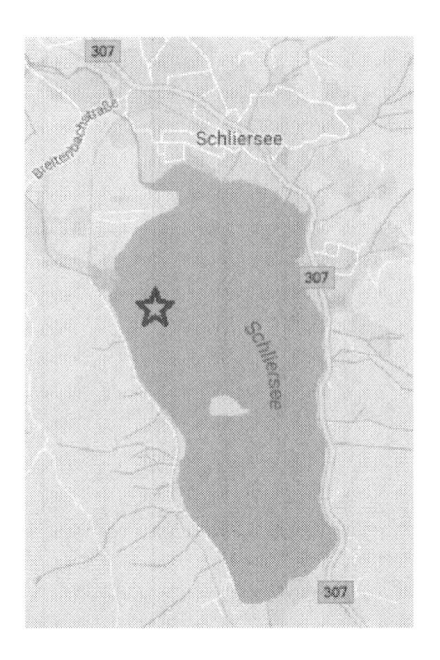

Approximate location of diving operations at Lake Schliersee.

The next day the team, with the assistance of some engineers, took soundings and discovered that the depths in the target areas ranged from 20 to 50 feet. A more detailed survey by a navy diving officer resulted in the recommendation that the job was within the capabilities of the Army pier divers from Le Have.

Talbot-Ponsonby and Fehl made a trip to the Bad Aibling prison camp to investigate a rumor that a score of section heads of OKW/*Chi* had been held there but a search of the camp's records produced no information. On 17 August, Talbot-Ponsonby returned to the UK leaving Fehl in charge of the operation. Fehl then made other trips to the Freising P/W cage and to Unken, Austria to interview a former translator for GdNA, both visits leading to dead ends.

A week later, a small party of Army engineers arrived with pontoons and began building a raft for use in the diving operations. The leading group of the 1051st Construction and Repair Group, the pier divers, began to arrive on 2 September, with the rest of their party arriving with equipment a week later.[199] Diving operations began on Tuesday, 11 September and lasted for a week. The first area worked was the site of the recovery of the original box, and although the murky water complicated diving operations, the site yielded 28 boxes, most found below the slope in 30 to 50 feet. It appeared that the materials had been hastily dumped from a boat. The second area explored, near the landslide, recovered seven boxes of discarded equipment from the local German SS artillery school, but produced no signal intelligence material.

Army pier divers at work in the Schliersee, August 1945. (NARA)

7. Mopping Up

The recovered boxes were transported to the Third Army Signals Intelligence Battalion at Camp Goulette where they were stored in a vault. There they were sorted, non-relevant equipment discarded, re-boxed, and sealed for transport. This resulted in 19 boxes, totaling 188 cubic feet and weighing 8162 pounds. No attempt was made to dry out the documents, instead TICOM wanted the materials moved to England as quickly as possible. Fehl arranged for an airlift, and on Friday, 5 October, two C-47s landed at Biggin Hill where trucks met them to carry the cargo to Bletchley Park. The search for OKW/*Chi* was complete.

* * *

While Team 1 concluded their mission and returned to the UK, the "Russian FISH" equipment, all 7 1/2 tons, was left in the care of Major Rushworth at Augsburg. Delays prevented the shipment to be flown to the UK until June 5th when it finally left accompanied by Rushworth and Captain Carter.

The GdNA Groupe VI men were also delayed at Augsburg, where Seventh Army wanted first crack at interrogating them on Soviet order-of-battle information. They were then sent by road to the jail in Wiesbaden, accompanied by Paul Whitaker, where they were held temporally in protective custody. This gave the TICOM committee the chance to sort out their prisoners, and six were selected for further interrogations in England. In addition to Suschowk, Hempel and Karrenberg, this group also included Unteroffiziers Erdmann, a specialist in NKVD traffic, Grubler, an electrician and radio mechanic, and Schmitz, an intercept operator.

Finally arriving in England on June 29th, they were sent to a site at Steeple Clayton, a village some 15 miles southwest of Bletchley Park that was a decommissioned CGCS outstation. The captured gear, sent down to the site by TICOM in the previous two days, awaited their arrival, and the party was immediately sent to work reconstructing the intercept equipment. Despite a few technical delays such as fitting the proper type heads to the printers and a lack of some test meters and tools, the 9-channel universal set was set up by the next evening. In addition, the intercept receiver, a wide band Fu. H.E.c. was set up and two antennas, one 30 meters high in a tall tree and the other an 18 meters on a mast were erected.[200] As an initial test, some loud and clear Russian signals were picked up by the German operator.[201]

The next day, July 1st, the printers were connected to the intercept unit and operations began. By mid-day, some traffic on a two-channel circuit around 8 MHz was intercepted, and by evening, the 9-channel Baku station (at 12.6 MHz) was picked up. Karrenberg kept busy preparing charts and index headings to begin the documentation of the intercepts. The Baku

7. Mopping Up

traffic was unencrypted and provided data such as locations of factories, the names of their managers, imports, shortages and various types of commercial information.

Over the next few days, these circuits were printing solidly. The Germans PWs had attempted to set up the six-channel machine to monitor traffic on a Rostov-Moscow circuit, but had experienced trouble due to jamming from an American commercial transmitter. The efficiency of the six-channel set was questioned, but the prisoners insisted that it was their best set; having been built in 1939, it had served them in Russia.

At this point, the TICOM officials debated the question of priority. The engineer Mr. Kenworthy[202] wanted to limit operations in order to do an in depth examination of the machinery, pointing out that there were many reception problems at the current site, there was a lack of directional aerials and facilities for diversity reception, and the few sets operating could not provide adequate coverage anyway. However the traffic analysts Captain Jack Magilavy and D.R. Uzielli, wanted copious traffic. The operation's commander, Captain Carter, felt that they had a unique opportunity to observe German interception and traffic analysis technique firsthand, rather than learning about it through interrogations. Since TICOM had shown a deep interest in the nature of the Soviet traffic, a decision was made to let the Germans practice their craft since 'example was better than theory'. A compromise was reached in the usual manner and it was agreed to continue to collect traffic, but put an increasing importance on the technical considerations.[203]

"On subsequent days therefore, the operators worked under the general direction of the evaluator (Karrenberg); they picked out the circuits which would give him the TA data he required, held them for as long as he wanted and then left them."[204]

Finding that the propagation conditions were much better in the evening, an evening shift was added to the workload. By this time, some ten to twelve 2-channel links were discovered, but most of them were sending only synchronization signals. The Baku circuit continued to transmit unencrypted traffic of no great value. Work continued in setting up a second 2-channel set, and the Germans were assisting in translating technical instructions.

However, the activity at Steeple Clayton was beginning to attract attention. The Post Office delivered a complaint that there was interference with local reception of the BBC. Also, the amount of equipment the group was powering was exceeding the local 15 amps limit. Captain Carter bought time by requesting the local authorities to investigate the trouble from their end and to let them know the results.

Over the next few days work continued, with both the engineers and the evaluators gaining confidence over their mastery of the system. A second 2-channel machine was up and running in a separate hut by British personnel without German help. The TA effort was yielding results. However, the Post Office authorities were still concerned and reported that the trouble was in the electrical mains and asked if the group had any unusual electrical machinery. A non-committal reply was given.

The next day, July 6th, Captain Carter along with the engineers Kenworth and Mason, reported to Bletchley Park to brief TICOM officials. The technical challenges of the site along with the unwanted attention from the GPO resulted in the decision to cease operations in the next 24 hours. The Carter party was asked to write recommendations for both the short-term disposal and the longer-term future of the equipment and POWs.

The following day, final tests of elements of the last 9-channel sets were completed in the frame of the original while the rest of the equipment was packed up. The 6-channel set was

7. Mopping Up

finally made to work satisfactorily. An interrogation team from TICOM also came down that morning to conduct the first formal interview of Karrenberg. It was also learned that Unteroffizier Erdmann, the NKVD specialist, had a wife and five children in the Soviet zone, and would be unable to go home. Carter and the rest of the TICOM officers, always sensitive about the morale and motivations of their prisoners, were concerned.

The collection effort of Karrenberg's unit, GdNA Groupe VI section 1b, was specifically targeted at the interception and evaluation of Russian Baudot traffic.[205] Its work could be broken down into three phases; interception, decryption via key recovery, and supporting traffic analysis, all of which were demonstrated during its week at Steeple Clayton. However, Karrenberg and his fellows could not explain everything; the output of Groupe VI had been sent to GdNA Groupe IV, the cryptanalytic division, whose section 3, under Leutnant Alex Dettmann, did the actual analysis and evaluation of the Russian materials. Gaps in this knowledge were filled in piece by piece by TICOM over the next few months by careful examination of captured documents and further interrogations of other German personnel.[206]

The technology behind the interception of "Russian Fish" can be traced back to 1874 and the efforts of the French telegraph engineer Jean-Maurice-Émile Baudot. In a desire to increase the speed, amount and accuracy of transmitted text, Baudot adapted principles of the Hughes telegraphic printer and a five-unit code devised by Gauss and Weber to invent what would now be described as a synchronous time division multiplex system.

The heart of his system was a distributor, which rotated brushes over a set of contacts, which connected a series of transmitter and receiver circuits into a single line. This allowed up to four channels to operate simultaneously.[207] The transmitted characters were interleaved so that the signal occurred in different time slots. Further development of multiplexing by Western Union allowed for the simultaneous transmission of eight channels by 1913. By 1936, further Western Union development of a system called the Varioplex increased capacity to 72 channels of transmission.[208]

The code Baudot devised for this system represented letters of the alphabet with five electrical impulses, the unit representing either a pulse (mark) or its absence (space). This resulted in 32 combinations, 26 representing the letters of the alphabet and 6 that could be assigned as control characters, such as a shift to a number or a page feed. In contemporary terms, it can be described as a five-bit code.

The transmission was generated by a skilled operator manipulating a series of five piano like keys in the proper pattern to generate the character signal, which could be printed out at the receiving end. In 1902, Charles Krum, a cold storage engineer, devised a "start – stop" code sequence to add to the Bardot code that allowed automation of the transmission. Both the transmitter and the receiver were now cued as to the start of the next 5-bit sequence, allowing a standard typewriter device to become the keyer. In 1908, the Morkrum Company developed the first commercial printing machine, and by the First World War this technology was being adopted by cable companies, railroads, and other corporations that had a need to communicate large amounts of textual data.[209] By this time, paper tape readers had been devised which allowed the message to be punched out ahead and then run through a reader for transmission. The communication demands of the war led to military interest in teletype, but they also had to contend with the additional difficulty of security. Gilbert Vernam, an AT&T engineer, developed an automatic means to encrypt the Bardot code punched onto the paper tapes. By creating

7. Mopping Up

another tape of randomly generated letters (a key), and running it in step with the plain text, the two message streams could be added together with Boolean "exclusive or" (XOR) function to create a cipher of the original message. Thus, a space + space = mark; a mark + space = mark; a space + mark = mark; and a mark + mark = space. By reversing the logic at the receiving end with an identical key, it would automatically recover the original plain text message.

However, this system had a weakness, as identified by US Army Signal Corps officer Major Joseph Mauborgne in 1918. The key tape had been formed into a loop and run continuously through the reader. If the message was long enough, this key sequence was repeated, creating a critical clue that would be exploited by a cryptanalysis. Mauborgne's solution to this problem was to utilize a key sequence that was as long as the message, thus never repeating. This created an unbreakable one-time pad system.[210] However, this system was logistically difficult to manage, it required that two copies be produced of the key tape for each message and could only be used once.

Teletype systems continued to develop throughout the 1920 and came into common use by both commercial and military users. By the beginning of World War II military communications services were replacing the paper key tape with a Hagelin style rotor machine to produce the key sequence used in encrypted teletype messages. The German Siemens T-52 Geheimschreiber and the Lorenz SZ-40/42 devices were based upon this design. Ironically the US was rather late in getting into this game, not producing a similar crypto device until 1944 when it came out with the SIGTOT.[211] Multiplexing also continued to develop among the belligerents with the British early in the war developing a pulse-modulated microwave (UHF) radio relay known as the No. X10A. The US Army Signal Corps also developed the AN/TRC series of VHF/UHF multiplexed transceivers utilizing up to seven channels, primarily for radio relay[212]

Vernam encryption and multiplexing of teletype signals became a common practice among the major powers. The ability of RTTY to cover long distances without the need for landlines, and the capability to transmit vast amounts of detailed texts without the need for highly trained Morse code operators were ideal for the Soviet Union. By the mid-thirties, the use of Baudot communications was extending across the USSR, and the Germans realized that they needed a means to intercept it. In 1936, the OKW contracted with the Berlin firm of Lorenz to design and build a receiver that could convert the transmitted Baudot impulses into printed text. The Germans first intercepted Russian traffic of this nature in 1940 in Warsaw, however other priorities, including a reorganization of the intelligence effort giving the Army responsibilities for the military and diplomatic intelligence on Russia, followed by the increased workload of the invasion put a low priority on the monitoring of Soviet internal communications.[213] In 1942 a Baudot interception unit was created as part of the Intercept Control Station, East (HLS Ost) at Lötzen, East Prussia. It was equipped with the Lorenz technology, two nine-channel, two six-channel, and five two channel sets. According to the intelligence section chief Alex Dettmann, there were numerous problems with reception at Lötzen and half of the intercepted material was unreadable because of distortions, 35% of the material was of some value, and 15% were private messages dealing with family matters. Much of the evaluated material was of industrial and administrative matters, such as manufacturing requirements, plant completions, personnel training, and routine reports. Nevertheless, the material also included military matters such as special announcements from high military command and coded messages between the General Staff and various front staffs. Most of the Baudot circuits regularly covered included those links

7. Mopping Up

between Moscow and major regional centers such as Baku, Leningrad, Sverdlovsk and others; along with inter regional circuits, including coverage of shipping, airline and rail traffic.[214]

On 18 September 1943, in a very rare meeting between 'Goering's Research Bureau' the Forschungsamt (FA) and the Army cryptanalytic service was held at the FA headquarters in Berlin. The purpose of the meeting was to pass on technical information from Dr. Martin Pützel, the head of mathematical research at the FA to his counterpart in the Army, Dr. Pietsch.[215] Pützel reported that for some time the FA had been intercepting Russian Baudot traffic and had made some progress on its decipherment. Traffic analysis indicated that these circuits were between Moscow and the high staffs at their Army fronts, communicated on one or two channels. FA cryptanalysis determined that it was machine-generated cipher with a particular anomaly; at every pause, it transmitted a compromise of seven characters of apparently pure key before shutting off. This of course produced a major crib for the cryptanalyst. The deciphered text yielded a plain (non-enciphered) five-digit code.[216]

Later Dr. Otto Buggisch, who had worked for both GdNA and OKW/*Chi* during the war, related to TICOM what he knew of the matter: "(I) ...heard in 1943 that the FA had claimed some success on a Russian teletype machine and had reconstructed the machine. It was a machine with a very long cycle being not prime but the product of several smaller cycles like the SZ 42." ...He heard this from Doering[217] "who was then doing his research on the T 52 but liaison with the FA was bad anyway ...." and the next Buggisch heard was that the traffic found by the FA had stopped. Buggisch was again questioned about this teletype machine success of the FA and answered in written homework that; "... the FA had analyzed a Russian cipher teleprinter system in 1943, and recognized that it must have been based on a machine having certain similarities with the German SZ-40. After a short time, the Russians altered the system.

The FA then communicated its results to my unit ... This was one of the very rare cases where the FA and In 7/VI (the Army predecessor to GdNA) exchanged results. I did not study the FA results at that time, as I was not responsible for work on cipher teleprinters, and hence can give no details. At all events the Russian machine (just as in the German types SZ-40, SZ-42 but in contrast to the T-52 a, b, c, and d) gave only 32 different substitution alphabets, the succession of which became periodic only after an astronomically large number of steps. This succession was given by a system of pin wheels the peripheries of which were prime to each other at an estimate lay between 30 and 90. In any case there was no complicated mutual influence of the pin wheels on each other (as for example in the T-52 d)." [218]

Buggisch also added that: "The Mathematics section of In 7/VI ... worked on it and at the end of 1943, there was a "Kompromiss," (compromise) and a depth of 8 messages with the same setting was created. The section was able to recover 1400 letters of pure key, and to determine that the traffic was derived from a 5-figure code. The Germans postulated a machine like the German T-43, but was not able to prove any theories they had."[219]

Sometime after September 1943, the Army took the project over from the FA and assigned their Baudot station to the interception of this Russian traffic.

The haul of gear later captured at Rosenheim included three different types of intercept receivers. The WA PRUF 7/IV, a six-channel machine built by Siemens-Halske, distinctive in its use of a cams mounted on a rotating shaft functioning as the distributor. The Gerät1313 or the "HZFS" was a two channel receiver, and the Greät 1309, or "HMFS", was a larger, 'universal' set that could be configured to operate with 2,3,4,6 or 9 channels. Both the HZFS and the HMFS functioned similarly:

7. Mopping Up

1. A standard radio receiver fed the intercepted RF signal into the machine. The signal was similar to a standard carrier shift teletype circuit, except that the shift was of 5000 Hz rather than the standard 850 Hz, indicating that it was probably generated by two separate crystal oscillators, a feature that in the post-war era could be described as 'spread spectrum'. The standard teletype start/stop pulse had also been deleted from the signal and each individual pulse compressed to 10 milliseconds, most likely to increase traffic carrying capacity.

2. An automatic Volume Control and a rectifier unit changed the voice frequency into direct current.

3. A double mechanical distributor on a single shaft, utilizing brush contacts, synchronized to regenerate each channel. Synchronization, accomplished via the use of an oscilloscope, could be locked in with automatic circuits. With the HMFS, different distributors could be inserted into the machine to configure it for the different number of channels.

4. The output was sent into a pulse regenerator as a final stage that inserted a start-stop signal into the data flow and then stored it in a band of five relays that acted as short-term memory buffer (a "Speicher") before being transmitted to a corresponding teletype printer. This was necessary to expand the compressed Russian signal back to the standard 20-millisecond length.[220]

After the Russians went on the offensive and HLS Ost was forced to retreat out of East Prussia in the fall 1944, the Army's signal intelligence service was reorganized into the *General der Nachrichten Aufklarung* (GdNA). The Baudot intercept section moved from Lötzen to Zossen, and a few months later to Jüterbog in an attempt to improve reception, and was redesignated as Groupe VI, Section 1b, under the command of Captain Rowder.[221] Unteroffizier Karrenberg was the technician primarily responsible for this traffic. The two channel enciphered military traffic (codenamed 'Bandwurm' by the Germans), was determined to be high-level circuits from Moscow to the Front Armies. There were also one or two links to the Air Force, and one possible link to the Far East. Moscow acted as the net control station and traffic from one Front Army to the other routed through this central point. [222]

Information derived from operator chat, message externals, and the study of frequent depths in the traffic led to some German assumptions about the system. Karrenberg stated to TICOM that the system contained two elements: a Baudot teleprinter producing 32 characters made up of the Russian alphabet along with a figure and a letter shift, and a cipher attachment consisting of five small wheels driven by one large wheel, creating a cipher with a period of 43. Despite this knowledge, the Germans made no effort to reconstruct the wheel patterns.[223] The cipher attachment had two settings, a 'large' setting that gave a simple one-letter substitution for the key, i.e. the wheels of the cipher device did not move. A 'small' setting that engaged the gears of the cipher device producing a seemingly endless stream of non-repeating key. The Russian teleprinter operators used the large setting to establish contact and test the mechanism.[224] This was probably done to simplify the process of setting up the circuit, the operators only had to refer to a table of the 'letter of the day' to establish contact. This letter, sent in the clear, was repeated three times to ensure that the receiver had his machine set up correctly.[225]

Experience with the traffic, specifically close study of preambles, initial contacts, and operator chat, provided many clues into the cipher. Preambles of messages were always enciphered but their stereotypical format and content provided cryptanalysts a clear insight into the beginnings of the cipher text. Contact traffic of the operators, in the 'large' setting, often gave the setting away. When the key was not revealed in the set up chat, the Germans could often relay on depths, that is, repeated messages, where the same plaintext is transmitted more

7. Mopping Up

than once at different positions in the key stream, giving cryptanalysts a means of comparison. Depths were due to bad reception, sometimes requiring repeating the message three or four times. Depths were also caused when the reciprocal station got out of phase with the sending station and the key sequences did not synchronize. Karrenberg commented:

"When traffic is running smoothly, and on a day when a lot of material is transmitted, one can count on key-identity being given away by repeats."[226]

As to the unencrypted nine-channel traffic, Karrenberg stated that the Russians had introduced two modifications during the war. First, the impulses of channels 1-2, 3-4 and so on were interchanged, thus leaving the ninth channel clear. Later channels 1-4 and 4-8 were scrambled, again leaving channel nine in the clear. Karenberg felt that the Russians assumed that this was enough to secure the system, but that a depth of 2000 letters was enough to enable him to reconstruct it.[227]

The traffic analysis study by Magilavy and Uzielli at Steeple Clayton showed that the bulk of the traffic was two-channel military, with commercial traffic passed in the clear on 6 and 9 channels. The message preambles and endings, such as originating station, serial numbers, group count, dates, address, routing and priority and indicator were mapped out. In addition, some internal police (SMERSH) traffic was identified in the two-channel system. The frequencies used varied between 8 and 11 MHz and were changed at irregular intervals, which were easily tracked from the simple code used in the operator chat.[228] The Russians had a lack of security discipline when tuning and operator chat often revealed the identity of the net. The call signs of all Soviet ground stations were made up of three letter characters, or a combination of three letters and figures.[229]

Once the key was recovered and traffic deciphered, there were further challenges. Although commercial traffic was in plaintext Russian, military traffic was encoded in a variety of systems, including 2, 3, 4, and 5 figure and five letter codes. A postwar TICOM chart lists 35 three-figure, over 40 four-figure, and at least 15 five-figure Russian codes attacked by the Germans.[230] How many of these codes were successfully read is not certain, but at least a few were. The highest level, most secret communications were 5-figure codes enciphered by one-time pads, a common practice of the Soviets, which the Germans did not even bother to attack.[231] The rest of the enciphered traffic was judged medium grade, which "The German cryptanalysts state…readily yields a solution while the One Time Pad messages are used only for traffic analysis. In general the Russian cryptographic and communications security is very poor, in fact, incredibly poor."[232]

However, this German effort against Russian Baudot communications was not without its problems and limitations. The war effort took many of the most experienced and talented operators and evaluators into other assignments, leaving less qualified and less motivated personnel in the unit. A post war US Army intelligence report concluded:

"It can be conclusively stated that the possibilities of the intercepting and evaluating branch were not fully utilized. The ease with which important results could have been obtained in unlimited quantities and in the shortest length of time was not recognized, or it was not properly valued. If the Russians now maintain operations in the same fashion, in less than half a year there could be important results in evaluating, if a sufficient number of Baudot receivers are used."[233]

7. Mopping Up

Groupe VI remained at Jüterbog until the deteriorating situation forced them to again retreat, first to Stuttgart, finally to Rosenheim in southern Germany, where they set up shop in the Poinier Kaserne, and awaited their fate.

After the week of demonstrations at Steeple Clayton, the Karrenberg party was transferred to the Combined Services Detailed Interrogation Centre (CSDIC, the 'London Cage') for further interrogations, which continued through October, November, and into December. They were questioned about the German effort against Soviet communications, NKVD signals and German knowledge of Allied cipher machines, while Karrenberg was questioned about the specifics of the Baudot intercept effort and his knowledge of "Bandwurm".[234]

After the conclusion of the testing, the British moved the operation to its intercept station at Knockholt. Established in May 1942 at Ivy Farm, Knockholt, Kent, it was an outstation of GCCS designed specifically to intercept German teleprinter traffic. It housed the Foreign Office Research and Development Establishment (FORDE) created to intercept Fish traffic and transmit it to the cryptanalysts at Bletchley Park. By May 1945, it had a staff of 815 civilian and military personnel. With the drying up of this traffic on VE day, Knockholt, with its specialized rhombic aerials, receiving huts and trained operators, was looking for a new mission. As station director, H.C. Kenworthy boasted in a November 1945 report "The Research Station, Laboratory and Workshops authorized by the Director especially for Non-Morse is able to tackle any problem put to it, and is able to arrive at solutions in a very short time."[235]

Armed with their newfound knowledge and technology, the British went into production under the codename CAVIAR. Hoping for quick success, the British built up the program throughout the summer and fall. An example of their work can still be found in the archives, a collection of some two score intercepts from the Berlin – Moscow Baudot circuit reporting

Soviet 'Y' service data. These reports of wavelengths, bearings, station callsigns and identities, and content (probably plain language), shows that the Soviets maintained an active intercept and D/F program after the surrender and were now targeting the western allies. This data was sent in a code the Russian called 'SANATORIJ', a three-digit code written in 5 digit groups that was being read in part by the British.[236]

Shortly after VE day, negotiations began between GCCS and the US Army-Navy Communications Intelligence Board to continue their wartime cooperation by targeting the Russians. From the American perspective, as laid out by OP-20-G chief Captain J.N. Wegner, cooperation with the British would provide a greater volume of raw traffic, increase the overall effort, and increase the collection of collateral information and physical possession of code books, translations of messages and other related materials due to the worldwide presence of the British intelligence network. However, Wegner also expressed concerns about lack of American security control over these British assets and the possibility of high policy complications due to deviations between American and British foreign policy, such as on colonial issues.

Internal discussions and negotiations with the British continued through the summer. Details of the exact nature of the material to be shared and the liaison channels to be set up were completed by the end of July. The code name BOURBON was adopted for this program and exchange of this material began on August 15th. [237], the CAVIAR material was a large part of the exchange.

The existence of Soviet RTTY was not unknown to American intelligence, in early 1945 Lieutenant Louis W. Tordella (who later became the Deputy Director of NSA) , the officer in

7. Mopping Up

charge of the OP-20-G unit at the Navy radio receiving station at Skaggs Island, CA. was given a new mission.

"About April or early May I received a message from OP-20-G requesting that we find and intercept a two-channel Russian printer signal frequency unknown with a synchronized pulse of 180 to 210 times per minute. We looked for such a signal for a week or so and I had the good fortune to find it idling one morning about 0330 local time ....We immediately began undulator tape interception of the signal and organized teams of two WAVES each to read the material out in thirty-one-letter Baudot code. I later was able to get Russian typeface for the RIP-5 typewriters, but we continued to read out in Baudot code so as not to be overheard by uncleared personnel who were in part of the intercept station building ..."

After an analysis of the signals, and problems with fading, Tordella recommended that the equipment be moved to a site nearer the source of the signals, either Adak, AK or in China. [238]

Tordella then learned that the Army SSA station at Two Rock Ranch had also begun to take Russian printer traffic.

This effort was obviously added by the TICOM captures. The Russian FISH booty had been divvied up by the end of July '45. The British sent one 9-channel unit and two 2-channel units to the US for use by the Army and Navy. Receivers, teleprinters and associated spare parts were also sent along. By early 1946 the ASA had developed a series of Bardot intercept sets for two-channel (codenamed PEBBLE), 2, 6 and 9 channels (ROCK) and a universal multiplex receiver (BOULDER), all based upon the captured Russian FISH equipment. [239]

By September, OP-20-G, under the leadership of former TICOM officer Lieutenant Joseph Eachus, was attacking the CAVIAR machine. But by the following year, CAVIAR began to run into difficulties in both the British and American intelligence services, mainly due to personnel shortages caused by demobilization. The war diary of OP-20-G4-A noted that in April 1946 "the big problem now coming up is CAVIAR. The British and the Army have both dropped it temporarily, leaving us with the whole responsibility. The greatest need is more long key, which is only available by reading depth." The following month, in relation to CAVIAR "some progress has been made on this, just how much will not be clear until the smoke blows away." Yet by early August Commander Howard Campaigne noted, "CAVIAR is being put to bed by Blankinship as comfortably as possible. This is because lack of personnel forces us to temporarily abandon this project."[240]

8. Postscript

All documents and captured materials shipped back to Bletchley Park were registered and processed, given a library number according to a standard classification, given a suitable title in English and German, and if necessary, a synopsis was written and attached. For example, seized OKW/*Chi* documents were numbered in the TICOM 'DF' series; interrogation reports or translations of the 'homework' produced by German personnel were published in the 'I' series. German translations of decoded traffic were in the 'T' series. Ascension lists, which cataloged the captured documents, were produced and then distributed to the various intelligence originations that had an interest in such materials. Units could send a representative to inspect the selected document and services were provided for translation. A US Navy microfilm unit copied documents intended for Washington.[241]

TICOM officers wrote their final team reports and, for the Americans at least, headed home. The TICOM committee officially dissolved on November 25, 1945. By that time Colonel Bicher had rotated home where he took up the duties of Deputy Chief of The Army Security Agency, and continued to serve in that capacity until his untimely death from cancer in January 1949. ASA continued to collect and evaluated its TICOM materials and in May 1946 published a nine-volume study, *European Axis Signal Intelligence in World War II as Revealed by TICOM Investigations*.....[242] TICOM investigations continued in the ASA Europe office, primarily by Captain Mary Lane, into the early 1950s.

The conclusions were reassuring. The primary concern among the allied high command dealt with the security of their communications. Was the Axis able to penetrate the codes and ciphers of the allies in any way compatible to the ULTRA effort? TICOM documented that the German effort against Allied high grade machine ciphers, the Type X, SIGABA and Combined Cipher Machine were miserable failures. After a few months studying these signals, the Germans concluded that the massive effort to attack them could be better spent on more productive lower level systems. Unfortunately they concluded that the same must be true of the Allies effort and therefore their own Enigma and Geheimschreiber systems must be secure. It wasn't as if the cryptologists within Germany were ignorant of the Enigma's weakness, theoretical studies within OKW/*Chi* by Doctor Fricke on the Enigma and Doctors Lindmayer and Stein on the SZ 40 teleprinter showed that these machines were vulnerable.[243] And suspicions over the issue were raised by as high a personage as Grossadmiral Dönitz, but his experts convinced him that the U-Boat defeats in 1943 was due to the development of airborne radar, not cryptanalysis of the Enigma. The sheer practical difficulties of a mass changing of cryptologic systems in the middle of the war encouraged German denial of the problem. However, researchers within Germany were on the verge of producing a new generation of systems by the end of the war, including the Cipher Device 39 and variable notch rooters for the Enigma, which BP later determined could not have been broken with their current resources. Had these devices been introduced a year earlier, they could have changed the outcome of the war.

However, the TICOM investigations weren't all-encompassing. The investigation of the Forschungsamt seemed lacking as it focused almost entirely on their war time role and seemingly ignored their role in Hitler's consolidation of power in the 1930s. Perhaps this can be attributed to the lack of documentation. Between the bombings of the FA's headquarters in November 1943 to the disappearance and probably destruction of their archives in April '45, what documentation that was found in Kaufbeuren was a small set of working papers relating to the current situation. However, TICOM did eventually capture a number of the FA's leading personalities, including

8. Postscript

their chief Gottfried Schapper, and it is curious that their interrogations contain no specific questions about pre-war Nazi activities. Other aspects of the German intelligence effort, such as the role of the Abwehr and RSHA as SIGINT producers or consumers, got short shrift. Although the German Reichpost *Forschungstelle* Research Station was mention in conjunction with the interception of allied scrambled telephone calls, no other investigation of this organization was conducted.

But the collective efforts of TICOM were valued enough to generate a turf war within American intelligence. According to a 1950 memo the Army's collection of TICOM reports numbered at least 200, many with multiple parts, totaling approximately 10,000 pages. Furthermore these documents provided not only historical context but also operational value. Another memo listed a number of codebooks and keys captured by TICOM which were (as of 1952) still of immediate value."Identification of these compromised codebooks with actively used systems has resulted in inestimable sums of money in bookbreaking personnel, and of months or even years of valuable time in reading the traffic and getting the intelligence to interested customers." This Army collection was transferred intact to the Armed Forces Security Agency upon its formation and soon came to the attention of its new intelligence division, headed by a naval officer, who demanded that they be turned over to him to be inspected for current intelligence value. A back and forth battle over who was suppose to index and who would be allowed to process them broke out between these supposed unified AFSA sections. Much time was spent debating the meaning of the term "operational intelligence" and the fine points of the AFSA Organizational Manual, along with some insults and threats. The situation became serious enough that AFSA chief Cryptanalysts William F. Friedman had to intervene.[244]

TICOM: The Hunt for Hitler's Codebreakers

Fortunately internal bureaucratic disputes did not completely occupy AFSA's energy. They also found time to focus on the Russians. Throughout the war, the Soviet Union had been a forbidden target for the Anglo-American SIGINT agencies, by orders of the President and Prime Minister. With the bulk of effort directed towards the Axis, spying on an ally fighting to the death with Hitler was deemed unnecessary and a waste of resources. The British had a long history of intercepting and breaking Soviet communications, dating back to 1920. However, the American agencies of the Army and Navy had little interest in Russia, given the distance and contemporary concern with Japanese aggression. As the war progressed, the leaders of Anglo-American intelligence became suspicious Soviet intents and rightly perceived that Stalin would become their chief rival for power in Europe once Germany collapsed. The high level orders pertaining to Soviet communications were interpreted liberally by ASA and a small capability was developed. In 1942 Soviet encrypted weather broadcasts out of Siberia were broken and this weather data was used by the USAAF in planning bombing missions against Japan. Also, war time censorship laws allowed the American government to copy outgoing or incoming international telegrams, and a large collection of Soviet diplomatic material was turned over to the Army, and a small secret cell was set up to begin analyzing these telegrams in 1943. This led eventually to the post war effort known as Venona, which permitted the identification of Soviet espionage rings in America. About this same time the Russians requested that the US establish teletype landline between their Lend-Lease office in Washington and their liaison officers at Ladd Field, Alaska. When this line was established, it was tapped by ASA.[245]

This and some initial success in reading Russian low level military codes was the basis of what was soon dubbed "The Russian Problem" after V-E Day. The TICOM materials, especially the treasure trove of tactical codes, ciphers and intercepted communications from

8. Postscript

KONA 1, must have appeared like manna from heaven. The fruits of three years of German effort under combat conditions provided an open door into Soviet communications. Despite a slow start, due mainly to manpower problems, by 1946 breaks into higher level systems (codenamed 'Coleridge' and 'Longfellow') were being accomplished.

The legacy of the Russian Fish and CAVIAR lived on into the Cold War. ASA collection and exploitation of Russian plain text teleprinter traffic began on a part time bases in 1946, probably utilizing the ability of the Russian Fish to intercept nine-channel traffic. This program was expanded in May 1947 when new teletype intercept devices based upon the Russian Fish were deployed to the field. This effort was placed under the direction of Jacob "Jack" Gurin, an ASA Russian linguist, who had the insight that even the plaintext traffic, although individually not of much value, could in the aggregate track strategic trends in the Soviet economy. Thus ASA adopted the same mission that was tasked to the FA years before. This program, a sideshow at first, became crucial after "Black Friday", August 25, 1948, when code and cipher changes by the Russians dried up the traffic that had been exploited since the end of the war. For many years, this traffic provided the only SIGINT insight into the Soviet Union.[246]

However, information about the extent and importance of the "Russian Fish" in the cold war is still obscured in the mist of classification. Much of the cryptanalytic data provided by Karrenberg in 1945 are still redacted.[247] Many questions are still unanswered in the archives: Did the Anglo-American SIGINT agencies produce their own (perhaps improved) version of the "Russian Fish"? Did the allies ever reconstruct the Soviet cipher machine? How much of the Soviet two-channel military traffic was read in the immediate post-war era? Apparently, 70 year old technology and cryptology a quarter century after the end of the cold war, is still a threat to the sensibilities of the NSA.

TICOM: The Hunt for Hitler's Codebreakers

By the 1950s, the TICOM files, along with all the other wartime ULTRA materials were safely locked away in the archives of the by-now NSA, assumed to never see the light of day, forever safe from the prying eyes of the uninitiated. But by the 1970s historians began nipping at the great secret. David Kahn's monumental *The Codebreakers* managed to hint at the possibility of ULTRA but skirted any specific mention of it, perhaps under the pressure from the NSA. But he provided a rich background to the history of code breaking which provided fertile ground for anyone wanting to ask questions. Anthony Cave Brown, conducting research for what was to become his first book *Bodyguard of Lies*, utilizing his own interviews and some limited documentation provided through the new American Freedom of Information Act, was on the verge of blowing the whistle when he was suddenly beaten to the punch by an old UTRA hand,

Group Captain F.W. Winterbotham who had served in the war as BP's architect of the ULTRA distribution system wrote his history/memoir *The Ultra Secret* from memory without the benefit of any official documentation, but it was the first account in English revealing the details of the Allied code breaking effort. Despite its flaws as a history, it shocked many conventional WWII historians, forcing them to reassess the decision making process employed by Allied high command and its now honored generals.

What followed in the next few years was a flood of authoritative accounts from many sources, including a number of former practitioners who themselves were professional historians. This in turn raised a number of questions which could be asked through the mechanism of the FOIA, creating pressure on the NSA and other intelligence agencies to reluctantly acknowledge their past. Why the British allowed Winterbotham, who after all was still bound to secrecy under the Official Secrets Act, to publish his book has never been satisfactorily explained. One theory was that all the old Enigma machines handed out to Britain's former colonies at the end of the

8. Postscript

war had by now worn out, and a new generation of electronic based code machines had made the ULTRA secret redundant. Or perhaps it was just a fit of common sense deep within the bowels of the British government that keeping the secret was no longer worth the effort and let history have its say.

The Americans for their part weren't eager to reveal the secrets, but under the 1972 FOIA executive order, government agencies were required to declassify documents that were thirty years or older unless the department head certified that declassification would adversely affect the security of the United States. NSA considered that any cryptologic information affects the security of the nation, but the Winterbotham publication had generated pressure to declassify ULTRA. NSA facing a 1980 deadline from the Secretary of Defense, created a declassification program in 1975 that hired retired annuitants to return to work part time to review the materials. Of course as information about ULTRA was released, historians had clues on what to further request. This drip, drip, drip of information continued into the next two decades.[248]

However, TICOM continued to be held close to the vest. Reporter James Bamford wrote that "In 1992 the director of the National Security Agency extended the secrecy order until the year 2012, making TICOM probably the last great secret of the Second World War."[249] This was probably a reference to a loophole, buried deep in the various presidential declassification guidelines that allow the Director NSA, after passing through various levels of review, to seal certain cryptologic records for 75 years. Why this was necessary at the conclusion of the Cold War, decades after the Soviets changed their codes en masse, and technology made its technical details obsolete is a mystery?

In 1998 Congress passed the Nazi War Crimes Disclosure Act and the Japanese Imperial Government Records Act mandating the release of millions of WWII government records. In anticipation in April 1996 NSA declassified and released a set of 4,923 entries comprising some 1.3 million pages of WWII crypto documentation. This collection, now known as the Historic Cryptographic Collection, contains some TICOM files, although they are not explicitly identified as such. However, the astute historian can find some obvious TICOM materials, including interrogations and translations of German documents.

Around this time the first information about TICOM was published in public. In 1986 Thomas Parrish published *The Ultra Americans*.[250] His history of the American role in Bletchley Park's Ultra program included a chapter about the TICOM mission and the capture of the Russian Fish. It was the earliest published account of TICOM in the open literature. The following year, former TICOM officer Paul Whitaker teamed up with cryptology historian Louis Kruh and published an article based upon a series of unofficial photographs taken by Whitaker on the mission, including scenes of the discovery of the 'Russian Fish'.[251] Later, the aforementioned James Bamford published a book in 2001, *Body of Secrets: Anatomy of the Ultra-Secret National Security Agency*, which included a chapter containing the most complete account of the TICOM mission available up to that time. That same year Richard J. Aldrich's *The Hidden Hand: Britain, America, and Cold War Secret Intelligence*, provided more details about the TICOM mission including additional information on German Signals Intelligence officers captured and held for debriefing.[252]

Another release by NARA in April 2011 provided a further 4,923 items, many of them TICOM documents; this time NARA divided them into a series of specialized entries such as P-4, "Historians' Source Files Relating to Target Intelligence Committee (TICOM) Interrogation Reports", entry P-3 "Historians' Source Files Relating to Wilhelm Flicke,", and most importantly

8. Postscript

entry P-11 "Archival and Historian's Source Files, 1809-1994". This has provided a boom to serious study of the TICOM operation, opening up the bulk of the archive to the public.

A handful of TICOM documents have still not been released, apparently clinging to the 75 year exemption granted by the director. A dozen detailed technical reports pertaining to the Feuerstein Laboratory are still classified, along with a number of interrogations and homework assignments from some of the leading cryptologists such as Huttenhain, Fricke, and Dettmann. TICOM's interrogation of Walter Schellenbarg, head of the RSHA'a Amt VI has never seen the light of day. In addition, many of the documents pertaining to Italian Signals intelligence are still in the vault. Whether this is intentional, just a byproduct of priorities in the declassification process, or perhaps just lossed in the shuffle over the last 70 years, is unknowable at this point.

Despite some of the conspiracy theories that have popped up over TICOM, no political bombshell has been found in the released materials. Most of the secrets hidden by TICOM are technical in nature, communications patterns, types of codes and ciphers, names of German sources, all highly sensitive in the immediate post war era. The overall story of German intelligence moreover, was told in detail in David Kahn's *Hitler Spies* published in 1978, based upon his own research and reporting, rather than declassified documents. Why TICOM remained classified into the 21st century is perhaps its greatest secret

Appendix:
The codes and ciphers of WWII

Codes consists of assigning specific words, phrases, names and terms that make up a message and assigning them to an arbitrary *code group*, usually two to five letters or numbers. For example a three figure code group would have up to a thousand placeholders (000 to 999), whereas a three letter code group gives a total of 46656 (36 x 36 x 36) combinations. Codebooks were written to cover most situations and complex common messages could be communicated with a relative small number of code groups. Due to the rules of commercial cable companies which defined a "word" as five letters or figures, five place codes became common. As long as the code was restricted to the senders and receivers, messages were protected from eavesdroppers.

Codes groups must be randomized, but how they are organized in the codebook can vary. With one part codes the plaintext is organized in alphabetical order then matched to the code groups randomly. This **"hatted code"** allows the same codebook to be used for both encoding and decoding. This however, can lead to some predictability, an aid for the cryptanalysts. The two part code (also known as a semi-hatted code) was then devised to make up for this weakness, by providing no predictable relationship between the code groups and the ordering of the matching plaintext, but usually ordered the plaintext into subgroups to facilitate looking them up.

Cryptanalysts' soon discovered that by collecting and studying coded messages the meanings could be derived from the context. For instance, suppose a ship in mid-Atlantic receives a coded message "PBNSX DFQZO" and that ship subsequently changes course and

Appendix: The codes and ciphers of WWII

enters the port of Càdiz, Spain. A few weeks later, another ship using the same code system receives the message "PBNSX AKRPQ" and that ship changes direction and sails to Lorient, France. The cryptanalyst can then hypothesize that PBNSX is an order to change course and that DFQZO means Cadiz and AKRPQ represents Lorient. Continued observations of these types of messages will confirm the meaning and derive new meanings. Messages studied in bulk over time will reveal the meaning of their codes: a process called "breaking the book". Cryptanalysts engaged in this type of work were often linguists familiar with the language, its technical terms and experienced with the context of the type of message studied; maritime, diplomatic, military, or commercial. Perhaps the most important, and consequential example of this type of attack was the British breaking in 1917 of the German diplomatic code communicating the Zimmerman telegram.

    Laborious and time consuming to break, intelligence agencies sometimes resorted to what became known euphemistically as "practical cryptanalysis"; i.e. the acquisition of enemy codes by devious means, usually theft, bribery or capture. The Italians had a reputation for this; at one point in August 1941 they acquired a copy of the American diplomatic BLACK code (which was used by military attaches) from the embassy in Rome. This provided decrypts from the reports of the military observer in the Middle East, Colonel Bonner Fellers, which outline British plans in fighting Rommel. In1937 the BROWN diplomatic code and the M-138 cipher device were photographed in the American consulate in Kobe by Japanese intelligence agents.[253]

    However, the Axis powers were not the only ones to descend to such devious means. In a series of black bag jobs in 1920, 1926 and 1927, the US Office of Naval Intelligence broke into the Japanese consulate in New York City to photograph the Red naval code. They made a less successful attempt in 1935 in a break in to the Washington DC apartment of the Japanese Naval

Attaché while he and his wife were at dinner, seeking to photograph a new cipher machine that had just been issued.[254]

Experience soon taught cryptologists to increase the security of codes by use of **superencipherment**[***] which came into practice between the world wars. The code groups were disguised by adding a random number from a table separately issued by using none carrying addition or subtraction, the result was an enciphered code group that was transmitted. At the receiving end, an identical copy of the random numbers sequence was used to decrypt the message back into its original code. For letter codes, some system was devised to convert code groups into numerical equivalents and some type of indicators were devised and embedded in the message to identify the starting point of the additive. Common or repeated terms came out as different numbers, nullifying a typical approach to breaking the book. By frequently changing the additive tables, security could be increased without having to change the underlying codebook. Superencipherment, and increasing use of RTTY which allowed for the rapid and accurate transmission of numerical data, led to increasing popularity in the use of figure codes.

This security improvement soon drew the attention of the cryptanalysts. Sophisticated statistical analysis of enciphered groups, such as the Index of Coincidence invented by US Army cryptanalysts William F. Friedman in the 1920s, allowed the comparison of two texts side by side to see if identical letters in the same position in the texts was by coincidence or by intent. This helped identify the key length and the language of the plain text. Once reassured that a series of messages were probably encoded with the same code and in the same language, the difference between each pair of code groups could be calculated, this reflected the relationship between underlying additive groups. Matching these intermediate values in one message with identical intermediate values in another message would allow the additive of two messages to be

---

[***] Also referred to as enciphered codes, or additive or subtractive tables.

aligned in columns. This created a "depth", which allowed for further comparisons. The more depths identified in a group of messages the better the increased statistical probability for accuracy calculating the true value of the additive. This followed an often-intense application of deduction to identify the true additive value, which was then subtracted from the message text. This got the cryptanalyst back to the underlying code groups, which were carefully recorded and compared to future messages. Hopefully the underlying code groups had been already solved to a certain degree by breaking the book. When the enemy changed additive tables, the entire process had to be started over. This was a very labor-intensive effort in these pre-computer days and helps explain the tens of thousands of personnel employed by WWII Cryptanalytic agencies.

In **ciphers** the primary unit of meaning is the letter, as opposed to the code in which the primary unit of meaning is a term. A cipher conceals meaning by substituting a letter for another letter, with a key determining the substitution. Ciphers have some advantages over codes; they do not require the lengthy compiling, printing and distribution of codebooks, and they provide the writer with greater flexibility in expression. During World War I many codebooks were captured, requiring time and labor intensive effort to revise them to regain security. With a cipher security can be regained by changing the key.[255]

A **Caesar shift** is a simple cipher in which each letter of the message is shifted alphabetically to the right to create a jumbled result. Thus the message "DOG" with a Caesar shift of 3 would come out as "GRJ". In modern terms the plaintext (the message) has a key (the shift to the right of 3), resulting in the cipher text (the jumble). As the name implies, it was used by the great man himself during his heyday. However, once the nature of the cipher became known it was easily broken. Just take the first handful of letters of the cipher text and shift them in turn one step to the right. Since there are only 25 possibilities of letter substitutions, the result soon comes out looking like a word, and you have discovered the key.

This approach was soon improved by abandoning the shift as a key and replacing it with a unique randomly jumbled alphabet; this became known as a **monoalphabetic substitution cipher**. However the desire to keep secrets is always matched by a desire of someone else to discover them, and cryptanalysts soon devised techniques to break them. Since each letter in a substitution is always enciphered in the same way, cryptanalysts developed the use of frequency analysis to identify the substitutions in a cipher text of a language's most commonly used letters. For instance in English, ETAONRISHDLF account for about 80% of the letters used in a typical text. By counting the most frequently used letters in a cipher text and comparing their percentages to the most common letters in English, you can then begin to guess the substitutions and unlock the cipher.

Every advance in cryptanalysis ultimately leads to an advance in cryptology in the never ending quest to secure communications. By the renaissance ciphers were developed in which a different substitution alphabet was used for every letter of the plain text. This was based upon the concept of a Latin Square, a 26 X 26 square with letters in alphabetical order across the top and down the side. By incrementing each row by one letter the result is a tableau in which in no row or column a letter appears more than once. This became the bases of the **polyalphabetic cipher,** with the first row as the key and the left column as the cipher text. Starting with column A, the cryptographer went down the column to look up the first plaintext letter, and then went across the row to find the corresponding cipher text letter. Thus, "DOG" becomes "DNE". Note however that the first letter of the plaintext is always identical to the first cipher text letter. This problem can be solved by simply mixing the order of the alphabets on the top and side; this

Appendix: The codes and ciphers of WWII

however requires that copies of the cipher be provided to the senders and receivers, rather than reconstructed from memory. The 16th century cryptologist Blaise de Vigenère recommended using a simple keyword that was easily remembered by the participants to build the tableau. Repeating the keyword across the top allowed for the creation of a tableau wide enough to contain the entire message. For example "BALTIMORE" as the key and the alphabet as the cipher text would create a 9 X 26 table for encoding. Repeating the keyword as "BALTIMORE BALTIMORE" would give you an 18 X 26 table, and so on. [256]

Variations of the polyalphabetic cipher kept cryptographers busy for the next three centuries. One variation, the **Playfair**, in which the keyword was not repeated but rather the rest of the alphabet was formed from the remaining letters, and then formed into a square that was the basis for enciphering each pair of letters of the plaintext, was popular among British government officials in the Victorian era.

Mechanization of cryptology was a concept established as early as the 1800s when Thomas Jefferson developed a **cipher wheel**, a device consisting of 25 disks engraved with mixed alphabets, which could be mounted on a bolt. The order that the wheels were mounted became the key; each wheel was turned to spell out a 25 letter message, then the whole device was tightened and another row was selected at random to be copied as the cipher text. The receiver of the message revered the process, aligning the wheels to spell out the cipher text, and then revolving the whole device to find a line that spelled out the message. A more modern version of this device was adopted by the U.S. military, known as the **M-94**; it was used into the middle of World War II. Another variation of this idea was developed into the **Strip cipher**, which was used by the U.S. military and State departments into WWII. Instead of disks, the randomly mixed alphabets were printed out on paper strips, 50 to a set, of which 30 were placed into a metal rack, the order determined by a daily changing key. The strips were moved back and forth to spell out a message in the first column and then the sender picked out another column and transmitted it. Like the Jefferson wheel, the receiver ordered the cipher text into a column and then looked for a corresponding column in plain text.

Another approach to the problem gave rise to the development of **transformation ciphers**, which rearranges the plaintext letters to form the cipher text, rather than substituting letters. The letters of the message are rearranged without actually replacing the letter and the frequencies of each individual letter are not altered by the encryption. A common example is the word scramble puzzle found in many newspapers. However, these puzzles are easily solved by anagramming; any real transposition cipher needs more complex patterns to provide security.

A better method was to construct a tablet of various rectangular shapes and to superimpose a pattern to be followed by the text. A common type of transposition that became popular is known as the **"rail fence"**. Create a rectangle of any number of rows, and then expand its columns in width to ensure that enough cells are created to hold each letter of the message. For example, a message of 60 letters could be fir into a 5 X 60 grid. Write the message out by placing the first letter of the first word in the upper left grid box, and then put the second letter in the next row one column to the right. Continue to place the letters vertically below each other forming a diagonal until the fifth letter is at the bottom of the grid, then start an upward diagonal with the sixth letter. Keep placing the letters of the message in this up and down diagonal pattern until completed and the text will look like a rail fence. Then take the first row, which will have 12 nonconsecutive letters and copy it out horizontality. Do this for each row in the message and transmit the whole now scrambled message to the recipient. The key to this cipher is the knowledge that the transposition is a 5 X 12 grid arranged in a rail fence pattern. Any number of shaped grids with any number of differ patterns can be used for transpositions. Another way to make the transposition more secure is to write the message out in a grid, then number the columns in a non-sequential manner. Transmit the columns in the order defined by the non-sequential numbers and the message will be thoroughly scrambled. The recipient must know the non-sequential sequence of the columns in the original grid in order to reconstruct the message. This then becomes the key for what is known as a **columnar transposition**.

A cryptanalytic approach to attacking these transpositions is to factor the total number of letters which will then result in all the possible variations in the grid, as in the example above, 2 X 30, 3 X 20, 4 X 15, 5 X 12, and 6 X 10. The message can be written out column by column for each grid and then anagrammed until the results until they make sense. Labor intensive, but it only requires pencil, paper, and time to solve.

To overcome this weakness the **stencil cipher** was developed. As its name implies, the basis was a cardboard stencil of the same size and shape of the transformation grid. Random squares were cut out of every row, and these blanks were used to write in the message horizontality. The number of blanks was arbitrary, but should be less than half for the grid, and an odd number of total blanks made the cipher more difficult. Columnar transposition was used to order the columns; the stencil itself was used as the key. Only the recipient, holding the same stencil as a key, could reconstruct the message. Easy to use but difficult to solve, these became popular during the Second World War for use as tactical codes in the front lines.

Vulnerabilities in conventional ciphers and codebooks, combined with a massive increase in communications during WW I, motivated a number of inventors after the war to develop sophisticated machines that could produce massively complex polyalphabetic ciphers. Perhaps the most well known of these machines was the **Enigma**, developed in the early 20s by Arthur

Scherbius based upon a patent by the Dutch inventor Hugo Koch. Originally rejected by the German military and foreign services, Scherbius attempted to commercialize it and market it to international firms as a means to secure their commercial transactions. The machine design was based upon the wiring of three interacting wheels. When the keyboard letter was depressed, its impulse was sent to the first wheel and scrambled by its cross wiring, then sent through the second and third wheels for a further permutations, reflected by the machine with another scrambling, and then sent back through the wheels again. The result was 26 X 26 X 26 X 26 X 26 X 26 X 26 possibilities for the resulting cipher text. The wheels stepped with each letter, rotating the internal wiring, and created another set of permutations. The Enigma proved to be a commercial failure, but not before French, British and American intelligence agencies had a chance to buy copies of the machine for evaluation. By the late 1920s the German military began to see the value of a cipher machines and reconsidered their earlier decision. Starting with the Navy, they reequipped all the armed forces with the machine and saved the Enigma firm from dissolution, while also modifying the machine with a plug board to add another permutation at the input. Later the Kriegsmarine created a model that added a fourth wheel creating yet another X26 permutation. The massive British, and later American, effort to break the Enigma was code named ULTRA. The story of this effort is now well known and since the mid 1970s it has spanned a plethora of books and studies.[257]

Also, around 1925, the Swedish businessman and engineer Boris Hagelin took control of the firm Aktiebolaget Cryptograph which was producing machines based upon Arvid Gerhard Damm's 1919 patent for a wired rotor machine. **Hagelin** was more successful in the limited market than Scherbius and managed to survive the depression. In 1935 he devised a machine based upon a pin-and-lug mechanism which was sold to the French military. Known as the **C-36**,

Appendix: The codes and ciphers of WWII

it was small, rugged, lightweight (less than 3 pounds), didn't require batteries and could fit in a pocket. With war clouds gathering over Europe, Hagelin moved his company to Switzerland, where he continued to do business internationally. During WW II he made a massive sale to the U.S. military where a modified C-36 was fielded as the **M-209** cipher machine (Navy designation CSP-1500). Although not as secure as full size machines, it was secure enough for front line use where it was only necessary to delay the enemy's reading of your messages by 48 hours. This machine was used by the U.S. Army well into the Korean War.

The master American cryptanalyst William Friedman, director of the US Army's Signals Intelligence Service, fully aware of some of the weakness in existing cipher machines, invented a rotor machine that utilized two sets of five rotors each to generate pseudo randomness for the stepping mechanism. This machine, developed into the **SIGABA**, was never broken by the enemy. The British also developed a 5 rotor-machine, the **TYPEX**, which was adopted for their highest level, most secure communications. The Germans captured one at Dunkirk, but its wheels had been removed and destroyed, and they never were able to break it.

Although the German Enigma machine eventually became well known to the public, another mode of communications was to impact the cryptologic efforts of the Second World War, **the encrypted teletypewriter**. TTY communications were based upon the telegraphic code invented by the French engineer Émile Baudot in 1870. It was designed on a pattern of impulses modulated into a fixed unit of time, rather than the standard Morse code dots and dashes. The Baudot code was the first binary code consisting of what was called "marks' and "spaces", named for the pattern punched into the perforated tape that fed the reader. In modern terms it would be considered a five bit code, resulting in 32 unique combinations. Twenty six of these combinations were assigned to the letters of the alphabet and the rest represented control characters such as figure shift, line feed, etc. This system was developed to allow the multiplexing of more than one message at a time over a circuit; another advantage was that it did not require an operator trained in Morse code. Its ability to directly encode letters and numbers accuracy made it useful for business communications, and it was adopted early for use in the stock market.

In the First World War the U.S. government was seeking methods to communicate the vast amount of information necessary to support the war effort in Europe, but the major challenge was to devise a method to secure the transmissions from eavesdroppers. Gilbert **Vernam**, a young AT&T engineer was given the problem. He realized that the five bit pattern of the Baudot code could be transformed mathematically into an encoded version, and transformed back to the original automatically through the use of specially designed circuits. This not only secured the communications but automated the time and labor intensive efforts of code clerks. In the early 1920, telecommunication engineers developed radio transmitters to transmit Baudot code over the air, and the technology caught on commercially, freeing the sender from the constraints of crowded land line cables. Press Associations were early adopters, sending their dispatches from the far corners of the world.

Governments too found the technology useful, especially Britain and the US which had worldwide interests, and the Soviet Union with its vast landmass and low level of infrastructure. Vernam's original approach, which relied on feeding a tape of random letters for the key was replaced in the 1930s with cipher machines for the key source, relieving the logistics burden of supplying key tape to the recipients. The Germans, although relying heavily on the Enigma for the bulk of their communications, developed two different teletype machines, the **SZ 40 and 42**

Appendix: The codes and ciphers of WWII

models developed by Lorentz as an teletypewriter attachment, and the integrated Siemens & Halske **T52**, known as the ***Geheimfernschreiber***; both using Vernam's principles to encrypt the messages. These systems were used for the most important strategic communications from the high command to the major military commands such as naval headquarters or Army Groups. Originally relying on landlines, Hitler's war of expansion soon outran the established networks and these communications began to be sent over the air via RTTY. These signals began to be intercepted and studied by the British in 1942. Hard work, brilliant insights by some of the bona fide genius at Bletchley Park, and strokes of luck led to a cryptologic break in into this system that was technically more challenging than the Enigma cipher. Over the next few years new devices were invented to assist with the breaking of these signals, now codenamed FISH, including the world's first truly electronic computer, the COLLOSUS. Critical intelligence from this source was vital during the Normandy invasion and the breakout across France.

Notes

Introduction

[1] Pidgeon, Geoffrey *The Secret Wireless War; The story of MI6 Communications 1939-1945*.Arundel Books, Richmond, UK, 2008.
[2] Winterbotham was the author of *The ULTRA Secret,* London, Weidenfeld and Nicolson, 1974, the first public revelation in English of the breaking of the German Enigma cipher.
[3] Quotes are from Hill, Marion. *Bletchley Park People*. Stroud, Gloucestershire, U.K. The History Press.

Chapter 1. Beginnings

[4] F. H. Hinsley and Alan Stripp, *Codebreakers: The Inside Story of Bletchley Park*. 1993, Oxford University Press.
[5] Memo War Department to Eisenhower, August 7, 1944; Memo Commander in Chief U.S. Fleet to Commander TWELFTH Fleet, 6 September 1944. National Security Agency (NSA). *European Axis Signal Intelligence in World War II as Revealed by 'TICOM' Investigations and by Other Prisoner of War Interrogations and Captured Material, Principally German*. WDGAS-14, Chief Army Security Agency, Top Secret/Cream report, 1 May 1946. Nine volumes. (Hereafter referred to as EASI), *Volume 8 – Miscellaneous*, p. 55-58. http://www.nsa.gov/public_info/_files/european_axis_sigint/Volume_8_miscellaneous.pdf (accessed June 15, 2010).
[6] "Personal memo to Commander Brute Roeder, 23 September 1944." Ely TICOM pinch file, NARA, RG 457, Entry P-11, Box 114.
[7] TICOM/1 Memorandum concerning Signal Intelligence Targets. Minutes of the Second Meeting of Target Intelligence Committee held at Station X at 2:30 p.m. on Friday, October 13, 1944. Both contained in RG 457, Entry P-11, Box 55, folder 'Establishment of TICOM'.
[8] Sean Londgen. T-Force: The Race for Nazi War Secrets, 1945. 2009. Constable Robinson. Kindle Edition.
[9] PRO WO 219/2694 Organization & Personnel "T" Forces. Memo SHAEF to Chief of Staff, Organization of "T" Force, "YULETIDE".
[10] Information from the following memos "TICOM Personnel, 28 January 1945";"Annex I"; "Annex II"; "DD(NS) Memorandum Number 64" all from TICOM Reporting Officer's Personal Training Folder. NARA RG 457, Entry P-11, Box 55.
[11] PRO HW 50/71"Dossier Captured Documents"
[12] "Guide to Docket NID 01865/45" in TICOM Reporting Officer's Personal Training Folder. NARA RG 457, Entry P-11, Box 55.
[13] Ely,TICOM pinch file. Memo: Special Procedure Captured Signal Documents, 22 November 1944. NARA RG 457, Entry P-11, Box 114. Guy Allan Farrin, (ed). *History of 30 AU*. "Section 7 Notes on NID24 and Section 12a Bletchley Park.. http://www.30au.co.uk (accessed Dec. 1, 2010.)
[14] "Message Traffic Bicher – Coreerman, 12 May 1945" RG 457, Entry P-11, Box 55, folder 'Establishment of TICOM'. Farrin, *History of 30 AU*. "Section 7 Notes on NID24 and Section 12a Bletchley Park.
[15] NARA, Operation Eclipse Airborne Operations. RG 331, Entry 268, Box 71. Memo, First Allied Airborne Army, Office of the Acting C of S G-3, Subject: Airfields. January 31, 1945. Memo, Assistant C of S G-3, SHAEF, Subject: Troop Carrier Type Aircraft for FAA "Eclipse" Airborne Plan, 13 March 1945., Memo, H.Q. First Allied Airborne Army, Subject: Troop Carrier Type Aircraft, 22 February 1945.
[16] NARA, Operation Eclipse Airborne Operations. RG 331, Entry 268, Box 71. Memo: EXFOR Main to SHAEF, Operation ERUPTION, 29 March 1945.

Chapter 2. Spoils of War

[17] Yes, that Ian Fleming, the author of the James Bond books.
[18] Gimbel, John Science, Technology, and Reparations: Exploitation and Plunder in Postwar Germany. Standford University Press, 1990. p. 4.
[19] The other members were British Lieutenant Howard J. Lorton, Sub- Lieutenant Edward Morgan, and two

Notes

Americans, Lieutenant (J.G.) Milton Gaschk, and Ensign Pearly Phillips. Lieutenant Commander Leonard Griffiths and Lieutenant Lorton of the Royal Navy later augmented them

[20] Rankin, Nicholas (2011-09-07). *Ian Fleming's Commandos: The Story of the Legendary 30 Assault Unit* (Kindle Location 4412). Oxford University Press. Kindle Edition. See also The British National Archives (TNA), *History of 30 Commando (latterly called 30 Assault Unit and 30 Advanced Unit)*, PRO HW 8/104.

[21] Longden, Sean (2009). *T-Force the Race for Nazi War Secrets, 1945*. Constable Robinson. Kindle Edition.

[22] Ibid, p. ???

[23] TICOM I-9 Notes on the 'Kurier' Communicatiosn System. NARA RG 457 ???; Kurier system of U-Boat Communications, RG 457 ????; The Kurier problem, RG 457 ????; Ralph Erskine, Kriegsmarine Short Signal Systems – and How Bletchley Park Exploited Them, Cryptlogia, January 1999 Volume XXIII Number 1. Like many examples of German advanced technology, the Kurier system reappeared for use in the Cold War, when the Soviet Navy in the early 1960s developed burst encoding systems for their own submarine communications. See W. Craig Reed, Red November, Inside the Secret U.S. Soviet Submarine War. New York: William Morris, 2010.

[24] They were Dunstan Curtis, Brian Connell, Geoffrey Pike, an American ALSOS (nuclear intelligence) officer Captain A. G. Mumma;

[25] Kapitän zur See Wolfgang Lüth, and Dönitz's chief of staff, Korvettenkapitän Walter Lüdde-Neurath

[26] SG 41

[27] Narrative and Report of Proceedings of TICOM Team 6, 11th April – 6th July, 1945. p. 13. NARA, RG 457, Entry P-11, Box 131.

[28] Ibid, p. 14.

[29] Ibid, p. 15.

[30] Ibid, p. 17.

[31] Kahn, David. *Hitler's Spies: German Military Intelligence in World War II*. New York: MacMillian Publishing, 1978. P. 213.

[32] Thanks to Ralph Erskine for clarifying the nature of British Naval codes and Cyphers.

[33] TICOM Team 6 report, p. 19.

[34] The party also included Captain Alfred George ("AGR") Royffe, also of the BP Research Section, and three RNVR officers, Lieutenant Commanders Davenport and Forster and Lieutenant Morley.

[35] TICOM I-38 *Report on Interrogation of LT. Frowein of OKL 4 SKL III , on his work on the security of the German Naval Four Wheel Enigma.*

[36] See R.A. Ratcliff, *Delusions of Intelligence*, Chapter 8, for an in-depth discussion of these matters.

[37] The experts in this field were Kapt. z. S. Beremann, head of 4 SKL II General Referent IIc, responsible for production and distribution of keying materials, and his assistant Amsrat Pitzer, in charge of the printing machine.

[38] The German cruiser SMS Madeburg ran aground in a fog near the island of Odensholm in the Gulf of Finland and sunk on August 26. Its codebook was dropped overboard in shallow water before being abandoned. Russian divers were able to salvage it and a copy was forwarded to the British Admiralty, allowing its Room 40 analysis to read the German Navy's coded radio traffic, to Britain's great advantage. See Patrick Beesly, *Room 40, British Naval Intelligence 1914-1918*, New York: Harcourt, Brace, Jovanovich, 1982.

[39] John Jackson, *Hitler's Codebreakers* and EASI, *Volume 2 – Notes on High Level Cryptology and Cryptanalysis*, 46-47.

[40] EASI, *Volume3 — The Signal Intelligence Agency of the Supreme Command, Armed Forces*, 105.

[41] TICOM I-16, *Notes on the Interrogation of Amtsrat Schwabe and Obfkmstr. Warzecha on Russian Naval Cyphers.*

Chapter 3. TICOM in Burgscheidungen

[42] Bamford, *Body of Secrets*, p. 11.

[43] NSA. Oral History Interview with Paul E. Neff, NSA OH 01-83, 26 January 1983, p43.

[44] Kahn, The Codebreakers, pages 436 -437. Also, TICOM I-172.

[45] This system was codenamed GEE by the Allies. See *European Axis Signal Intelligence...* Vol 2 , 34-35; *European Axis Signal Intelligence...* Vol. 6, 63; Friedrich L. Bauer. *Decrypted Secrets: Methods and Maxims of Cryptology*. Heidelberg New York: Springer, 2007, 164-165;.TICOM I-22 "Interrogation of German cryptographers of the Pers ZS Department of the Auswärtlges Amt".

[46] EASI — *Volume 6 – Foreign Office Cryptanalytic Section*. p. 1, 4-6.

[47] TICOM Team 3 Report, page 27; Neff Oral History, p. 42
[48] TICOM Team report, page 30.
[49] Nuff, Oral History p44.
[50] TICOM Team 3 report; TICOM I-22; EASI Vol. 6, p. 12, 16.
[51] Roy was later reported by Selchow to have spent time in a prison camp and then turned over to the Russians.
[52] Nuff Oral History p. 46.
[53] Ibid, p. 45.
[54] Kahn, *The Codebreakers*, p. 446.
[55] TICOM I-22, p. 7-8.
[56] Budiansky, *Battle of Wits*, p. 84.
[57] TICOM I-22 "Interrogation of German cryptographers of the Pers ZS Department of the Auswärtlges Amt" paragraph 19.
[58] In an interesting irony, the Germans developed a practice where Pers ZS worked on traffic from even days and OKW/*Chi* solved the traffic from odd days, a system identical to that later devised by the US Navy and US Army prior to Pearl Harbor in their attacks on Japanese diplomatic traffic.
[59] EASI, Vol 2, p. 70
[60] These messages, classified "Magic", were intercepted and read with delight by the Anglo-American intelligence agencies.
[61] Paschke, quoted in TICOM I-22, paragraph 120.
2 Robert Louis Benson and Cecil Phillips, *History of Venona* (Fort George G. Meade, MD: Center for Cryptologic History, 1995, p. 51 Available at http://www.gwu.edu/~nsarchiv/NSAEBB/NSAEBB278/01.PDF. Accessed June 11, 2013,
[63] For further details See TICOM I-172 "Interrogations of Hagen and Paschke of Pers ZS",
[64] Bauer, p. 77.
[65] Weber, Ralph E. United States Diplomatic Codes and Ciphers, 1775-1938, p. 254; TICOM I-22, page 10.
[66] Christos, http://chris-intel-corner.blogspot.com/2012/05/us-diplomatic-codes-a1-c1-gray-and.html
[67] TICOM I-22, p. 10.
[68] Kahn, The Codebreakers, p. 493; Wrixon, Codes, Ciphers and other Cryptic & Clandestine Communications, p. 245. See also *Special Instructions For Using The Strip Cipher Device (1945)* This is available from NARA; NSA Historical Collections 190/37/7/1, NR 2288 CBLL35 12804A 19450205 (Box 798, F: 2288, pp 12).
[69] The team also included Dr. Hunke and Klaus Schultz.
[70] In fact, on that date the state department switched from the O-1 to the O-2 version of the strip cipher.
[71] For a more detailed and technical account, see Hans Rohrbach, "Report on the Decipherment of the American Strip Cipher O-2 by the German Foreign Office', Crptlogia, #;1, 16-26, 1979.
[72] Bauer, p. 123.
[73] Rohrbach, op cit. p. 16.
[74] EASI, Vol. 6, p 1-2.
[75] History of Venona, NSA, p.56.
[76] Commander Bull, Memo: Disposition of German Nationals, June 23, 1945. TNA: HW 40-180.

Chapter 4. Fruits of Victory

[77] TICOM I-208 "Interrogation Report On Kurt Selchow Former Head of the Pers ZS Department of The German Ministry of Foreign Affairs"
[78] After the war Kirby was to go onto a long career in the NSA, and was later inducted into the NSA Hall of Honor. He died in 2009.
[79] EASI, *Volume 3 - The Signal Intelligence Agency of the Supreme Command, Armed Forces*, p. 3.
[80] TICOM IF-165 *Special Report by O. Kirby on TICOM Team 6's relations with OKW/Chi personnel*. NARA RG 457, Entry P-11, Box 115.
[81] After the war, Hüttenhain became the chief cryptanalyst for the Gehlen Organization, with the cover name "Studiengesellschaft für wissenschaftliche Arbeiten" (Study Group for Scientific Investigation). From 1956 until 1973, he was head of the Federal Government's Zentralstelle für das Chiffrierwesen ('German Cipher Board') in Bad Godesberg.

Notes

[82] TICOM DF-187E *Comments by Fenner on the Austrian Cryptologic Bureau and Former German Colleagues*, DF-187A *Organization Of The Cryptologic Agency Of The Armed Forces High Command, with Names, Activities, And Number Of Employees Together with a Description of Devices Used.*
[83] TICOM IF-165, p. 4
[84] Ibid.
[85] TICOM DF-187E, EASI Vol 3. p.4.
[86] This was the Petsamo codebook; the Soviet reuse of one-time pads was rediscovered a few years later by the ASA and was the key to unlocking what became known as the Venona materials.
[87] See TICOM I-60, I-15; EASI, — *Volume 4 - Signal Intelligence Service of the Army High Command.* Chapter 4.
[88] TICOM DF-187C *Relations of OKW/Chi with other Cryptologic Bureaux*, TICOM I-201 *Interrogation of Franz Weisser.*
[89] TICOM I-202 *Interrogation of Min. Rat. Victor Wendland of OKW/Chi.*
[90] David Alvarez. (2007) 'Wilhelm Fenner and the Development of the German Cipher Bureau, 1922-1939'. *Cryptologia*, 31:2, 152 -163.
[91] David Alvarez, "Wilhelm Fenner and the Development of the German Cipher Bureau, 1922-1939". *Cryptologia*, 31:2, (2007), 152 -163; EASI, *Volume 1 – Synopsis*, 18.
[92] TICOM I-202, 4.
[93] Oral History interview Oliver Kirby.
[94] Roder's identity is from History of Venona, p. 58-59, however Kirby remembers him as a member of the Forschungsamt. Kirby may have written the name down incorrectly in his notes as no Roder is listed as a member of Pers ZS, however there was a Dr. Schroeter who was a mathematician who worked on Japanese ciphers. Furthermore, there was a Georg Schroeder who was the head of the Codes and Cipher department of the FA, who was in a position to have access to this type of material if it was in the possession of the FA.
[95] This was the "Russian Fish", see chapter ?? for details.
[96] TICOM I-2 "Interrogation of Huettenhain and Fricke"
[97] See "Rasterschluessel 44 (RS44)" at the Crypto Den website http://www.cryptoden.com/index.php/21-intro-raster. Accessed August 14, 2013.
[98] Issued as TICOM I-36 and TICOM I-37.
[99] Appendix A: Josef Triembacher, p. 3-4, from PRO HW 40-186 RLM/ Forschungsamt.
[100] TICOM I-22 Interrogation of German Cryptographers of the PERS ZS, Department of the Auswärtlges Amt, and TICOM I-54 Second Interrogation of Five Members of the RLM/ Forschungsamt.
[101] TICOM IF-165, p. 10.
[102] Ibid, p. 12. See c NARA, RG 457, Entry P-4. Meugge, still suffering from his wound and illness, expressed a desire to emigrate to Sweden, where his wife, a Swedish citizen was residing. He was released from custody in July.
[103] This was another German technology that was later adopted by both the U.S. and Soviet Navies.
[104] TICOM Team 6 report, p. 21.
[105] NSA "Oral History: Oliver Kirby" OH-20-92. Available online at
[106] TICOM I-39 *Organization of OKW/Chi.*
[107] EASI, Vol. 3, p. 19.
[108] EASI, Vol. 2, p. 18 -27.
[109] EASI, Vol. 3, p. 55.
[110] TICOM I-201, see also 'US diplomatic codes A1, C1, Gray and Brown', Christos Military and Intelligence Corner (http://chris-intel-corner.blogspot.com/2012/05/us-diplomatic-codes-a1-c1-gray-and.html) accessed September 27, 2013.
[111] TICOM I-201, TICOM DF-187B *The Cryptanalytic Success of OKW/Chi after 1938.*
[112] EASI Vol. 3, Chapter 4. TICOM DF-187B.
[113] TICOM Team 6 report, p. 24.
[114] See the TICOM DF-187 series.

Chapter 5. Success

[115] After the war Oeser headed the German personnel research branch of the Control Commission, assessing the suitability of locals for leading roles in a reconstructed Germany. Having married an Australian, he moved there to take the foundation chair of psychology at the University of Melbourne, where he help establish the field of social

psychology. He served as dean of the faculty of arts and retired as professor emeritus in 1969. He stayed active in his field in retirement until his death in Melbourne in 1983.

[116] Compaigne went on to a long career at NSA, pioneering in its development of computers and serving in research and development. After retirement he served as chair of the mathematics department at Slippery Rock University, PA.

[117] Thomas Parrish, *The Ultra Americans*, New York: Stein and Day, 1986. 279

[118] Norland, conservation with the author, October 7, 2011.

[119] Levenson went onto a long career at NSA.

[120] NSA, Oral History Interview with Arthur J. Levenson

[121] TICOM M-5, Demonstration of Kesselring 'Fish Train'.

[122] The Urh (*Umkehrwalze*) was an add on box to the standard three rotor Enigma that allowed the plugboard connections to be changed by simply adjusting a switch. This allowed the operators to change the plugboard settings hourly rather than daily. It was introduced in July 1944 by the Luftwaffe but was broken by GCCS Hut 6 within days of its introduction.

[123] Unknown to Ōshima, his lengthily and detailed reports on German strategy and capabilities, transmitted back to Tokyo in the Purple cipher, read by both the British and Americans, became a prime source for Allied intelligence.

[124] IN 7/VI conducted high level cryptanalysis for the Army, the Control Station for Signal Intelligence, LNA, evaluated the materials passed to it from IN 7/VI. Both were located in Berlin but the IN 7/VI headquarters was destroyed in the November RAF bombing and was forced to relocate to Jüterbog. HSL OSt, the Intercept Control Station East was responsible for all cryptanalysis and evaluation from the Eastern front, and east located at Loetzen, East Prussia. See EASI, Vol. 4, Chapter 2.

[125] TICOM IF-5, Notes On Field Interrogation Of Various German Army and Air Force SigintPersonnel.

[126] Mark A. Tittenhofer, The Rote Drei: Getting Behind the 'Lucy' Myth. CIA: Center for the Study of Intelligence, September 1993. Available at https://www.cia.gov/library/center-for-the-study-of-intelligence/kent-csi/vol13no3/html/v13i3a05p_0001.htm. (Accessed November 6, 2013).

[127] TICOM I-13 Interrogation Oberst Lt. Friedrich, p. 2

[128] TICOM IF-5, pages 7 and 8.

[129] TICOM DF-9 Captured Wehrmacht Sigint document.

[130] James Bamford, *Body of Secrets: Anatomy of the Ultra-Secret National Security Agency*. New York: Anchor Books, 2001. 16.

[131] Whitaker, quoted by Parrish, *The Ultra Americans*, New York: Stein and Day, 1986. 283.

[132] Quoted from TICOM IF-5, page 9.

[133] NSA. IF-162, Evaluation of Multichannel Teletype (HMFS). FOIA case #64093, 29 March 2011.

[134] A photograph of the "Russian Fish" can be found in Parrish, 1986, and in Paul Whitaker and Louis Kruh. "From Bletchley Park to Berchtesgaden." *Cryptologia,* XI (1987): 129-141.

[135] EASI — *Volume 7 – Goering's Research Bureau.* p. 2.

[136] David Kahn, Hitler's Spies: German Military Intelligence in World War II. (New York: MacMillian Publishing, 1978), 178.

[137] EASI Vol. 7, p. 6-9.

[138] TICOM Team 1 Report, Appendix 2, p. 17-18.

[139] One of those recruited from OKW/*Chi* was Hans –Thilo Schmidt, the spy employed by the French who was responsible for passing along data that allowed the Poles to make the initial breaks into Enigma. See David Kahn's *How I Discovered World War II's Greatest Spy*. Boca Raton, Fl. 2014.

[140] EASI. Vol. 7, p. 22.

[141] Ibid., 74.

[142] Ibid., 72.

[143] Ibid., 39.

[144] Kahn, 180.

[145] EASI Vol. 7, p. 73.

Chapter 6. Captured Intact

Notes

[146] NARA. Final Report of TICOM Team 2, 9 May 1945 to 5 July 1945. RG 457, Records of the NSA, Entry P-11, Box 131, P. 3

[147] TICOM IF-177 Seabourne Report Vol I, p. 1-4.

[148] Ibid, p. 5-7. Among this group were Voegele and Major Ferdinand Feichtner, CO of LN 353 regiment, who were interrogated by TICOM at "Inkspot" interrogation center at Wandsworth, London on September 12th. See TICOM I-112.

[149] The Seabourne Reports; Vol. I Introduction and Report, Vol II Biographies of Contributors, Vol. III The Radio Defense Corps, Vol. IV. Biography of Major Ferenand Fichtner, Vol. V The Chi Stelle, Vol. VI History of Operations in the West, Vol. VII Technical Operations in the West, Vol. VIII. Miscellaneous Studies, Vol. IX History of Operations in the South, Vol. X Technical Operations in the South, Vol. XI History of Operations in the East, Vol. XII Technical Operations in the East, Vol. XIII Cryptanalysis.

[150] Kahn, *Hitler's Spies*, p. 212.

[151] TICOM IF-5, p. 3.

[152] TICOM I-112, p. 5.

[153] The Syko was a manual strip cipher device used in aircraft by the British. It consisted of a box consisting of 33 strip alphabets ordered according to the day's key. Because it was used in the air to send encrypted Morse messages, it was cryptologically fairly simple.

[154] TICOM I-112.p. 3-4.

[155] NARA. Seabourne Report: The Signal Intelligence Service of The German Luftwaffe (Vol I Thru Vol XIII). RG 457 HCC Boxes 974-976.

[156] KONAs were technically, not a regiment, but rather a commander with an extensive staff. It was organized this way to avoid the bureaucratic delays and difficulties of formally organizing a new regiment within the German army. See 'Final Report of TICOM Team 2', p. 10.

[157] TICOM I-23 Interrogation of Major Ernst Hertzer of German Army Signals Intelligence Service.

[158] EASI, Vol, 4, p. 18

[159] FESTEs (abbreviation for *Feste Nachrichten Aufklaerungsstelle*, i.e. Stationary Intercept company) were developed form the pre-war Army fixed intercept stations that were dismantled and moved out of the Reich to follow the army's invasions of foreign territory.

[160] Later renamed Army Group Center, it had fought on the middle of the Russian front retreating back into Galicia by the end of the war.

[161] Its other NAK, 953 had been transferred to the western front in September 1944

[162] EASI, Vol 9, German Traffic Analysis of Russian Communications, p. 22

[163] TICOM I-62 Field Interrogation of PAUL RAATZ of the German Army Signals Intelligence (1933 -1945), TICOM I-19b and EASI Vol. 4, p. 70-71.

[164] A "hatted " code was when in the encoding section the plain text groups are arranged in alphabetical or other significant order, accompanied by their code groups arranged in a nonalphabetical or random order, i.e a two part code.. A semi-hatted code was one hatted within definite, and usually small, sections.

[165] TICOM DF-112 *Survey of Russian Military systems* by Alex Dettmann, p. 65, 81-82. This extensive essay is the most complete German analysis of Russian Codes and Ciphers in the TICOM archive.

[166] EASI Vol 4, p. 100. Gerlich, a Russian code and cipher expert had been attached to NAAST 1, a SIGINT evaluation center in Cracov.

[167] A stencil cipher…

[168] TICOM I-75 Report on the Interrogation of Ltn AUGUST SCHROEDER, 11 Aug 45. p. 4.

[169] TICOM I-19b, Report No. 7. P. 13

[170] Inspectorate 7/ section VI of the Army High Command (OKH) was that service's central cryptanalytic agency for non-Russian traffic. In 1944 it was reorganized and merged with HLS Ost, the intercept control station East that broke the Eastern front traffic, and the LNA, the central evaluation agency to form the GdNA.

[171] TICOM I-19c Report on Russian Ciphers, p. 12.

[172] Ibid, p. 8.

[173] EASI, Vol 4, p. 105; also see Chris Triantafyllopoulos's essay *Soviet 5-figure codes*, from http://chris-intel-corner.blogspot.gr/2012/01/soviet-5-figure-codes.html . . (Accessed on January 14, 2014) for a list and description of these five-figure codes.

[174] Ibid, and TICOM I-19c p, 12.

[175] TICOM I-19b, Report No. 27 and 28, p. 46-49, and TICOM DF-112 Survey of Russian Military Systems b b Alex Dettemann. See also Christ Triantafyllopoulos's essay *NKVD Operational and High Level Codes* at http://chris-intel-corner.blogspot.gr/2012/05/nkvd-operational-and-high-level-codes.html. (Accessed on January 14, 2014.

[176] TICOM DF-112, p. 7.

[177] EASI Vol. 4, p.116.

[178] Arno Graul and radio finger printing: EASI, Vol 4. p. 71; Team 2 report bottom p. 13; TICOM I-47 POW Sitrep:"Originally requested back in U.K. but released upon recommendation of Bundy's party."
TICOM I-7 Statement of Major McIntosh concerning Underoffizier Graul; TICOM I-59 Interrogation of Unteroffizier Graul at Revin; TICOM message traffic 16, 17 1nd 18 June 1945.

[179] TICOM I-19 a-g *Report on Interrogation of Kommandeur Der Nacer. Aufkl. 1 (KONA 1) at Revin, France, June 1945.*

[180] Chef der Heeresruestung und Befehlshaber des Ersatzheeres, Amtsgruppe fuer Entwicklung und Pruefung des Heereswaffenamts, Waffenpruetung, Abteilung 7, Army Ordnance, Development and Testing Group, Signal Branch, Section 7. Its Group II was responsible for developing new radio, teleprinter facsimile, television and ciphony and cipher equipment. Group IV was its counterpart, developing, intercept, D/F and decoding equipment. It is interesting to note the relative low ranks of those cryptologic experts in the Army, Buggisch, a Ph.D. in mathematics, was a Sergeant. Compare this to an equivalent American, Dr. Howard Compaigne, also a Ph.D. mathematician, recruited into the Navy Signals Intelligence as a Lt. Commander.

[181] The cipher device 39 was an irregularly drive Enigma utilizing four variable notch rotors. This would have made it invulnerable to BP's standard cryptanalytic approach to the Enigma. A small number of test models were built, however bureaucratic delays caused in part by a lack of focus delayed the introduction of this device, which is used widely earlier int eh war, would have blacked out BP. The cipher device 41was a mechanical, hand cranked machine similar to Hagelin devices like the American M-209. However, its interacting, irregular cipher wheel motions made it difficult to cryptoanalyze. A few Gerät 41 signals were intercepted in 1945, but luckily mechanical problems due to its engineering delayed production. The Geramns had originally planned to order 11,000 of these machines for the Army, Air Force, and weather services. Teleprinter T-43 utilized a crystal controlled circuit developed by the Feurestein Lab allowed for the electronic synchronization of the sender and receiver units, a one-time key tape system generated by a T-52 running a 50 meter long tape loop to generate the key stream. This allowed the T-43 to transmit continuously all day, thereby defeating enemy traffic analysis because there was no break between the messages. These devices demonstrated that the Germans had the technology in their hands, which had the war lasted a few months longer, would have completely secured their communications.

[182] This device was the AN/GSQ-1 SIGJIP voice scrambler. Coupled with the SCR-522 VHF radio it could provide secure voice transmissions up to a range of 50-80 miles. It functioned by dividing the speech signal into 37 segments of a ½ millisecond length, then rearranging the order according to a key inputted by a punch card device. Despite the SIS warning that the system did not meet their security standards, it was deployed to the field in July 1944. Mounted in P-51 reconnaissance aircraft, one was almost immediately shot down near Berlin. As OKW/Chi cryptanalyst, Dr. Hüttenhain later testified to TICOM, the key was repeated every two seconds and an intercept operator could progressively adjust the signal until it could be deciphered by ear. He estimated that it would take up to two hours to decipher it. However, within a few months, the system was abandoned by the reconnaissance groups when the pilots preferred that he space in the airframe used by the system could be better used to house a tail warning radar. For further information see "The US AN/GSQ-1 (SIGJIP) speech scrambler", *Christos Military and Intelligence Corner* (http://chris-intel-corner.blogspot.com/2014/03/the-us-angsq-1-sigjip-speech-scrambler.html) accessed May 7, 2014; 'The Achievements of the Signal Security Agency (SSA) in World War II', 1946, p. 45; TICOM I-31 "Detailed interrogations of Dr. Hüttenhain, formerly head of research section of OKW/Chi, at Flensburg on 18-21 June 1945"; 'Performance Speech Equipment AN/GSQ-1 AN/GSQ-1A SIGJIP-SIGMAR'.NACP RG 457, Entry 9032, box 792. 'Information security: An elusive goal' by George F. Jelen available for download at *www.pirp.harvard.edu/pubs_pdf/jelen/jelen-p85-8 pdf.* accessed May 7, 2014.

[183] See TICOM I-46, *Preliminary Report on Interrogation of Wachtmeister Dr. Otto BUGGISCH and Dr. Werner LIEBKNECHT*; TICOM I-58, *Interrogation of Dr. Otto BUGGISCH of OKW/Chi.* TICOM I- 64, *Answers by Wm. BUGGISCH of OKH/Chi to questions sent by TICOM*; TICOM I-66, Paper by *Dr. Otto BUGGISCH of OKH/In. 7/VI and OKW/Chi on TYPEX;* TICOM I-66; Paper by *Dr. Otto BUGGISCH of OKH/In. 7/VI and OKW/Chi on Cryptanalytic machines;* TICOM I-92 Final Interrogation of *Wachtmeister Otto BUGGISCH.*

Notes

Chapter 7. Moping Up

[184] NARA, *Report of TICOM Team 4 visit to Southern Germany and Austria, 14th June – 12th July 1945*. RG 457, Records of the NSA, Box 168, p.6
[185] ibid, p. 17.
[186] Robert D. Farley. 'Oral History Interview with Dr. Howard CAMPAIGNE'. NSA-OH- 20-83 http://www.nsa.gov/public_info/_files/oral_history_interviews/nsa_oh_14_83_ campaigne.pdf, 25. (accessed May 15, 2010). Robert D. Farley. op. cit., 22-23.
[187] NARA, *Report of TICOM Team 4 visit to Southern Germany and Austria, 14th June – 12th July 1945*. RG 457, 570, 69, 4, Box 168.
[188] Robert D. Farley. op. cit., 22-23
[189] http://120years.net/wordpress/tag/oskar-vierling/
[190] For further details see TICOM I-43 *Report Written by Vierling*; TICOM I-57 *Summary of Enciphering Devices worked on by Dr. Liebknecht at Wa Pruef 7*; TICOM M-2 *Major Barlow's Report on Dr.Vierling's Laboratory*; and EASI Vol. 2, p. 22-23.
[191] Ibid. Note that this was the "Little Baustein" (Der Kleine Baustein). A Big Baustein was designed which utilized ring wobbling to alter the voice frequency, but difficulties in creating an autokey to control it made it too hard to control for the receiving equipment.
[192] TICOM M-1 *Vierling's Laboratory at Ebermannstadt*.
[193] The Series of TICOM reports E-7 through E-19, *Detailed Feuerstein Technical Project Reports*, is the documentation of this exploitation. As of this writing, most were still classified and held by NSA.
[194] TICOM IF-14 *Vierling Library*.
[195] http://www.vierling.de/de/ (accessed November 8, 2014)
[196] NSA, *IF-167 Final Report on the Visit of TICOM Team 5 to the Schliersee Area 3rd August to 7th October 1945*, 1. Freedom of Information Act, September 2010, case #62136A.
[197] TICOM, Vol. 3. p. 8.
Robert E. Button, a SIGINT liaison officer with 12th Army Group claimed that he was the receipent of this box. "It was about six feet long and three feet high. They had found it at the bottom of the Schliersee, a lake in Bavaria, while dragging it for the body of the drowned soldier. They did not know the content of the box, but in line with their duties, they brought it immediately to high headquarters for intelligence analysis. With some effort, we pried the box open. The contents were well preserved and turned out to be volumes of German intercepts of the Vatican's wireless traffic with all of its church outposts throughout the world. The Germans had been monitoring this traffic and translating it into German from Italian and Latin. Word spread quickly around headquarters of this discovery. There was great sensitivity to the diplomatic implications that could well involve high politics and religion. Thus, when word of this chest (which was sitting under my desk) reached the State Department representative at Bradley's Verdun headquarters, it was instantly commandeered by the diplomats and disappeared from us in a flash. I never saw it again and have never heard it referred to in all my experience with the government and the military...." See Button, *Enigma in Many Keys*, Lincoln, NE. iUniverse, Inc. 2004. 117-118.
[198] Fehl was a specialist in traffic analysis and had worked in SIXTA and Hut 3 at Bletchley Park.
[199] The dive team consisted of 1st Lieutenant Ted Leland, M/Sgt. Daves, T/Sgt. Sonnengren, T/5 Cebula and Butler, and Pfc. Pugilise, all of the US Army Construction Engineers.
[200] Fu. H.E.c, Funkhorch Empfänger-c (Monitoring receiver), 3.5 to 25 MHz. For illustrations of this set, see http://www.laud.no/ww2/fuhec/index.htm (accessed May 30, 2011).
[201] Details about the operations at Steeple Clayton are all from *TICOM M-8, Diary kept by Capt. T. Cartes, I.C. of Tests on Baudot Equipment conducted in the U.K. June 29 to July 8, 1945*. NARA-CP, RG 467 Entry 9037, Box 44, Item #6862.
[202] Brief bio of Kentworthy
[203] ibid, 4.
[204] ibid, 3.
[205] This unit was part of the signal intelligence service of the army High Command, the *Oberkommando des Heeres/General der „Nachrlchtenautklaerung* (OKH/GdNA), not as Parrish stated, the Armed Forces High Command signal agency, OKW/*Chi*. For a description of the organizational structure of GdNA see *European Axis*

244

Signal Intelligence in World War II as Revealed by 'TICOM' Investigations and by Other Prisoner of War Interrogations and Captured Material, Principally German. WDGAS-14, Chief Army Security Agency, Top Secret/Cream report, 1 May 1946. Vol. 4, 12-16. National Security Agency.

[206] Matthew M. Aid, "The Russian Target: The U.K. – U.S. Cryptologic Effort Against the Soviet Union: 1945-1950". (Unpublished paper presented to the Annual Conference of the Society for Historians of American Foreign Relations, June 2003.)

[207] Alan G. Hobbs and Sam Hallas. "A Short History of Telegraphy, Part 2, Making a Record." http://www.samhallas.co.uk/telhist1/telehist2.htm. (accessed April 19, 2011).

[208] Bob Pollard. "Muliplexing History". http://sites.google.com/site/mdprcp/multiplexinghistory. (accessed April 19, 2011).

[209] Don Robert House. "A Synopsis of Teletype Corporation History." http://www.baudot.net/docs/house--teletype-corp-synopsis.pdf. (accessed April 19, 2011).

[210] Fred B. Wrixon. *Codes, Ciphers & Other Cryptic & Clandestine Communications*. New York, Black Dog & Leventhal Publishers. 1998, 270 – 275.

[211] "T-52 Geheimschreiber". Crypto Museum. http://www.cryptomuseum.com/crypto /siemens/ index.htm. (accessed April 19, 2011); Friedrich L. Bauer. *Decrypted Secrets: Methods and Maxims of Cryptology*. Heidelberg New York: Springer, 2007. 386.

[212] George Raynor Thompson and Dixie R. Harris. *The Signal Corps: The Outcome*. Washington, D.C.: Center for Military History, U.S. Army, 1991. 499.

[213] *SI-32 German Signal Intelligence Branch for Intercepting and Evaluating Internal Communications (Baudot and W/T) of Russia, Particularly Communications Concerning Economic and Industrial Development.* Available from *Christos Military and Intelligence Corner.* http://www.scribd.com/doc/90475797/SI-32-Special-Intelligence-Report. Accessed July 7, 2012.

[214] Ibid, 2-3.

[215] The Forschungsam (FA) was the Nazi party's signal intelligence bureau, which reported directly to Herman Goering. They concentrated on internal monitoring and on foreign diplomatic and commercial communications.

[216] *TICOM DF-98, Russian Baudot Teletype Scrambler.* NARA-CP, RG 457, HCC, Box 1394, Item #4459.

[217] Mathematical researcher in GdNA, specialist in machine ciphers.

[218] *European Axis Signal Intelligence...* Vol. 7. 84-85.

[219] *European Axis Signal Intelligence...*Vol. 4. 111.

[220] *TICOM IF-162, Multichannel Intercept Teletype (HMFS).* RG 457, Entry 9037, Box 44, Item #6860 and *TICOM M-9, Report on German Multiplex Intercept Equipment.* NARA-CP, RG 457, Entry 9037, Box 44, Item #6862.

[221] *European Axis Signal Intelligence...* Vol. 4. 11-12,15,50,83-84.

[222] *TICOM I-153, Second Interrogation of Uffzo Karrenberg of OKH, on the Baudot-Scrambler Machine (Bandwurm).* NSA FOIA request, case #63702. 19 January 2011.

[223] *TICOM I-30 Report on Interrogation of Utfz Karrenberg at Steeple Claydon on 7th July, 1945 at 1100 a.m.* NSA FOIA request, case #64093. 29 March 2011.

[224] *TICOM I-169 Report by Unffz. Karrenberg on the Bandwurm.* NSA FOIA request, case #64093. 29 March 2011.

[225] *TICOM I-30.* 2.

[226] *TICOM I-169.* 3-5.

[227] *Final Report of TICOM Team 1.* NARA-CP, RG 457, Entry P-11, Box 114, item# 10248.

[228] *TICOM I-33, Report on Traffic Analysis of BAUDOT Traffic by Capt.Jack Magilavy, A.U.S. and D.R. Uzielli, SIXTA.* NARA-CP,RG 457, Entry 9037, Box 121, Item #11284.

[229] EASI *Volume 9 - German Traffic Analysis of Russian Communications,* p. 5,17.

[230] EASI *Volume 1 Synopsis,* chart 1-2, 101 – 104.

[231] The famous "Vennona" incepted Soviet diplomatic cables were of this type. See Matthew M. Aid, *The Secret Sentry*, New York, Bloomsbury Press, 2009. 6.

[232] TICOM *IF-162,* 3.

[233] *SI-32 German Signal Intelligence Branch for Intercepting and Evaluating Internal Communications...,* 3.

[234] See for instance, *TICOM I-30 Report on Interrogation of Uffz. Karrenberg at Steeple Claydon on 7th July 1945 at 1100 a.m.* NARA, Entry P **4** "Historians' Source Files Relating to Target Intelligence Committee Interrogation Reports", Box 1, Item #6889; *TICOM I-149 Report by Uffz. Karrenberg and Colleagues on Allied Cipher Machines.* Available from *Christos Military and Intelligence Corner.*

Notes

https://docs.google.com/folder/d/0B_oIJbGCCNYeMGUxNzk0NWQtNzNhZi00YWVjLWI1NmItMzc2YWZiZGNjNjQ5/edit?pli=1#docId=0B_oIJbGCCNYeMDlhNWZkZGItMzRlNS00MWRkLWFhNDgtMzY2MjZlY2ZiZTBl. Accessed October 16, 2012; *TICOM I-153 Second Interrogation of Uffz. Karrenberg of OKH on the Baudot-Scrambler Machine ('Bandwurm')*. NSA FOIA Case# 13586; *TICOM I-168 Report by the Karrenberg Party on Miscellaneous Russian W/T*. NSA FOIA Case# 63702; *TICOM I-169 Report by Uffz. Karrenberg on the Bandwurm*. NSA FOIA Case# 13586; *TICOM I-173 Report by the Karrenberg party on Russian W/T*. NSA FOIA Case# 63702; and *TICOM IF-123 Consolidated Report on Information obtained from the following: Erdmann, Grubler, Hempel, Karrenberg, Schmitz, Susdowk. CSDIC SIR 1717*, NSA FOIA Case# 63702

[235] *G.C.W.S. Ivy Farm, Knockholt Pound*. Kent & Sussex History Forum, Available from http://sussexhistoryforum.co.uk/index.php?topic=1471.msg4887#msg4887 (accessed November 1, 2012); Aid, *The Secret Sentry*, 14; PRO. "Peace-Time Interception of Non-Morse Transmissions." HW 14/137.

[236] 'Russian Y-Service Reports'. NARA-CP, RG 457, Entry 9032 HCC, Box 202, Item # 978; "Appendix D: Notes on Baudot Traffic" from folder "Baudot Charts Labeled Appendix A,B,C,and D" RG 457, Entry 9032 HCC, Box 1473, Item # 4903.

[237] 'RATTAN Liaison. NARA-CP, RG 457, Entry 9032 HCC, Box 1471, Item # 4870.

[238] Recovery of Intelligence From A Two Channel Multiplex Printer Curcult and modification of Commercial Equipment. NARA, RG 457, Entry 9032 HCC, Box #1381. Skaggs Island was a Navy interception station approximately 5 miles from Mare Island, where the modification to the equipment was made.

[239] NSA. *Candle in the Dark: COMINT and Soviet Industrial* Secrets, *1946-1956* Carol B. Davis. U.S . Cryptologic History Series VI, Volume 12. NARA. Recovery of Intelligence From A Two Channel Multiplex Printer Circuit and modification of Commercial Equipment. RG 457, Entry 9032 HCC, Box #1381. Skaggs Island was a Navy interception station approximately 5 miles from Mare Island, where the modifications to the equipment were made.

[240] OP-20G4-A War Diaries, September 1945, April, May, and July 1946, and Campaigne, handwritten note dated 7 August 1946. The author wishes to thank Ralph Erskine for bringing these documents to my attention.

Chapter 8. Postscript

[241] Guy Allan Farrin, (ed). *History of 30 AU*. http://www.30au.co.uk (accessed Dec. 1, 2010.)

[242] National Security Agency. *European Axis Signal Intelligence in World War II as Revealed by 'TICOM' Investigations and by Other Prisoner of War Interrogations and Captured Material, Principally German*. Army Security Agency, Top Secret/Cream report, WDGAS-14, Chief Army Security Agency, 1 May 1946. http://www.nsa.gov/public_info/declass/european_axis_sigint.shtml (accessed June 15, 2010). The nine volumes are:
— Volume 1 - Synopsis
— Volume 2 - Notes on German high Level Cryptography and Cryptanalysis
— Volume 3 - Signal Intelligence Agency of the Supreme Command, Armed Forces
— Volume 4 - Signal Intelligence Service of the Army High Command
— Volume 5 - The German Air Force Signal Intelligence Service
— Volume 6 – Foreign Office Cryptanalytic Section
— Volume 7 – Goering's Research Bureau.
— Volume 8 – Miscellaneous
— Volume 9 - German Traffic Analysis of Russian Communications

[243] EASI, *Volume 2 – Notes on German High Level Cryptography and Cryptanalysis.*

[244] NSA. *TICOM activities of AFSA. Value of TICOM documents in Western Area Sections*. William F. Friedman Collection of Official Papers. Available at :https://www.nsa.gov/ public_info/declass/ friedman_documents/ index.shtml. Assessed February 11, 2016. The outcome of this dispute was not documented.

[245] Matthew M. Aid, "The Russian Target: The U.K. – U.S. Cryptologic Effort Against the Soviet Union: 1945-1950". (Unpublished paper presented to the Annual Conference of the Society for Historians of American Foreign Relations, June 2003.); Michael L. Peterson. *Before BOURBON: American and British COMINT Efforts against Russia and the Soviet Union before 1945*. Cryptologic Quarterly, Fall/Winter 1993 - Vol. 12, Nos. 3-4.

[246] Jeannette Williams, with Yolanda Dickerson, Researcher. *The Invisible Cryptologists: African-Americans, WWII to 1965*. NSA, Center for Cryptologic History, 2001.17-19. Available from http://www.nsa.gov/about/_files/cryptologic_heritage/publications/wwii/invisible_cryptologists.pdf. Accessed October 17, 2012.

[247] See for instance *TICOM I-169 Report by Uffz. Karrenberg on the Bandwurm.* NSA FOIA Case# 13586.
[248] Deutsch, Harold C. "The historical impact of revealing the ULTRA secret." *Cryptologic Spectrum*, Winter 1978 - Vol. 8, No. 1. .NSA. The NSA Declassification Program. *Cryptologic Spectrum*, Winter 1980 - Vol. 10, No. 1. Both available at: https://www.nsa.gov/public_info/declass/cryptologic_spectrum.shtml, accessed February 26, 2016.
[249] Bamford, James. *Body of Secrets: Anatomy of the Ultra-Secret National Security Agency.* New York: Anchor Books, 2001. 8.
[250] Thomas Parrish. *The Ultra Americans.* (New York: Stein and Day, 1986).
[251] Paul Whitaker, and Louis Kruh. 'From Bletchley Park to Berchtesgaden.' *Cryptologia,* XI (1987), pp. 129-141.
[252] Richard J. Aldrich. *The Hidden Hand: Britain, America, and Cold War Secret Intelligence.* (Woodstock & New York: The Overland Press, 2001).

Appendix I: The codes and ciphers of WWII

[253] Bauer, Fredrick.L. *Decrypted Secrets.* Berlin, Springer-Verlag, 2007.
[254] Budiansky, Stephan. *Battle of Wits,* New York, The Free Press, 2000.
[255] Wrixon, Fred B. *Code Ciphers & other Cryptic and Clandestine Communication.* New York, Black Dog and Leventhal Publishers, 1998.
[256] This became known as a Vigenère cipher although he did not actually invent it. What he did invent was the elegant idea of an autokey, in which a single letter "seed" can be used to build a key sequence. See Kahn, The Codebreakers, p. 145-148.
[257] In addition to the books mentioned in Chapter 8, see also David Kahn, *Seizing the Enigma*, Geneva, IL: Houghton Mifflin, 1991; Ralph Bennett, *ULTRA in the West*, New York: Charles Scribner's Sons, 1979 and his *Behind the Battle, Intelligence and the War with Germany 1939-45*, London: Sinclair-Stevenson, 1994; Ronald Lewin, *Ultra Goes to War*, New York: McGraw-Hill, 1978; Gordon Welchman, *The Hut Six Story: Breaking the Enigma Codes*, New York: McGraw – Hill, 1982; Hugh Sebag-Montefiore, *ENIGMA: The Battle for the Code*, Hoboken, NJ: 2000; and R.A Ratcliff, Delusions of Intelligence, Cambridge: Cambridge University Press, 2006.